The Naked Eye: New and Selected Poems, 1987–2012

Jack Grapes

Bombshelter Press
Los Angeles / 2012

Acknowledgments

Some of the poems in this book first appeared in the following publications, to whose generous editors grateful acknowledgment is made: *AfterImage, Alcatraz, The Alley Cat Readings, Amalgamated Holding Company, American Book Jam, Angel's Gate Review, As Each Unit Is a Constant, Bachy, Bellingham Review, Beverly Hills Playhouse Newsletter, Beyond Baroque Magazine, Bitterroot, Black Rabbit Press, Blitz, Blue Window, Border, California State Poetry Quarterly, Chattahoochee Review, Comic Spirit, CQ–Contemporary Quarterly, Cream City Review, culturalweekly.com, Deepest Valley Review, Earth, Electrum, The Fantastic, Foreign Exchange, Gorilla Extract, Gridlock, Gypsy, Japanese American Magazine, Kauri, Kaleidescope, Labris, LA Weekly, Lingo, Manic Press, Momentum, My Eyes All out of Breath, New Lantern Club Review, New Orleans Express, The New Orleans Review, Nexus, Olé, Orange County Poetry Review, The Outsider, Pinchpenny, Poetry East, Poetry/LA, Poetry Magazine, PoetMeat, rara avis, Rattle, Rufus, Scree, Shattersheet, Southern California Quarterly, Spillway, Stone Cloud, Sycamore Review, Tempest, This Poem Knows You, The Tiresian, Tsunami, Up:jut, Vagabond, Voices, Vol.No., Waves, The Willie, The Word, Wormwood Review, Yellow Fingers, ZYZZYVA,* and the following anthologies: *Anthology of Revolutionary Poetry, Gridlock, The Maverick Poets, Men of Our Time, News from Inside, Nueva Poesia de Los Angeles, Peace Among the Ants, Poetry Loves Poetry.*

Second Edition

ISBN: 978-0-941017-00-8

Bombshelter Press
www.bombshelterpress.com
books@bombshelterpress.com
PO Box 481266 Bicentennial Station
Los Angeles, California 90048 USA

Printed in the United States of America

Cover art by DeLoss McGraw
Author photograph on back cover by Lori Grapes
Trees, Coffee, and the Eyes of Deer photo by Samuel Grapes
and the running form, naked, Blake cover art by Jack Grapes
Breaking down the Surface of the World cover design by Judith James
Photos in "The Big Wake" by Naomi Lieberman

for

Lori

lifesaver

Contents

Trees, Coffee, and the Eyes of Deer

Breaking Down the Surface of the World

Lucky Finds

The Naked Eye

Afterword by Bill Mohr

Trees, Coffee and the Eyes of Deer

What counted was mythology of self.
. . . . until nothing of himself
Remained, except some starker, barer self
In a starker, barer world. . . .

He came. The poetic hero without palms
Or jugglery, without regalia.

It purified. It made him see how much
Of what he saw he never saw at all.
He gripped more closely the essential prose
As being, in a world so falsified,
The one integrity for him, the one
Discovery still possible to make,
To which all poems were incident, unless
That prose should wear a poem's guise at last.

—Wallace Stevens
from "The Comedian As the Letter C"

All the Way Back

All the way back, all the way back and start over,
start over, go all the way back and do it again,
over there, by the tree, go over there, stand over there,
by the tree, walk on over, go all the way over, by the tree,
not by the rock, over by the tree, all the way back,
past the rock, go past the rock, go all the way over and
start again, from the tree, slower, start again slower this
time all the way over past the rock and do it again, without
flinching this time, slowly and without flinching, get your
hands out of your pockets and do it barefoot this time, without
flinching, from the beginning, from the start, from the very
beginning, all the way back without flinching past the rock
slowly and barefoot by the tree and get your hands out of
your pockets, drop the knife, drop the coins, drop the string,
leave them by the tree with your shoes, with your fingernails,
in the box that holds the fire without flinching, that burns
so slowly the flames seem frozen, glittering like swords in
light, without a trace of blood, ice, so dry your skin sticks
to it and comes off, without flinching, from the beginning,
all the way back from the start, go all the way back, and slowly,
as slowly as possible, so slowly you appear to remain still like
that without ever beginning, as if you hadn't yet begun,
when in fact you had begun from the beginning, all the way back
from the start, all the way back, all the way, without flinching.

The Picture

I am five
but that's
not me
in the picture
that's some
one else
who looks
like me
but isn't
me I'm be
hind him
telling
him what
to do with
his mouth
so he'll
look like
me to some
one who does
not know me
if you know
me you know
I look com
pletely diff
rent with
my mouth
shut tight
and my eyes
wide open
and both hands
covering up
my ears so I
won't hear a
thing or say
what I see
when I see
so much
and I'm five,

not even that
yet not until
September
eleventh then
I'll be five.
Imagine when
I'm ten

I Am the Darkness

I am the darkness
Within you all.
I will get you.
Cheat not, tell no man
Lies.
Love those you can
And reserve the others
For boredom
But not pity
And not hatred.
Do not cover your face.
It only becomes
What you are.
Give children pennies
Especially in the winter
Or a candy bar.
Don't cop a feel on a bus
Of a woman
And whatever you do
Don't forget to feed me.
I am the Darkness
Within you all.
I will get you.

Midnight in the Kitchen

The stiff finger of the wind—
no, it doesn't come here anymore.
We used to have eggs stacked in the ice box,
two seltzer bottles,
my father's favorite salami and cheese
to snack on after midnight,
when you were you.
You could see
how the mustard spread on the hard bread
by the light of the refrigerator,
the closing door that put the light back in
to keep it cold and stiff
where all the light you need at midnight is
in the ice-box
and you are you
and your mouth tastes the food,
elbows on a Formica table top,
fat sad eyes in the dead of night
chomp chomp   tick tock
light dark
and you think and you think.
The mouse under the floorboards
breaks a leaf and is gone
knocking a mud-caked coke bottle
against a piece of slate,
and you think and you think
chomp chomp
tick tock
and you are you
getting fat and getting full,
my old lost father
sitting in that midnight kitchen,
1946,
a slow sweep of the hand
and the salt is off the table,
this white rain
spreading on the floor.

Greenhouse Effect

If there is a sound, it is not crying.
To tell you the truth, no noise
comes from the house across the street
where rain collects in the bird bath
on the front lawn, though no bird
ever drinks from it there's so much scum
and floating objects thrown there
by kids walking to and from school.
But where are the children?
We haven't seen any in years,
and the school's been closed,
boarded up, as a matter of fact, burned down,
razed to make a harness factory that shut down
after the strike and sits in disrepair.
That's right, it's not a school at all.
But I take the quiet as a blessing.
What's vanished into the asphalt's
best left where it belongs.
No one around here wants any kind of new life.
I lose a shoe, I wear another that doesn't match.
What's the difference. I see a flower,
I snap it off just like that.
Down the street, Eloise invites the weeds in for tea.
The old bushes rake and rummage across the front yard
like the crippled monster from one of the tales
we used to tell the children with a wink. No one winks now.
We are the thing told and like it. Last year a young decorator
working the neighborhood with his red leather briefcase
and white shoes made the mistake of knocking
on one too many doors. We did everything but
eat his bones. Threw them in the bird bath
to rot and stink up the place so they'd never be noticed.
The sun's our only enemy. But we can wait.
Let it come just a little closer.

What the Leaves Make That Turn in Autumn

What the leaves make that turn in autumn
is pinched from the wind.
On the front porch of my uncle's house
we watched the pony named Pinto
ride down the neutral ground
up and down Elysian Fields Avenue.
What the water tower painted green was green for,
high on its legs, a fresh god,
and I was that child that water
has not come to again.
The hurricane's coming, Aunt Bea said.
Moaning of the dead surrounded the house.
What the windows exed with masking tape faced;
that rags were wrapped for the freeze;
Uncle Charles gone to the store for flashlight batteries;
and the horse called to me,
he was my horse wasn't he.
What the Indians rode when I wished I was with them
to have bare legs against a blanket
and threaten the hills that turn black
when the sun goes behind them.
How did it work, I wondered,
and waited for the work to begin:
The lightning froze our faces first,
then thunder inside steel boots pranced on the roof,
and the rain filled the water tank
where Pinto could drink the next day
after we rode him in the air of a fall afternoon,
where Elysian Fields and Esplanade Avenue meet,
where I want to go again,
to feel that pony's teeth on my hand,
to climb the ladder to the top of the tower
and pick splinters from a green god's hand.

Mardi Gras, 1950

Dressed in a Superman costume,
I fly over them.
Karl is Daniel Boone.
Louis is Davy Crockett.
Charlaine is the baby in the gypsy outfit.
I fly over them.
Beer in the streets.
Is it a man or a woman
my mother asks
as it swishes by and flips up
showing crinoline
and a bare ass.
I fly over him.
King Zulu goes by, throw me a coconut
we scream, running after the floats.
Beer in the streets beer cans.
Flambeaux carriers dressed in white robes, struttin'
where 'ya at, mutha!
Harem girls, spacemen, monkeys
in monkey suits.
I fly over them.
Sick in the streets, wine in the streets.
The floats go by throw me something mister!
Music the bands drunks singing.
I fly over them.
The Indian princess kisses Dracula.
Don't step in the vomit! my mother yells.
Frankenstein's holding a glass from Pat O'Brien's
filled with pink punch and rum;
he sips from a long pink straw.
The Devil with his pitchfork gooses Buck Rodgers.
Broken glass and confetti float down the gutter.
Someone steps on the pink hot dog bun.
Dad sneaks a drink as he hugs
the lady in the cowboy suit.
Raiders from Mars!
Black leather jackets and boots!
Flowers out of the magician's mouth!

I fly over them.
Gangs with razor blades snug in the tips of their shoes.
Faces with knives.
Police shoving the crowd back.
Drunks singing in the beer streets.
Pissing in the streets.
Faces in the streets.
Throw me something, mister!
Throw me something, mister!
Throw me something.

Boom goes the drum.

What Drove Damon Down

A short thunder is what drove Damon down,
and not meant to be confused, he stood on the corner
of Pico and Alvarado until the rain was in his pocket
next to the bumble-bee (how he loved anything that bumbled,
Damon was that kind of a guy)
and cried himself to sleep.
His mother came by once,
and in Africa he saw himself a huge rhino
(when are rhinos small, I know)
snorting in a pool of water.
Once in Woolworth's Damon took a toy airplane
trembling it under his coat
and all the way home on a bus
even under his pillow trembling
then finally down in the dark corner of his closet
where it stayed until he was past his third wife,
the plane was gone,
Damon never knew who took it.
"I want meat!" he shouted, pounding his chest
with one clenched fist holding a fork.
Damon liked pigeons.
Damon fixed flat tires.
Damon was in love with women.
Damon kept looking for things that would change his life.
A book, a poem, a stranger on the streetcar.
The end came in July.
Damon was in bed, smelling the hot okra sidewalk
and listening to the rain.
This is old, he thought, looking at his skin,
but if I was never young
why do I remember my pet turtle, hollow in the sun;
the hard washcloth my mother rouged against my cheeks;
no one's moon but my own
outside the window next to my crib?
Then thunder came in, and
Damon said it was too short,
and he went down.

Someone in the Next Room Goes Mad, 1953

Aunt Adela is pushing fish into the grinder.
Aunt Fanny swings around the dining room
talking and bumping her ass
into the table set for Passover.
On diet pills, she's a 45-year-old speed freak.
My mother sits in the kitchen
on her fat hams, fat thighs, fat arms,
cheeks in a bulge,
like a moored battleship unfit for tourists.
Bernice in white maid's uniform
understands the Yiddish passed
between these women, why not,
she was there when my grandmother
shriveled in her wheelchair, yelling in Yiddish,
"Too much noise, the children
make too much noise."
We ran around her wheelchair whooping like Indians.

This is the exhibit at the World's Fair
next to the Disney version of frontier life:
Mrs. Boone does the wash out back;
Abe Lincoln's father drags home a deer.

In the next panel is the home of the future.
There's me and my family wearing red jump suits,
staring out the windows—magic panes
that do not break and keep out the cold,
where nothing freezes or burns or rusts or goes crazy,
and you're forbidden to remember the past.

In the next panel
strapped to a chair,
someone is writing this down.

Nothing Left to Chance

Begin with fish,
smack their heads off with a mallet
or tear through the entire phone book
sheet by sheet
and digest the lives listed
five hundred to a page.
You don't remember one old phone number
but all the addresses
for each home you've lived in
bob like little boats
on the ocean of your daydreams.
You can't understand why poets
write lines like that,
or what makes a car go,
and when you see those steel girders
going up on the vacant lot,
the exposed elevator shafts,
glass and concrete not far behind
you wonder how so much can be built
one piece at a time
and nothing left to chance.

Arms That Take You In

She does not climb
the star of lion,
had nettles put in place
and takes your face
home in a bag.
Now she was clever, all right.
Each night she removes
her robe, butchered
ankles with one swoop
and the flapping trips
the alarm swarming
the place with cops.
This is it.
The face tucked safely
into her pocket,
she fades back and fades
to this day,
whether full-mooned
or in charge,
each arm takes you in,
without phony,
without pensions or blue playthings,
without kisses or kissing,
trumpets or slander,
without one sign or sure word,
a warning hiss—nothing.
I mean nothing at all.
She stands there
in clever home and opens her robe
flaps naked arms
and takes you in and to this day
she takes you in.

. . . . . .

She returns the turtle
with both legs open,
strokes the inside of her thighs
on a tie,

each knot passing
port cities and storms
above the oceans.
This is the wrong place,
but she waves the curtains back,
and shoves me down by the one light
on the bed stand,
uncertain headlights that circle
these walls in my sleep.
Crunch for one tabletop;
a breath that is good as gold.
By now, I am sweating.
I can slide off the muscles
of her skin.
Trombones.
Glaring spoons of bugles
where the flesh snarls glue,
butler, pussy, reingold,
shifting asses surfing on the bedspread,
fluctuate,
blaze down and into her,
she tuggles me in and bugles me out,
both legs open,
each knot passing,
she strokes the poor cities
on the inside of her thighs
and returns the turtle,
a breath that is good as gold.

. . . . . .

Who are we? Not noble.
We confuse structure with bear-traps
and bears for a song.
But there is no music,
just her humming by the dresser
as she returns each part of her panties
to her legs,
not a clasp notwithstanding.

The rhyme is with the lion.
A picture hanging crooked on the wall;

a window shade unpsrung;
the mirror on the closed closet door.
And the radio on.
I am only back where the old entrance
remains open,
the rest in hand.
A glacier that humbles Tuesdays
in my mouth and raises welts
if I suck too hard.
There is no sign.
There is only this turning,
this constant turning.
She adds a blouse,
a skirt,
a pair of high-heeled shoes
and hums,
what is the tune?
The tune is not the mirror
but one belt loop missed
is all I'd need to find her;
just this nickel in the palm of my hand.
Then she raises her arms like a dancer,
takes a deep golden breath of bars,
and goes.

Lizards, Backs, and Shoes As They Are

Someone's overturned the lake again.

I do not understand this one word here, he says.
Neither do I, which is why I keep it in.
But countless things escape so easily out of you,
he gasps.
Are you gasping? Actually gasping?
He apologizes, says he's been reading too much.

And someone's given birth to a brilliant lizard.
Perhaps you know the mother. Clues abound.
Geography is so bare: Like a wet fish
the thumbprint on the refrigerator
wiggles across the chrome.

You'll have to explain that other one, he says.
But we meet each other in so many different places,
I yell (yelling is allowed).
First you march up to the door and swing it open.
Then you learn the beast's language, full of eager notes
and Yippee! the soldiers are home!
Who minds their muddy boots.
Look at the moon how full it is.
My what a moon you say and see,
our problems are gone already.
Meet you at midnight with the fox of the evil evening,
backslapping summer mouth full of sucking flowers.

Ah, but a hundred miles away the city is being eaten.

Who's in charge of burning all these papers? someone asks.
Now this incessant questioning will just have to stop.
We'll never get anything done this way.
Count the bodies again. Are any new? Keep just few.
And Monday, the notary publics. The sheets
and the suits with no names attached,
false teeth still in their cup
and Wednesday too, missing with the rest
no one puts anything away, sheets of dead skin
hard and brittle crunching underfoot

static on the radio, fire drills, children
in the street hitting other children
with long crackling sticks.
Who is going to marry at a time like this?

There is so much and so much to do.
Let us be vegetables together or bubble gum.
Let's make love while the broccoli cooks.
Let's mail our shoes to the richest men on earth.
Who can ask questions with so much to be done?
And so many shoes piled by the door as we sleep.

Which Cup, Which Eye

The cup has come to his hand
and she says
which eyes
which eyes were you talking about?
He has begun to remove
her hands
which float up without complaint
each finger spread
apart
as if to say
no more.
A look out the window
reveals
the possibilities:
first the long black automobile
stranded with rust and bullets;
then the rubber knife beside
a leo lion puppet
and over by the trunk of the tree
crackling through the sidewalk
the book, stiff against the wind,
still wet,
covered with muddy footprints.

Which eyes,
she says again.
The eyes that approximate,
he says,
that remove tissue
without cutting bone;
eyes that
like your hands,
spread apart
as if to say
no more.
He opens the door and looks out
but there is no one, nothing.
Someone just a minute ago was listening.

He recognized the face.
They've seen us, she says.
Yes
and the skin
begins to come away
without a sound
from their heads.

And This Is My Father

Up
up
up.
Up through five green
hospital floors I run the
elevator up through five
green hospital floors
to where my father walks
along the clean halls
hands in his red robe
to meet me stepping out
to meet him.
A pale hand on my shoulder,
he takes me deep-dyed in ceremony
to the nurse's station
where all the work to be done
is flourished in rich flames
and slow thighs
that squeeze through the night shift.
"This is my son," he says
but I catch the stare of the red-headed
nurse turning her blood-dimmed face to mine.
It is the night shift;
she is the shadow of an indignant falcon.
My father spreads his thick pale hand
with me within it
down the halls into each living room
not staked with hanging vines
of water and blood.
"This is my son," he says to Mr. William
thickening in his heart.
"This is my son," he says to Mr. Butler
covered to the neck with a sheet.
"This is my son," he says
to whomever we pass in the hall.
The dying glide without glee
in their beds;
birds fly at the windows

and turn back.
"When are you coming home?" I ask.
My father smiles and his hand opens wide
without fear floating up to his ear, scratching.
The tall nurse catches him out of bed.
"What are you doing out of bed!" she thunders.
"Why, this is my son," he says to her
carrying off in astonishment
the fully mortal laugh of all his teeth.
And this is my father,
long after his death has died
haunting the night shift hospitals
with the relish
of a gypsy.

How Simple a Poem Is

it means to see to see the pitiful
handful of ashes you hold
as you move toward the horizon
singing and making a monument
on a road no one will pass
ever in your life time it means
to run against the wind mouth open
like a nut escaped from adjacent
territories of the interior the radiant
bedfellow of foolishness it means
to believe to believe that you
can be this far from the center
of the earth and still feel the fire
that washes up from the core it means
to stop to stop at once give birth
to whatever is handy that does
as it will do for no one
but yourself
for now

American River

A few birds
go into the fresh sky.

Someone sings gaily
along the black river.

It sure is a pleasure
California.

Look down upon the fork
of the American River.

Lie there in the sun;
a brown and fired look.

God, is that a peach?
Juicy as a watermelon.

Last night at sunset
I pointed out the pink sky.

This is the place to live.
Even at night, it's bright as day.

Pretend

Pretend you don't see me
behind the typewriter.
Pretend the words
were always just this way
on the page
before the face
of the one
who wrote them
in his underwear
on a cold November 5 A.M. Monday
morning
thinking about the commercial audition
he has today at 3:15
For Benson & Hedges.
Thinking should I shave
my mustache,
should I cut my hair,
should I wear a suit,
should I tap dance?
Thinking my sister lives
two thousand miles away
and at 20
hasn't what it takes
to live the next 30.
Thinking why was my wife crying
over the toilet when I walked
into the bathroom.
Pretend I have no face,
no name, no history.
Pretend
the poem's
the thing
that dies.

Holding On

It's been such a long time holding on.
I die with the ones I love
and they go on without me.
Is that me in the photograph?
Jack, do you see me looking at you?
Do you know that camera is the future,
and there is nothing out there
but me, looking back at you,
wondering whether to rip you out
as if you were the imposter.
I have forgotten what you seemed to know,
smiling as you climb out of the pool,
sliding hair out of your eyes,
no rush to get your medal,
just a pause to let your tan body glisten.
What did you know that you could wait
a winner at the lens.
I am tired of your marvel.
I dare you to leave that picture
and walk with me now and remain beautiful.
I'm the one who has marched backwards
to keep you where you are.
I'm the one who holds onto all the family movies and pictures,
boxes and boxes of beanstalk seeds.
My body dies to keep you alive.
My spirit dies in your name.
I'm the one who writes this
unable to hold on.

Feeding Time

The horse
in the house
is not dead
but he pretends to be.

"Get that horse out of the bathroom!"
my wife screams.

The crows beat on the doors.
"We want our money!" they cry.
My five buck friends I call them.

I am in the attic—
the giraffe—
sticking my head out the window.
"No one's home," I shout down.

And you know what's in the belfry.
My wife complains.
"Move out," I say, "if you don't like it."

She moves out, taking
Morgan the canary,
Trigger the cat,
Bruce the dog,
and Lassie,
our pet hamster.

So it's the horse and me.
One of us pretending to be dead.
The other, stretching his neck out in a dry season,
reading leaves,
cleaning ash trays on the coffee table,
cooking up a roast in the kitchen.

The tigers are coming for dinner.

Listen

Listen, what are you reading this for?
Haven't you got bills to pay,
a movie you've been wanting to see,
a woman to love or a wife to ignore.
I'm here because it's raining,
and poets write poems when it rains—
at least that's what I read once somewhere.
(Listen, I'm lying to you. It's not raining.
I just said that because it sounded good.
It's a beautiful day. There's liable to be a law
or a proverb dealing it a blow from which
it may never recover that's how beautiful a day
it is and you should find a girl or a football
and a field of clover
to take them both
around around around.)

Are you reading this to feel better?
Do you think writing this makes me feel better?
Let me tell you something.
You know what'll make me feel better?
A million dollars. A million million dollars.
I want to be corrupted by money and fame
so bad it squeaks my socks.
I want to be filthy with money
to buy filthy men out
and sell their souls
for a bucket of paint.
I want to have so much money
I'll be able to rob my own bank,
buy my way *in* and *out* of jail,
cook omelettes from golden goose's eggs,
send every starving poet
a twenty-dollar cook book
and laugh in their faces
saying:

I don't need your words!
I don't need your poems!

I don't need your books or your dreams.
I don't need your aches and pains
and sensational sufferings!
I don't need your visions
your eyes your goddamn poet's eyes!
I've Got Money, Baby!
I'VE GOT ALL THE MONEY
IN THE WORLD!
I OWN THE EARTH AND THE SUN
AND THE PLANETS
AND THE STARS I DON'T OWN,
NO ONE CAN BUY!
I CAN BE GOD! I CAN BE GOD!

. . . . . .

Listen, I didn't mean what I wrote.
I got a little carried away.
You'll forgive me because it's raining.
I get carried away when it rains.
I don't want money.
I don't want power.
I don't want to own men's souls.
I want just to be poet.
To write words of startling beauty
to fill the universe
of emptiness
in your soul.
To make the trees dance
and the winds curl back upon themselves
like confetti off a ship.
I want your tears.
I want to reach
the dept of such beauty—
I want the universe to suffer
because beauty is a pain beyond pain
that dies in the willow
as well as in the wars of men.
I want all men to own my soul,
the poet's soul,
for it's always for the asking.

I want to belong to all the nations,
and all the oceans.
I want to belong to the earth,
the planets,
all the stars,
and all the spaces
beyond all spaces.
I want to be God.

How the Stranger Is

How is the stranger?
He's okay.
See him eating in the kitchen.
Dirty boots full of mud.
But he likes the ham sandwich.

How he got in
I don't know.
It was so early when he knocked.
Go take a peek.
Is he still eating?

Now the mailman comes for a coke
and the two of them chat.
Perhaps they know each other.
I walk around the house
thinking what to do.
The stranger comes out
and asks me what I want.
What *I* want? I say.
But he laughs and punches my arm,
then sits in front of the TV
and watches.
Should I talk to him?
Three paintings by van Gogh
on the wall I got at Sears
he likes, says they remind him of home.
Are they still fixing the street? he asks.
I go out and look, but nothing's there.
He laughs when I come back.
Tricked again, and he punches me on the arm.
He punches me again, harder.
Then again, harder, and again
on the other arm, with his other hand.
What's for dinner, he asks.
He asks to see my maps, all my maps:
The close-up of the Salton Sea
and Lake Pontchartrain.
He punches me again, harder.

Hey, I yell, that was pretty hard.
He smiles, takes the salami and cuts it in half
with the large bread knife.
Want to cut, he asks,
big teeth showing in his smile
and he hands me the knife.
Go ahead, he says. Cut.
Tonight he throws all the pillows on the floor,
takes the chairs and sets them
against the walls.
He stomps around the house
with those big boots and leaves mud tracks
in the kitchen and on the carpet on the stairs.
He goes about dumping everything on the floor,
sweeping his hand around the cabinets and cupboards.
Bam-bam, he one-twos me in the stomach
with each fist,
then *slap-slap* in the face.
Big meaty hands.
Slap-slap again.
Chairs through the windows.
Kicks in the TV.
Books topple from the shelves.
Hurls the telephone into the bathtub
that is already filled with water
and overflowing.
Have a cigar, he says.
Have a cigar.
The stranger lights it for me,
and watches me puff on it
and lights one for himself,
and gestures me to sit down with him
next to the overturned sofa
and we sit
blowing smoke above our heads.
Real fine, he says, dontcha think?
Yep, I say.
Real fine.

Lights in the Museum

My brother wears long-sleeved shirts
that cover the tracks on his arms.
He lives alone now in the big house;
we've all married and moved out
or died.
Louis stalks the rooms like a walrus
and forgets to turn out
the lights.
I come home for a visit and hear
the ghost of my father complaining
about the light bill.
"Louis, turn out the lights
when you leave a room," I tell him.
As he leaves each room, he remembers
and lurches back,
slamming his arm
on the wall,
hoping to find the light switch;
and this is how I see him
after I've gone:
lurching from one room to another,
lights on,
lights off.
The lights in my home back home
go on and off
day and night
all year long.

My brother could hop fences
like a deer
and my father once took his picture,
a freckled face covered with dirt
and peanut butter and jelly
smeared on his chin;
a photograph that once hung
in the Delgado Museum for a month.
It was titled *The All-American Boy*
because the confederate hat he wore

had “The All American Boy”
written across the top band,
but with that face and freckles,
there was no mistake that here,
under the hat,
was the real thing:
the all-American boy.

That photograph hung with others
along walls full of light switches
and someone going from room to room
turning out the lights—
a woman giving tours through the museum.

My home back home is like a museum.
In it my brother is a photograph
that moves down the halls,
meaty hands and shirt tail hanging out,
freckles and tracks on his face and arms.
Everything about that photograph
my brother has become
moves like the flesh
of an old lake.
Everything moves but his eyes.
They stare without direction,
and it is hard to tell
whether behind them
the light
is on
or off.

Another Poem

The simmered center of your life
hardens on a teaspoon.

You do not begin
at the beginning.
You begin at the end
of a brutal whiteness
when the heart has lost its nerve,
the incomprehensible hand
that reaches for the incomprehensible razor
waits for the death of the body
that follows the death of the heart
which refuses
in spite of its name
to die,
and if you don't know this already,
it will take more than poetry
to teach you.
After all, life is a tomato,
whatever that means.
It is also a wristwatch, and by and by
a pencil.

In the middle of watching *Beloved Infidel* on TV,
a movie I've seen four times and know by heart,
I come here to do this, to write,
to stir up the soup of my life, as it were.
My wife and I are not living together now.
I wonder how my brother is,
eating up the skin on his arms,
trying to save his life, his tomato,
his wristwatch.
The high point of my day these days
is getting a peach at Farmer's Market.
These facts are only of my life;
like yours, elegant as they are dull.

But I come here to write this
to save my life, when it is a tomato,

a wristwatch, and by and by a pencil.
So what's to save?
On channel 9 Victor Mature is an Indian;
On channel 13 Matt Dillon kisses the girl
and carries sacks of flour to her house;
On Channel 4 they're dancing to Isaac Hayes.

It's about time I end this poem,
wrap it up like laundry to drop at your feet.
I know you need these loose ends tied up.
When a man sits down to save his
tomato,
as it were,
it's the least he can do.
And the truth of it is, I can do it.
I'm a good enough poet to do it.
I know how to begin and end a poem.
But just now,
on the edge of a pain
I can't point to or name,
I don't feel like it.
My life is not a tomato.
My life is not a wristwatch.
My life is not a by and by.
I'm going to watch *Beloved Infidel* end
the same way it always ends.
My ends will all be different.

And this poem?
I'll end it
in another poem.

Burial

Plucking the light above me
I dream in the darkness
of my black mother
a running splash of rust
whose head grows immense
in my arms.

Dazzled and green-eyed
from the streets
I watch brown stockings
fall to her feet.
Coffee blossoms
amazed at the armpits,
to come home
hung by a thread
the brown carcass of my black mother
who has strangled the tired voice
whose head grows immense in my arms.

She says your mother means well.
I do not tell her
that she is my mother
brown my black mother
asleep in white calico
who rocks with the voice
whose head grows immense in my arms.
You are not from my country
she says
but I am brown your black mother
I pass fingers through your hair,
come here
high on the tree
to sit when it rains
overgrown with coffee blossoms
my boy   my boy   my boy
I am brown your black mother
my head
grows immense
in your arms.

The Count's Lament

There are not too many ways
to drink the blood.
Thick and slightly warm
like pureed vichyssoise.
Sometimes I roll it around,
what little there is,
in my cheek between tongue and palate,
just to get a taste again
of what I've forgotten the taste of,
drinking it so much now out of desperation
that perhaps even this sip
is not enough anymore.
Perish that horrible thought!
I go now from neck to neck,
throat to throat,
reeling, scratching with my fingernails,
flapping against invisible mist
that issues from their mouths
as they walk about the streets
in a cold that lies above the ground,
a cold you can wave your arms in
should you need to.
Not the cold darkness I bask in.
A darkness that has a taste,
a dull texture that grinds in my sleep.
It's all the same:
Flamingos!
Daffodils!
To dream of a blazing sun,
just think of it,
to dream of that burning
and be unable to touch it,
suck its fire into my own veins,
down the gullet where it boils
the substance of my flesh—
then to wake, biting at splinters.
It's no life for a Count, believe me.
Were I to drive drunken

down one of your neon streets
what breath test would you give me
when even the flesh turns thin and white
at the end of a century.
A century!
It's like a snap to me.
All I vomit is blood.
That sickness comes out of my throat.
To be drunk again for fear of the waste.
The indignity!
Just to stand at the sideboard
with a scotch and ice in my hand
and clank the cubes around the glass
and finish it off with a puff.
The worms. The rats. The beetles.
The spider spinning its web
for the unwary fly,
tiny cracks of blood I've long disdained.
And now all there is left
is you,
your own meager supply
that brightens with my pulse.
Imagine what it might be like
to flow in my veins
for centuries without end.

Ask the Bulls

What are you sure of?
Ask the bulls.
The kill must be easy,
quick if you can
manage it,
but easy if nothing else.

So you're outside Mexico City.
The local boys torture the bulls.
Their silk is full of sweat and dust.
On wooden benches
you sit watching
and crack pistachios
between your teeth.
You don't see blood
until the black animal
is dragged through the dust
on ropes and chains
like a stalled truck.
The *banderilleros* push
from behind, churning
their thin legs.
Flies buzz lazily
in the plaza.

Now you know
you are going
to write a poem about this.
Down the aisles the kids
had yelled all afternoon—
"Piece da cheese! Piece da cheese!"
waving little bags in the air.
Why are they selling
pieces of cheese, you thought,
but finally buy,
and as the bull
is being dragged through the dirt
you crack the "piece da cheese"
between your teeth,

spitting shells into the ring.

You look around,
at the fat *afficionado*
displeased with the slow kill.
The bull's neck hanging
to the ground.
The matador stands over him,
hands above his head
like a dancer in fifth position
to drive the blade in.
He thrusts six, seven times
and the bull is weary
and no one watches.

You see this all
taking place
not just now,
but later,
in the poem,
in the poem you will write:
the flags and the ceremony
and the fat *picadores*
grunting in the saddles
of their horses;
the hot sun, the animal smell,
fierce ladies in yellow hats
shaking their fists for blood.

You sit back, smug and grateful,
the empty page of the poem
folded in your back pocket.
You know just how it will go.
There's no need to rush it.
Anytime you need it,
the poem's yours.

An easy kill.

Suspect

Suspect
the poem
that is not
a matter
of life & death.
It is like
all the other
poems
that are not
matters
of life & death.
When a man
talks to you
without
blinking an eye,
when a man
listens
without glancing
over his shoulder,
his hand
is on a knife
and he knows
what he wants.
He wants
your crippled mother
clutching that
foolish poem
in her
wheelchair
hands.

I was much further out than you thought
And not waving but drowning.

—Stevie Smith
from "Not Waving but Drowning"

Invisible

Dispatch: Blue baby left
in back seat
outmaneuvers rat
for rattle.

Sun goes down. Sun comes up.
No one touches me.
Even in plain sight: hiding.

They come to my room
These are his things.
a dozen pipes;
five thousand books;
pennies by the jarful.

Just what is too much to ask
when you're invisible:
that they leave you alone?

She Fucks and I Fuck

She fucks and I fuck
and both of us are fucking.
Now I'm up,
I'm thinking I'm fucking
then I'm not thinking
I'm fucking
I'm just fucking.
Then I'm telling her how good it feels
then I'm feeling how good it feels.
I want to come and I don't want to come.
She wants to come and she doesn't
want to come, oh not just yet,
you can't fuck and think about fucking
all at the same time,
your leg is in
her cunt all of a sudden
and you want
to be her cunt all of a sudden,
to be fucked, not to fuck,
to include, not to penetrate,
to be killed, not the killer
Oh and it's always moving,
it's going to be over
suddenly you think and then you don't think,
A tongue licks your closed eye
and it licks your closed chest
and you lick back, thinking of licking,
then just licking
and your heart breaks, it breaks,
you're fucking the woman you love
and it breaks your heart.
You're deep and full
in pity and in pain,
coming up from life
for air,
and yes, I love me now,
I am plunged and raised,
set down and risen,

the inside breaks against the bone,
and God, dear God,
if You could fuck the woman You love
when You are loving her,
everything that hurts
in Your heart
would come true.

State of the Union

Me, Tarzan: You Jane.
This is how physics
gets at the nature of things.
Once I thought I'd see everything.
Then be able to show it.
Like I could love you,
and solve everything.
A philosopher told me
not to use the word *thing,*
that it was vague,
meaning among other things,
affair, event, deed, act,
possession, accomplishment,
circumstance, detail,
individual, and especially,
person.
Sleep is a stabbed animal.
Life is out there.
I am in here.

Recitative

When the bottoms of tables re-embrace their
former students and the doorbells embark
upon stranger journeys inward,
keep this edge in your face that you know
which friend to love and lover to betray.

If there are words to be said to those
who threaten with their kneecaps
better to move against the wall sideways
like an animal in the zoo who keeps secret
which friend to love and lover to betray.

Certainly it's no use being skillful;
show your naked body to the camera even
when the background's similar; those
who look look back and fail to answer
which friend to love and lover to betray.

If you cannot sleep, sleep will pay no debts;
if your hands are shamed into motionlessness
take care that your feet scrape
the proper mud from your shoes and lead you to
which friend to love and lover to betray.

I've got no answers. A coat or sweater
works as well as a shelf though a bed
unobserved is no place to dream or cut your
wrists. Cut your eyeballs out if they know
which friend to love and lover to betray.

Never mind. This is taller than you are.
A movement to the window. Out there the name,
walking on its fingertips, at the edge
of the face, on the tongue of each friend
who loves you and each lover you betray.

The Beast and the Dreamer

There is a beast
in the bed with you.
You'd rather pretend
it's the dream
or the overcoat
you forgot to hang up
or that person
you share space with
on the sheets.
When you roll into him
during the night
and his teeth fly up
to the ceiling,
you hold still,
listen for a sound
to explain it,
look for the book
you fell asleep reading,
then roll back over,
and the beast settles
down again beside you
like a black balloon.

I know about this beast.
He does not sleep
and he does not dream.
To himself, if asked,
he is more a beast,
knows his ugliness
to become more ugly.
Swamps dry up in his mouth.
The death of ships
under the ocean
slide in slime on his skin.
His arms are the broken
bones of asteroids,
his eyes
the open ass of Krakatoa.

And though he's never died,
his death is all he truly remembers.
Condemned to the light within the dark of sleep,
he is not permitted his own,
but puts one arm
behind his head
and thinks through the night
with you,
avoiding the beast of thoughts.
He lies beside you,
envious of your slow breathing,
wishing your dreams
were his to dream,
wanting just one
of your nightmares
to wake from.

This Storm, and the Next One

All of this pain
is an envelope.
Look what upsets you:
a spilled glass
of apple juice
and your kids,
why worry about them?
Where are your parents now,
now that you tie your shoes
and ignore your wife
who locks the doors
when you go.
An envelope, a chair,
a dish of almonds,
that ridiculous $40
hand-painted
waste-paper basket.
Today the city is under mud.
The sun comes out
and everyone's back
to buying hamburgers and gum.
I'll bet your suit is pressed.
My shoes are wet
and still I wear them
but no big thing.
Was that a neighbor of yours
who carried a bag of valuables
into the den
just before the water
swept his bedroom down the hill?
An envelope.
A chair.
A plate of cheese.
Did you read about the winter Olympics
with transit strikes and Soviet medals?
This Lake Placid is that what you mean
by pain?
An envelope.

A chair.
A line of tanks and bombs.
And what of that Greek
who burned the enemy's fleet down
by reflecting sunlight off the shields
of his men.
And that shoemaker in the lava of Pompei,
still bent over his workbench.
Envelopes, chairs, shoes, shields.
The sky is getting dark again.
They say the next storm is 200 miles
off the coast, due later tonight.
Well, it's me reaching up and dragging
all that rain down.
That's my hand going up black
behind the bushes.
Remember this storm years from now
when you are swept into the cities
by the cities,
and into the sea by the sea.
This one: an envelope,
a chair,
a line of hands
reading your own hands' future.
Stay in tonight.
Lock the doors.

Strange Visitors

I believe I have seen
whole houses lift right up
and fly off, without
a sound.

Now, the doorbell rings
and I pull my pants
up my walking legs
to get there
before my miracle goes away.

But it's just two tall girls
of the Jehova Witness—
clean and fresh flesh
under thin summer dresses
and they put into my hands
lit-ter-a-tchure, instead of their own hands.

"Look," I say, "I'm an atheist,
thank you anyway."
But they keep their smiles
and come right back.
"An atheist! Well, we can fix that.
See here on page ten
where the light
came out of the sky
and the face of the void was full?"
And I listen to their talk
full of bloom and bubbles,
shaking my head, "Ahuh, ahuh..."
Then finally:
"Look, I was beating off
when you rang the bell.
Could you come back in about ten minutes.
I'm almost finished."

I believe I have seen
strange visitors from other planets
unwrap salami sandwiches

in the park, plastic forks
in cups of chopped liver.
I believe I have seen strange faces
disappear in supermarkets.

My sister called today, long distance,
to tell me my brother's
shooting up again.
"We haven't seen him in weeks, Jack,
and I'm scared."
"Charlaine," I say, "maybe he just
went to visit that girl in Houston.
Maybe he just had to get away,
fly off somewhere."
"Maybe," she says.

The light in the sky goes away
and the night comes now
in one large, slow footstep.
I have been feeling ancient lately.
Something in me wants to go back.

I look out the window.
There goes another house.
In the distance, it looks
as it rises
like a kite.
And the doorbell rings.
And the phone rings.
And my hands,
blooming with fingers,
ring,
waiting to be answered.
And my hands, strange visitors,
fly off,
and take me
with them.

Copernicus

The whale at the extremity of the nose
the most eastern of the three in the jaw,
begins to the south at the first bend in the water
greater than fourth magnitude
and brings it to the mouth of the southern fish.

To the west and on the dark
at the head of the arrow
the more obscure on the left shoulder
the goat remains three in the middle of the body
the brighter of the two
and heel.

The dragon
in the tongue
on the jaw
above the eye
in the cheek
above the head
the most northern in the first curve of the neck
and the unconstellated between the thighs
which they call Arcturus

On the head
on the breast
on the girdle
above the seat, at the hips
at the knees
on the leg
at the extremity of the foot

at the mouth
on the head
in the middle of the neck
in the breast
the most brilliant in the tail
in the elbow of the right wing
in the flat on the wing
the middle one

the more western of the two

the greater   the smaller   the obscure

the star which is the first of all and the more
of the two on the horn
the bright one at the extremity of the river
in the hollow of the right foot

neither at rest nor in the center
at the point that makes the center,
unmoving.

Break Down

Of course, you're alone.
In America, on a Texas highway
watching the last smoke of the sun
grow black.
Without oil, without gas,
without a pay phone that works,
Tonight, you'll be killed:
that, you know.
A drunk pick-up does it as a joke,
or the night swans
who prowl for your kind,
who leave your shoes,
and take the camera,
the luggage, the money.
You're alone, you're going
to be dead, if you walk
toward the closed Texaco station
one mile up or sit it out till morning,
you're going to be dead.
Where were you going? El Paso?
On the map, for some reason,
you circled Carlsbad and Sonora.
The last for gas, you thought.
Then:
A pair of tail-lights turn
on the gravel shoulder
and slowly become headlights.
You begin to laugh,
make an outstretched gesture
with both arms wide
as if sending aloft
a dazed insect
from the palm
of each hand.

The Long Poem

The long poem
has brought seven friends
to help carry in
all his luggage

Buzzard

Buzzard makes the mountain
and says to me:
"The light. I made the light, too
and cracked those rays in my throat,
tasted what you call flesh
but was plaster, then copper,
then rusted pipe,
the blade of a knife still sharp.
Is this what your people
have come to?"

The snows melt and take with them
the cave raging of the buffalo.
My first dance. Will she dance
with me? If I squeeze her hand
will she squeeze back, and if that,
then what?
Buzzard flaps in my chest.
He wants out.
He wants to follow the trains
but to meet no train
that stops.
He wants to trust the trees
and melt the cities down
to mercury and sulphur.
Buzzard says:
"I can eat my own kind, too.
It wasn't easy, but you taught me.
And I make the light;
I go up and lay the killing
at the feet of the father
and bless its food.
Reason will justify anything
but bless the poetry
and the light will bring you up."

He has a point.
Some days, we sit in the yard
and listen to the rain

shatter on the tin shed
by the plum tree
or watch it from the bedroom window
clog the backyard drain.

Buzzard shuts his eyes and takes
my hand.

"You have two homes," he says,
"but you can only die
in one."

My Rodeo

I'm ashamed of my cheap rodeo
so I keep it secret from my friends.
It's not even as big as theirs
and needs constant repair.
"How's your rodeo?" someone asks at a party.
"Fine!" they chirp up.
They jump at the chance
to extol the virtues of their rodeo.
Pretty soon a circle gathers
and everyone's discussing its size,
weather control, the acoustics, the peanuts.
If I stay in my corner someone will notice and ask about mine.
I don't want to talk about it.
So I join in, chirping up with *you-don't-says,*
and *isn't-that-amazings* and
what-about-the functional-glitter?

By the time I get home
I'm exhausted from avoiding the subject of my rodeo.
I get home and there it is,
not much on weather control, lousy acoustics,
Styrofoam peanuts.
There's no sub-culture, no glitz-trimming,
no contour illuminations, not even jacket hitch
where the top bolt exceeds the maintenance quota lining.
I'm embarrassed and ashamed of the damn thing,
give it a kick and stub my toe, then cover it with a sheet.
Maybe smother it.

I am a man who comes home depressed, lonely,
frustrated, who tries to smother his rodeo,
his cheap rodeo.
And I haven't even the courage to do that.
Imagine smothering one's rodeo.
The shame would haunt me the rest of my life.
So after a while I take the sheet off and go to bed,
hear its slight breathing throughout the night,
its occasional cough, the short low moan
just before daybreak. My cheap rodeo.

The Easy Part

The Eiffel Tower's on the cover,
cubist, prismatic, unshaven.
I watch the rain
shine up the earth, layer by layer,
Je vois tomber la pluie.
It's all one kind of rain
or another:
rain in the teeth,
rain in the palm of the hand.
It stops everyone from talking,
this yet and yet.
Once around the earth.
There is someone
who wishes to sleep beside you,
and you consent.
Because this is the easy part.
Just before sleep.
Just what your life has been
up to now:
a bird, a little bird;
so many things,
on their way to postage.

Butcher

Butcher sipping tea.
Butcher fishing with the cord tied round his neck
as he leans over the bank, thinking:
trout or shark.

Butcher notices his mother's getting old.
Cradles her wrinkled arm in his hand.
Takes a peek at the other arm in the
bottom drawer beside the bed.

Butcher's asleep now, so don't disturb him.
Tip-toe through this part, passing
his feet sticking out from under the sheets.
Stop! He's turning over.
The mountain rearranges itself and crawls
back into the dream, that deep mouth.

It's morning, he's off to work. His hands clean
as a baby's.

Butcher's in the bank. His desk neat: each pad,
pencil, loan request arranged geometrically
like a Mondrian. Here come the customers!

Butcher checks the vault. Smells new money.

Butcher's at his desk. His foot held above the button
on the floor. Sips his tea. Waits breathlessly
for the gun-wielding, stocking-faced, blood-thirsty
robber.

The First of Everything

The first hand
does not touch you.
It is a warning.
There is the breath of rocks,
a face that holds papers down.
And the first foot
does not step out.
It too is a warning.
You see it approach on a clear night,
its heel full of crushed berries.
A reminder, but of what?
The first eye has no need of seeing
and this too
in a way you cannot understand
is a warning.

These warnings slow you down.
Then, thumping your back door
like the morning paper
comes the first mouth
tied with string
and never mind what it says,
you take it as a warning.

The first of everything
revolves like a planet
around your mind.
Your standing at the front door
is a warning.
So is your walking out.
Your day is a road
broken only by bridges.

Giving the Names to Poetry

Birds uphold and princes fart.
Along the world and around it
runs a silver ridge.

Donald Zelanka,
Jerry Pinero,
Martin Shaprio,
you'll never read your names in this poem.
Maybe one of you is a lawyer
but I doubt it.
Your names go with your faces,
your lives.
One of you still wears white socks, I bet
with brown shoes.
And who still jingles coins in his baggy slacks
(God, who wore "slacks" in 3. grade?),
and one must work now
in his father's fruit stand on Carrolton Avenue.
I can just see you
Jerry Pinero
weighing a pound of peaches while you wonder
how your name got into poetry.
And that donkey laugh of yours,
Donald Zelanka,
do your kids own it now,
with that silver watch chain
half-mooned on your belt
(God, who wore watch chains in 3rd grade!), and
Martin,
Martin Shapiro,
I know you died of leukemia
three weeks before your bar mitzvah,
and I saw you in the coffin, too,
white, yeshiva face, and you still had dandruff.
What a big dope you were,
a big Jewish dope.
In a natural history museum
I'd figure to find you behind a glass labeled:

Rare Species—The Jewish Dope.

What is this
when the world gets suited up for winter
with slow moving skies
and the only sound I hear is the humming of the refrigerator
in the cold kitchen.
What is this that I think of you,
Donald Zelanka,
Jerry Pinero,
Martin Shapiro.
What is this that I wonder
what names like yours are doing now in the world,
names typed on credit statements,
traffic tickets,
letters from Shreveport.
What is this that makes me want
to give your names to poetry,
where a ridge is all there is
dividing birds from princes
and its world gives nothing away?

Mid-Leap

I used to know what I was
talking about.

Now I know what I'm
talking about.

Inflection changes the meaning of what you are
talking about.

Re-read the second stanza and you'll see what I'm
talking about.

You could overhear, for instance, someone talking about
his lover but would you know what he was talking about
if you'd never had a lover.

Does the fish, showing off,
suffocate mid-leap?

Imagine two strangers embracing in an airport.

Talk about tacky.
Talk about science.

Assume the world strays and somehow never returns.
Do you say, "Here boy! Here boy!"
or do you wait and examine your fingernails?

Anarchy depends on perfect communication.
Its bright stare fools us.
But we love to be fooled.
Those of us with lovers are constantly fooled.
It's a way of showing off.
In a situation like this you can always
talk about

something else.

The Short Poem

The short poem
comes in
perfectly dressed
long metallic heels
that click
click   *click*
until seated
and hands on each knee
the short poem
bends forward
opening
like a spy
a small black bag
and removes
first one
then two at a time
seven white marbles
which are rolled
on the floor
to your feet.

When you pick these marbles up
all seven of them
first one
then the next six
in pairs
and bring them to your mouth,
suddenly,
looking across the room
you see
that the short poem
has somehow,
without so much as a *click,*

gone.

The Lost Things

I lost my hiking boots.
And my green sleeping bag.
Maybe someone stole them.
Anyway, they're gone.
So is my copy of
Hear Us O Lord
from Heaven
Thy Dwelling Place
by Malcolm Lowry.
So are some of my other books.
Daniele left my red baseball cap
with the silver wings of Mercury
in the bathroom at Barbera's Pizza Parlor.
And I can't find my favorite pair of scissors
either, not to mention
my Bluit camping stove
and large cooking pot.
I loaned them to Karen Kaplowitz
coming out of the Cucamonga Wilderness
and she still has them.
She's a lawyer.
Now my mail isn't coming.
Someone put in a change of address form
and the post office
has been forwarding my mail
to the Graduate Department of English
at the University of Pittsburgh.
This is true.
"Why am I losing these things,"
I keep asking.
I keep asking this.
Out loud.
I'm driving Lori crazy.
"Something strange is going on here,"
I yell.
It's getting hard to concentrate on anything
for very long.
"Where are my boots," I whine

in the middle of a movie.
My favorite hiking boots.
It's very distressing.
Someone has my sleeping bag right now
and they're hurting it.
Someone's grimy hands are pulling apart
Hear Us O Lord from Heaven Thy Dwelling Place
and they don't even care about the underlines
or the notes I've made in the margins.
I'm not going to let it get me.
The red hat, with the silver wings of Mercury,
I plan to get back if it's the last thing I do.
I'll keep a look out
and someday whoever took it
will be wearing it in the May Co.
thinking I've forgotten all about it.
But I haven't.
I'll see it.
And I'll get it back.
I'll get all my things back.
My Bluit camping stove
and my large cooking pot.
And my mail, all my mail.
My sleeping bag.
My boots.
My broken-in hiking boots.
I've missed you all so much.
So very much.
The lost things are coming back.
It's all coming back to me.
And I need to feel that I deserve this.
I need to learn
how to open my arms
and take them in,
as I would myself,
lost
these many
many
years.

Nearing the Point

Nearing the point
where the point at center
and once on its own
transforms earth to water
and back up above the shore line
around the unnecessary eyes
of its fish.
And each too to have seen it,
this black eagle
that flies out from your throat
and refuses to sing.
In our twentieth century
not because of me
not because of you
love is denied
kept silent
touches in departing
brushes us with wingtips
in cornerless space.
And higher still,
each out of desperation,
in orbit,
a little weaker,
reckless,
sprung from the bedhead
where only yesterday
we stood
surrounded by the white ash
of our bodies.
So if not dead from the black water,
then dead from the frost,
from the window from the contrary idea
and so dead in fact from peace.
Convinced by the rooms we have loved in,
I get up from my chair
and walk toward the door
in this name flying up like a balloon,
while on the earth

there is time between points
to swim up from dreams
and smell your lover's shoulder
so deep in the earth's arms of sleep.

To Write a Poem

When I sit down to write a poem
I try not to think about anything.
Sometimes, I begin with a line
that just comes to me,
a line that might make no sense whatever,
and then I have to go on from there
making more lines that make no sense
until I've found a way before the end
to make it all make sense,
some kind of sense.
Now, I'm not know for being abstract,
so when Michael Ford asks me later
at The Lair where we all go for coffee
after the poetry workshop,
"Why are you writing so abstract?"
All I can answer is,
"That was abstract?"
I look down at the poem
and it doesn't seem abstract to me.
I read the beginning out loud.
"Nearing the point where the point
at center and once on its own
transforms earth to water and back
up above the shore line
around the unnecessary eyes
of its fish.—What's so abstract about that?"
I ask.
Michael tries an answer, but it's
abstract, too.
Bob says
I should cut the line
about my name flying up like a balloon.
And I agree with him.
Enough about my name.
My flying name.
Though, I think, the name too is abstract,
a rock I keep cracking into pieces,
or a balloon that does what balloons do,

and I wish it would make up its mind,
abstract flying cracking name.
Fist, rocket, staircase.
What's in an abstract flying name, anyway?
Did you know that *slug* spelled backwards is *guls*.
Thank about that
if you want to understand what abstract means.
And I find also that I tend to leave the poems
I write
somewhere in the middle and then have to come back
to them somewhere before the end.
Like now. Like here, in this poem.
And just what the flying hell is a poem anyway?
Huh?
Huh?
HUH?
(pause)
I didn't think you knew.
Well if you don't know
how come you're always combing their hair
and holding your hands over their mouths
and tying their shoelaces together?
I see all the poems we've strapped
and tied to straight-backed chairs
in cold basement rooms,
barely bringing enough water
and bread to choke on.
I'd set them all free—
hordes of all our poems
descending upon us
in rage.
And my own head hurts.
And I'm sick of seeing my body
fill with the death of poetry.
I'm fat and getting fatter.
I can't stop eating.
I'm sick of poetry and sick of being fat.
I'm sick of combing my hair.
Sick of wearing the one shirt that fits me,
sick of seeing my desk piled with mail

and paper clips and unpaid bills,
sick of sleeping all day
and eating all night
and sick of praise and sick of grief
and sick of misunderstandings
and sick of love
and sick of fucking
and sick of jerking off
and sick of poetry, that's for sure,
sick of my poetry and sick of your poetry,
sick of everyone's poetry,
sick of reading
and sick of baseball
and sick of movies
and sick of the horses—
I like Charlie Chaplin
but I'm sick of just about everything else
and that includes poetry
which includes everything anyway.
And I'm sick of this poem, too.
This poem that makes such sense,
that flies off, like my name.
It nears the point
where the point at center
and once on its own
transforms earth to water
and back
up above the shoreline
around the unnecessary eyes
of its fish.
And it's abstract.

Like a rock.

Like a slug
that spelled backwards
becomes a large white bird
that screams out in the air
and flies far
far away.

The Lover

A book with a picture on the cover
of a lady dressed in red on my desk.
This woman I love
trying her tennis shoes up on her feet.
A root-briar pipe,
straight-grained and carbon-caked
leaning on the rim
of the cork-centered ash tray.
A memory in the room
that settles like netting
as I enter,
the big house with winding
tunneled stairs.
These I own, these thoughts,
that book,
the woman I love,
my pot-bowled pipe.
And they own me,
they stretch and spread
and suck my flesh
not just into themselves
but out to air,
out above the hills and water,
in touch with
some-un-named holy voice
that calls me to my life.
And I am this one man
attached beyond beauty
to forms I cannot imitate.
And woman too,
I touch my nipples
and run my hands over the cool
flesh of my ass,
and I am woman too,
barely sensing that other beauty
I lost long ago.
And I touch each part of me
that walks in red dresses,

that thing smoked
those shoes laced,
these memories loved.
And I am open,
if not always,
then now,
to leave my hands on table-tops
and give up,
to let go,
to walk from my bed
in the morning,
open a window,
lean out,
open my mouth to speak
say nothing but song,
to flap my arms
and fly off,
to sail out
beyond the map
of my own
un-
traveled face.

Bodies

At first I am talking
about my body,
then something else.
What do you know
about bodies.
When Ben and I
have to move them
from one table to another
they're so heavy
and stubborn and clumsy.
Ben lifts the head
and puts a block underneath.
It's like lifting a broken desk lamp.
I swing the feet up
and straighten them.
Always under the cover.
When I go home
I sometimes think about
the part of my own body
I am soaping in the shower.
This hand holding *this* breast.
Why does touching myself here
feel better than touching myself
there?
Whose hands would feel better?
There is so much about bodies
I don't understand.
Sometimes, after we make love,
I discover that I'm bleeding.
There's a spot on the sheets,
and between my legs when I wipe myself
in the bathroom.
He comes in to watch, concerned.
Blood comes off in my hands
but after a bit the bleeding stops.
We're both naked.
There's a little blood on his penis.
I watch him wash it in the sink.

It's as if he were bleeding too.
Back in bed, lying side by side,
we talk about the bodies
then fall asleep.
When I wake during the night
I can hear his heavy breathing.
I lay my hand across his belly.
He turns and snugs his ass
up against my side
and I turn with him
throughout the night;
a kind of dance, a breathing,
a small exchange of words.
To wake in the morning
beside someone you love
is a miracle in itself.
Then the bodies get up
and have breakfast.

There is no insurmountable solitude.
All paths lead to the same goal:
To convey to others what we are.

—Pablo Neruda
Toward the Splendid City (Nobel Lecture)

Another Sentence

Every sentence is another sentence,
really another life.
Someone's always one step ahead.
The streets glow from the snow plow's blade
chipping up stone with a daylight flash.
From here, the same tree out back,
the same asphalt roof,
the same wounded clothes pins
shifting on the line.
Sometimes the man hanged is a hero,
sometimes a traitor.
Perfect sight and perfect blindness
when it suits our needs.
One day you realize
that you cannot break out
of your own bones.
There is snow-mush in the gutters
and along the edge of the highway,
melting here, turning to rock there.
Something's always a step ahead.
Every sentence is another life,
really another sentence.

The Surrealist Poem

Just a minute.
Can't you see I'm talking to someone.
Come back another time.
Or wait until I'm finished.
See that goldfish over there,
The one with the mag wheels
And carnation in its lapel
Right next to my copy of *New Directions.*
You can't miss it.
Where is your heart.
Why are you so sad.
Live a little.
There's still time.
You can't lose.

A Burning

Old cans full of sour milk
stacked in the back room,
his shoes, boxes of them,
not to throw anything away,
even shoelaces for sentiment
remembered in leaning cardboard boxes
once used to pack pillows before
the house burned down.
He smells that all the time:
the dry burning wood,
wet strips of ash and black puddles of water.
Sometimes he can trace the smell to something real.
Sometimes, to something else, coming or having come.
It will come again, he reasons,
and begins again to pack things away
so that what will burn will burn together,
each head in its proper place.

I remember his standing out back without tie or hat
looking up at the house, his shoes caked with mud
and the black marbles of charcoal he kicks with his toes.
The palmetto trees take up the sounds of the wind
and pass them down Elysian Fields Avenue.
A storm is coming
and I catch the bristle run up my back
as I watch him from the window
stoop to the burned pieces of wood,
the half-blackened fence posts,
a piece of metal covered with ash.
He stands and turns and sees me,
and I rise the man above him to him the boy below me
afraid to look at the unburned skin of his own hands.
Later, he brings the smell in with him to the table,
and leaves it on the chairs, and the sofa,
and the bed he takes for a month.
The last day with us he spends
talking to my father in the kitchen,
his hands flopped like fish in his lap,

and the burning and the burned
spread across the life of his back.
Had my father lived I might have yet remembered to ask
just who he was in his black coat,
this man with bad breath who looked at me in fright
as some other life unburned.
Had my father lived,
I might have yet asked just who he was:
A half-brother?
A friend? Another
Jew, passing through.
But I am not ungrateful of puzzles that grow strong
against the known and the sure,
nor the smell a man brings and takes with him.
I have that smell too somewhere.
I can recognize it from blocks away,
and sometimes days ahead.
I can look at you and tell if the smell of a burning in me
is the same as the smell of a burning in you.
I can tell who brings it in their hands,
how the bleach of their faces
wants one such burning to replace another.

Some Life

Some life that seems better than none
and all the beautiful women
who do their hair with Head shampoo
and never spill the ketchup.

inside the nightingale
the bat
and inside the leopard
the leopard

Now there are women
who sit with other women
or they sit alone
and I sit alone and watch them.
Just once I'd like one to get up
and come over to my table
and ask to sit and talk.
Give me that chance to show
that I am a man
who would make friends with women
and just that
and no more,
as if that were an honorable
place to stop,
an easy place to come to.

Some life is always better than none.
Inside each of us
that other animal,
as proud as hungry as fearful
as dangerous.

I think women are afraid of us
because we murder in ourselves
what they love too much in life to lose,
and there is no room now for love,
or friendship.

But I am not afraid of you.
I love your smells,

I love the blood that stains your underwear.
I love the rash under your arms
and the fat
below your buttocks & between your thighs
you pinch and wish away.
And that illusion of self
we both adhere to,
well . . .
we can forgive each other
for wanting this darkness
to see itself first in the eyes of the enemy.

Some life is all we have.
A marriage that lasts 10 years;
A love affair for 2;
A weekend with a stranger;
A voice on the phone—
wrong number.

and inside the nightingale
the bat
and inside the leopard
the leopard

Some men; some women;
some life.

Each one
inside
the other.

Poem without Picture for Picture without Poem

Dear *American Poetry Review.*
Enclosed are several pictures of me,
one of which
I would like you to consider
for publication in your paper.
I realize that along with each
poet's picture
you print a poem or two,
but I'm not sure I have any
that you would like.
Can I have a picture
without a poem
published?
I feel so different
with the camera.
The poem, of course,
is another matter.
I could just as well
fall flat on the page
and be done with it—
this creeping out
word by word
takes my breath away.
The pictures, though,
remain whole.
You can see where I gained weight
last summer
and the beard I grew
for a lover.
But smiling or not,
they're all just me,
arms open,
placing all that dumb trust
in this dumb world.
Sometimes, just looking at those pictures,
I want them to change me,
to give me back
the face I've been.

But, it's still my face
looking back at all of you,
daring you all to look back.
I've been looking back
at all the poets' pictures
you've published since you began.
They're good faces.
We've got such strong, healthy,
beautiful poets in this country.
It's time to face the poem
of all our faces,
and it's good that there's a place
we can look back at each other.
Thanks for considering *my* face.
Sincerely yours,

Jack Grapes

Trying to Get Your Life in Shape

It's like doing the roof.
Just when you've got the slate set,
the tacks in your mouth,
the tar hot and ready,
your foot accidentally
nudges the hammer
and it begins to slide away
from you
like a christened ship.
Down it goes.
You hear the crash below,
take a deep breath, say *shit*,
and turn for the ladder
just as it
catches a wind
and begins the long lean
away from your outstretched hand.
Aww, shit!
You look up.
Storm clouds from out of nowhere
belly over the setting sun.
The dark ice age is at hand.
And no one is home.
And the doors are locked.
Your baloney sandwich
has been pecked away by birds.
You sit back,
you contemplate this new richness
come into your life,
and shiver on the roof
knowing it could be worse.
Why you could be inside.
Warm by the fire.
Sipping sherry.
Shoes off.
Just
temporarily
alive.

End of Conversation Overheard on a Train

"... and so
his foot
was of no further
use to him ...

not as a foot
that is."

My Life

Now that's a log cabin if I ever saw one!
Someone else left that message.
I'm fishing.

Yet another silver fender blade.
See around the edges all those paper cuts.
But with summer this close, ear to jaw.
Lovers just don't care for politics.

You can wear any coat to the dance.
If all black then you must know something.
Each vest should contain a secret.
Who did you kill wearing those shoes?

I have this delicate relationship with my dreams.
Run for your life!
Will this gray rain ever stop!
The closer I look, the less I dream.

Some say there's method to one's madness.
Delirium is robbed of its meager truth
as madness if its called a *Work of Art.*
The chance to see being born, over and over.

After a while, even De Sade bores me.
Violence promises to recover the self,
but you can't limit the world that wounds you
any more than you can disappear into Nature
when Nature is invisible to begin with.

To lose everything at the movies
is an act of faith.
Scene. Close-up. Tracking shot. Dissolve.
You think that's something.
You should see my life.

What Is Wrong with the Weather

points of stars
small crabbed webs
if anything can gleam
a fall
hair brush
on my sister's
another morning
lap
and pencil
barely audible
testing memory
so much wrong
with the weather
he is inside
thinking
the time to get it right
is now
both hands
around both hands
look up
the stars
unable to breathe
till you do.

Why I Am Not a Sardine

After Frank O'Hara

I'm not a sardine, I'm a painting.
Why? I guess I'd rather be a
sardine, but I'm not. Well,

for example, Michael Ford
is cutting a poem into shreds. I drop in.
"Hang out the window and bleed," he
says. I hang; we bleed. I look
up. "You've got some poem there."
"Yes, it needs shredding THIS POEM."
"Oh," I go and the years fly by
and I'm still bleeding. I stop by.
The poem is still being shredded
into smaller and smaller pieces.
And the years go by, bleeding,
the two of us, almost finished.
"The poem's finished," he says.
"Where's the poem?"
All that's left is blood.
"It was too much," Mike says.

But me? One day I am eating a sardine.
A silver sardine.
I bleed into its mouth.
Pretty soon it's a whole fish of blood,
not even a fish anymore,
shredded.
Then another shred,
scale upon scale.
Lifesize to scale.
Wonderful silver.
Bloodthirsty.
There are more fish than sardines.
Life is horrible. Fish accept
the passage of time; the days
go by; years shredded into poets.
My meal is finished and I haven't even
mentioned I've been hanging out the window

all this time.
And one day, at a poetry reading,
Mike throws confetti over his audience,
and announces that it's not a poem,
but his old friend, Jack, a sardine.

The Serious Poem

There is no time.

And you can't win.

Confessional

I wish I could write it once and easy
to belong to me.
It always belongs to you.
And you never care to know
if it's once and easy
when it's yours.
What is going to grow in the heart
that is not ventured
or given with the hands open and up
to being within you again
when all you can say is how saddled horses
wait by the tent
or how mountains predict misfortune
or how your legs are the legs of a woman
and your breasts too yet you are afraid
of what you really know, believe only
what they tell you.
Everything you dare not say
truly yours
and so abandoned, like a viewpoint.
Will you count insults and grievances
or stand once and easy with the grief.
I wish I could write it once
and it would belong to me
and no one else,
but it always belongs to you.

To My Father, the Captain

In this wake
where blood separates me from midwives,
my father lies in his coffin,
engines cut,
his face done up,
still commanding me
not to exceed him.

But what excess, and whose?
I can go too far, I can not go
far enough.
Either way you win.
Dad, all I know in this life
is the way
through excess:
Too much pie in the face;
Too much flesh on the bone;
Too many words.

Power in the perfect ending,
in the gold piece
on the dining room table.
Power to make your son
frozen in his life,
the way you were
in yours.

You never thought
the gift of poetry
you gave like a meager token
would set me free.
I do this for myself, Dad,
not for you.
For you, I would
peel my flesh away,
inhabit stale bedrooms;
For you,
I would never try hard enough,
sell shoes,

look for my face
on the bathroom floor
where you told me it would be.
But look at the dream I am rising from.
For you,
I would chisel the stone
in my chest,
walk with my shoulders bent forward,
mumble my name.
For you, I would ride the whale down
to your ship on the reef,
not shine for myself
in his belly.

For me
I write this poem.
This is the power, Daddy:
that I will finish this poem
the way I want to,
with my name,
not the way you'd have liked,
with yours.

love,

Jack

On Raising the Hand

On Tuesdays I get up at 4:30 A.M.
to teach poetry in the schools.
My first class starts at 7:20—
it's called *zero period,*
which to me is very ominous
as if it were the final meeting
before the end of the world,
a final poetic countdown.
The students are tired, you can tell,
and drag on in without saying much—
to me—to each other.
When I read a poem and ask who liked it,
no one raises a hand.
"So how many didn't like the poem?" I ask.
Still, no one says a thing; no hands go up.
This is zero period. Barely out of sleep.
We sit drugged like flies at the screen.
I go home tired as well, feeling I've failed.
It's best to think of this as just a job.
I get paid for this, and that makes me honorable.
Poetry doesn't. Poetry gets me vacant stares.
And yet, from this thing we pay so little for,
we want so very much.
Sleepy, tired, educationally bewildered,
what they want is for me to set something on fire,
to open a door to another world,
to change them.
For a penny I'd throw myself at their feet
just as long as they'd embrace this thing
that sucks the blood from me and speaks always
in more voices that I can hear at one time
while the monotonous voice of the world drones on
about how to keep from dying in the cold of a strange city.
And then, today I come home and read the poems
they have written after weeks of treading
the waters of process.
Richard writes:
Was it you who used to look

people in the eye?
David writes:
This is not all that matters I like this.
Life it is not out this class.
Cindy feels she's being tortured and starved,
maybe for being beautiful, instead of useful.
Sam thinks
writing
is the first of all things
that builds up the world.
Charlie looks into the fish bowl and wonders if there is
loneliness in the unblinking eyes
of his guppy.
Bobby writes that
Dancing shoes that dive with desire
tremble with the fear they've failed.
And Tom ends his poem:
The glory that cloaks me is dying.

I read their poems in the early morning and raise my hand.
They've set something on fire.
They've opened a door for me.
I embrace their words, their courage.
In the cold of a strange city,
I keep from dying,
both my hands go up.

No Way to Break a Branch

This is no way to break
a branch.

The eels would not fear
you.

Imagine it is your neck.
Suck up your courage.
The juice of life calls.

Forget technique.
Go to it.   Dig in.

To Board the Bus

Just make enough sense
to board the bus,
he said.
I board the bus,
but I don't make sense,
I said.
Better to make sense,
he said, and stand in the street.
I stand in the street
but get nowhere for all my sense, I said.
For all your sense,
he said,
you don't have to go anywhere.
People will come to you.
They will board the bus?
I asked.
Exactly, he said.
Then let's stand
and make sense together,
I said.
Two of us making sense,
he said,
and the world will move.
Exactly, I said. I feel it already.
What you feel, he said
is the bus coming our way.
Then let it pass, I said.

The Children Look for Crabs on the Beach

There's a reason for this:
You put on your trunks and go stand by the water, watch
the guts of this planet wash up on the sand.
Two girls dig in the root-bones of a plastic-looking sea plant.
They say they are looking for crabs for their collection
and show you a half-filled paper cup stuck in the wet sand.
I'm not satisfied not knowing anymore
what is wrong with me,
what storm is tearing me apart
plank by plank on the rough sea.
I'm not satisfied anymore going from metaphor to metaphor:
a sinking ship,
a drowning sailor,
a beached hulk of a sea monster blinded on the beach
being picked apart by children.
I look out to sea and read the poets for comfort,
but if poetry is to save me,
it'll have to be my own, full of lies and mischief,
and the one paperweight of truth
that keeps everything from flying off.
I want to toss that paperweight out to sea,
that smug stone so breathless on my desk.
So I go back to my car,
shake the sand out of my shoes,
check the mirror to see if I've gotten any sun.
What do I need sun for anyway?
What do I need anything for anyway?
Why can't I fix the sink?
Why am I not more ambitious?
Why won't I come back to me?
I drive off down the highway
in my car that needs fixing everywhere.
God, I feel like a housewife
in someone else's soap opera.
Christ, I feel like laughing.

Orestes

Remember the truth
is all that changes.
Lies remain the same,
true to their cracks.
One degree at a time.
Oblivious to the mark.
Certainty is the lie
that lures us
once and for all
to be once and for all
true.
Made perfect by suffering.

Final Exam

Can you have a spree of cheese?

Would you loan a bank a flush?

Why is the back door of your house
  so morbid?

When you tie your shoes, do you
  indicate with word or gesture
  your preference for boots
  or do you have something
  to hide?

Say three words that don't dissolve
  or melt or evaporate or turn
  to powder and blow away
  without a fare-the-well or
  so much as a kiss.

Dillinger puts a nickel on the porch
  when he wants a newspaper
  but now he's dead. Some say
  he's alive still. Is this fair
  and why must the law
  protect the innocent?

Are you tired, listless, depressed, suicidal,
  rabid, loquacious, engaged, visionary,
  plastic, fiber, traffic, a kosher
  pickle, exact change? How could you
  stop this and change your life?

Would you rather live in New York or
  cash a ten-dollar bill?

What does the word *gaberlunzie* mean?
  Look it up.

Why is symmetry happy? How does grief expand?
  Is retribution a crystal?

Think of someone you've offended, grievously
wronged. Is there any way you could
make it worse? Is there any area that
remains unwounded? What are the prospects
for permanent injury? Is your day booked,
or do you have time to settle this matter?

How do you adjust?

Why does the broom whisk; is there any edge
to an elephant; what mystery burns your heart
the best?

Home Free

We're buying groceries for dinner
at the Vegas mini-mart,
so I plunk two quarters into the slot machine
stationed by the check-out counter
and on the second quarter hit a $12 jackpot.
The tin cup is designed to make it seem like I've blown up
Fort Knox and bells go off to let the customers know
there's a silver waterfall, one to a customer.
I'm hooked and I know it.
I give the money away, three bucks apiece to Vern
and Katharine and Lori, saying here's some lucky quarters
but I'm really just trying not to hoard the luck.
Too much might go off in my hands.
Too much might alert the gods.
This luck is stolen, and after all the other luck
that's come my way—well, I've got to be careful
is all. Now we're in the casino,
the big time. Vern hits a $50 jackpot.
I'm at the blackjack table losing my breath.
Lori and Katharine are in the bar picking up strangers
while UCLA loses on a field goal to Arizona.
I lose another $20 at blackjack waiting for my free drink.
By the time we leave I'm $60 down, probably $100.
Next day at the Crystal Bay Club I pick up $100
at blackjack. Lori convinces me to leave a winner.
But I know I'll be back. The next morning we're back
and I drop $120. By the time we get to Reno
I can't tell for sure if I'm up or down.
Quarters go into the machines as I go by.
I'm pulling handles down the way I'd strip bark
from a tree or rickety-rick a stick against a fence
when I was a kid. I walk by a blackjack table, bet $40
and win. Walk off and put chips on roulette and lose.
Fork up a few bills at another table and win on two kings.
Bells go off, lights blink.
All you have to do here is win one jackpot,
one big fat fucking jackpot and the rest is history.
Lori's grabbing my arm and Katharine's hungry

and Vern's walking slow and easy out the door.
This quarter, this next quarter, this $5 yellow chip,
this $25 black chip, this is the one that does it,
one more plunk, one more pull of the handle and it's done,
we're home free, we escape the pull of gravity,
we're off this rotten earth and heading for the stars.
"Lose here, win everywhere else," I say
as we get back in the car.
Merry Christmas, friends. Happy New Year.

I Just Had to Tell You

Listen I just had to tell you
I wrote five poems today.

Can you believe it—five poems!

Russia's still in Afghanistan
the hostages are still hostages
ah forget 'em
another storm coming
and other one for Sunday
fuck it
radioactive rain
the candidates on TV
elect 'em for all I care
we need ten presidents anyway
all those homes slipping into mud

destruction

death

one man looking for his wife
another girlfriend
hoping her lover is alive
and they're starving in Asia
and the blacks in Africa
are overrunning the white man's cities
well, come on,
drop the bombs here for a change
swarm up our black beaches
set fire to the whole Archipelago—
taxi A-bomb sewer rats parades
the tired and the hungry and the weak
up from the bottom of the sea
the molten core of the earth
and comets
strike us,
asteroids
planets
off their course

another sun
moving our way
fuck it fuckit fckit
I wrote five poems today.
This is the sixth.
Whoooopeeeeeee!

So Many

So many plays
and novels
and stories
and essays
and history books
and philosophy
and science fiction
and fiction
and science.
I thought once I was going to write them,
a novel, or a story, or a play.
I don't think so anymore.
It's so hard to write a novel.
You have to work at it every day
and you have to type up at least 200 pages,
even if you never go to a second draft.
And a play?
All those characters,
and scenes, and lights,
the changing sets,
and worst of all
the actors, acting.
Genghis Khan, Attila, Hitler,
Vlad the Impaler
are nothing compared to what
actors can do to a play
once they get to say the words out loud.
No, I won't be writing any plays.

And stories, fiction . . .
what can I say.
Men left the tribe and headed into the dark forest,
climbed out over the black mountains
and were gone for years. We were children
when they left,
but when our children mark off
a new boundary with boulders,
they come back, full of scars, jewels,

and strange women with shaved heads.
And they begin to tell stories.
And our children listen, and we listen,
and the weather and the seasons
and the sun on its way across
stop until the stories are all told.
That's what I think about
when I think about stories.
I won't be writing
any of those.

What, that's not in a play, or a novel,
or a story
can I possibly tell you.
How can I write enough and the kind of words
that conceal the lack
of anything true.

There is only this one,
true, utterly beautiful poem.
And each of us, possibly one time
in our lives,
can write it.
I would like to do that.
I would like to try that.
And when you write yours
I would like to hear it.
It's the same poem, each of us have to write.
So we'll know it when we see it.
So many plays, and novels, and stories.
But only one
poem.

I Like My Own Poems

I like my own poems
best.
I quote from them
from time to time
saying, "A poet once said,"
and then follow up
with a line or two
from one of my *own* poems
appropriate to the event.
How those lines sing!
All that wisdom and beauty!
Why it tickles my ass
off its spine.
"Why those lines are mine!"
I say
and Jesus, what a bang
I get out of it.

I like the *ideas* in them,
my poems,
ideas that hit home.
They *speak* to me.
I mean, I understand
what the hell
the damn poet's
talking about.
"Why I've been there,
the same thing," I shout,
and Christ! What a shot it is,
a shot.

And hey.
The words
Whew!
I can hardly stand it.
Words sure do not fail
this guy, I say.
From some world
only he knows

he bangs the bong,
but I can feel it
in the wood,
in the wood of the word,
rising to its form
in the world.
"Now, you gotta be good
to do that!" I say
and damn! It just shakes
my heart,
you know?

Shall we put in the heart now?

—Dr. Ernst Praetorius
The Bride of Frankenstein

The Poet's Funeral

Friends, we write the eulogy
and it is crap.
We praise the bird that barely
survives the rainstorm,
we make miracles of the poetry
written on, what?—paper!
and not the other kind
this is just her arms around me.
We believe the spirit
does not die with the man
when most often it dies before.
Shovel the bastard down, I say
and cover the pine with leaves.
A kick of dust and a what's for supper
will do any time.
Flesh!
Even now you're more concerned
with your itching leg
that sets the table and warms the palm
just midnight to a lover
and as it should be!
Talk to me for chrissakes! is what I say.
Toss the glass once in the air
and let it smash wine and all and say
good for that and riddance.
Stalk your own hearts and be ruthless about it,
swing each high in the air and wait
for the music to begin again
and when it does
with a hard hard heel and laughter
that fills a fist,
dance on, dance on.

Here's a Poem

Here's a poem that has not
been revised or rewritten
or read aloud or cut
or extended or given to a lover.
Here's a poem that
has no code word, no
name for something else,
no intended meaning,
no axe to grind.
Here's a poem inconsequential
as a thumbtack.
Give me a penny for it
and you've overpaid.
Lose it and it's still there
for all that it was worth.
Here's a poem less than
twenty lines.
Defend it.

Voyage

Now on the table
all my friends in ties
waving goodbye.
This voyage.
And so much time
taken to learn again
what we once knew
from each other
and forgot.
It's still daylight
but I can see the moon.
Almost
or so it seems
transparent.
Not even a full moon.
But a full moon.

Passing the Ketchup

She says pass the ketchup
and I grab the salt shaker
and stretch it across the table.
"The ketchup," she says.

The lawn chair's full of rust
and the nylon straps in straggles.
It leans in the corner of the garage.
"Let's throw it out," she says.
"Not yet," I tell her. "Maybe we'll find
something to do with it."

We come home from the beach
and a trail of ants
flow to and from
the sugar bowl
down the counter to the floor
and out the screen door.
"Look at them all!" she shouts.
So I do.

These men grow old in my body.
They take such slow steps,
and take all morning
to drink a glass of milk.
They find nothing familiar
in the familiar,
debate the eye of the city
and the hand of the country.
They fall asleep in the kitchen.

"Where are the car keys?" she asks.
"The car keys," I repeat,
unable to remember
what is a car
and what is a key.
Finally:
"In the car," I say.
"The keys."

I wake in the middle of the night
to answer the phone.
Hello. Hello.
Nothing but the sound of someone's breathing
coming from the other end.
It sounds like my own,
but I can't be sure.
"Who was it?"
"Who was what?"
"On the phone!"
"Me. I think."

Today I sit on the beach
and watch the waves come in,
break in a stiff white line
forty feet out,
and carry the boogie-boarders
to the edge of the sand still standing.
There is nothing on the horizon.
Not a storm coming our way,
not a black ship,
no land.
We are all stretched on beach towels
inching the white breast out for a tan.
We are all lying here at the edge
of a continent.

I get up and brush the sand from my body.
I take the napkins we brought
with the food in the ice-chest
and stick one each into my ears
and nose: wings of a sort.
Then another I roll for a fang.
Insert it under my top lip,
hunch over, and limp down the sand
like a walrus trying to dance
on the edge of the berm.
The kids step back at first,
then begin to mimic me;
finally, they join in, following me
as our footprints just above the water line

one on top of the other
change and grow larger, deeper.
A single new life form
come out of the water,
come out from the land.

“What do you think you’re doing?” she calls.

“Passing the ketchup,” I say.

A Deed of Light

My sister dies.
I am not born yet.
She barely strikes soul
and goes.
My Uncle Jack dies.
I am not born yet.
It is right
to give me his name.
Among other things
it means
something smaller
than the usual of its
kind;
a small stuffed puppet
set up to be pelted
for sport.
For years they call me
Jackie.
My father sneers.
What kind of name is that!
Uncle Charles dies.
Everyone in the kitchen
stands and cries.
A year later
on the kitchen floor
Uncle Lou dies
vomiting on the newspaper
under his head.
I bring him more newspaper.
My socks flap at the toes.
My name is Jack:
a small national flag
flown by a ship.
The next year
we move to the new house.
This time of brick.
Martin Shapiro dies.
My mother drags me to the wake.

In the open coffin
his face
can be seen
all the way from the back
of the chapel.
Applejack, jackknife,
jack-o-lantern.
Aunt Adela dies
all summer in the back bedroom.
Withers on the sheets of cancer.
Jackie, she says,
show me the movies.
My mother prances
with grief around the grave.
Sarah Bernhardt.
A year later, of cancer too,
she gets it down.
Hisses bitch at the nurse
the last two days.
When I leave for Europe
I forget to tell my father
goodbye.
In Italy the phone rings.
Come home, it says,
you're the man in the family
now.
Jacksnipe, jackstraw,
jack-in-the-box.
From tides to bushes
on Sundays,
each of us digs holes
in the backyard.
This growing further apart.
Karl who is my brother.
Louis who is my brother.
Charlaine who is my sister.
Jacksmelt, jackshaft,
jackpot.
I am Daniele's Uncle Jack.
I am Benjamin's Uncle Jack.

I am Ari's Uncle Jack.
My arms become trees
solitary with the base pale face
of a green kitchen door,
jewels for teeth to kill my father,
see me, see you,
see who dies on Tuesday.

No more of graves and names.
On the dead I spit on the dead of the dead.
The Jack deads and the Charles deads
and the mother deads and the father deads.
My name beats the bush
that sends up flocks of birds.
This lantern cut to look
like a human face.
The name looks out of my eyes.
The meaning looks out of my name.
Jack is a deed of light.

Another Sleepwalk

So severe and desperate is the heart's resistance
to cold crying sleep
that its one finger thrusts up screaming
at particles of separation
the dead cough up.
No, it says. No.
Those gods who walk on thin legs
and refuse to speak
counsel us to do the same.
A speechless bravery.
Well, tracks beaten in the canefields
are more determined in their course
than we with our nail of science
on the one hand,
a brief and perfect faith on the other.

I do not always sleep in peace.
She wakes beside me and pads off into the kitchen,
and I know how large out there is darkness,
a plain brown pillow thrown to the corner
of the room.
It is there for her, beastly in its fold of gray,
loving another deep death deep deep within her
and I am afraid that one can swallow the other
as easily as I fall asleep again,
passing so easily into dream.

What a lovely and beautiful and tingling thing
this fear is,
and I see my arms go out and take it all around.
And my fear in the night takes hold of itself
and dances back with the darkness.

How love can know from its losing
is beyond me,
but it does.
Yet the space grows to include us all.
We are big
for being so small

as to make the rest so large.

And we bring the light again
and say the words
and give the voice a shape
that says yes,
and again says yes.

Then:
lightswitch; footsteps; bedcover.

Then it is that her body slides up to mine
and the world
in its limping way
goes on.

Testimony

Why should I lie?
Ask any bed, the stutter gives it away.
One machine measures the heart beat;
others, more sophisticated,
the dilation of the eye,
the contraction of the pupil.
I still don't have a son
or for that matter, a daughter,
but loved as I am by children,
I wonder if I've not gone already
in some larger way beyond paternity,
the excessive transformation of my genes.
I am still here, and still there,
and already continuing in concrete and ash.
Why should I even think of lying?
The real killers are to be congratulated,
slapped on the back and toasted
for their inscrutable ingenuity,
the way a decision is sounded like an earthquake.
I'm always appalled by the ones
who pucker their lips and cannot laugh.
The pain,
to be humourless, tightly bound by logic,
the very idea that understanding
is not a killing, knowledge not a form
of asphyxiation.
It touches me that we whittle our lives down
to the smallest of entries in a notebook,
the notebook we carry with us on daily routine,
the notebook no one is ever allowed to read,
filled with one lie after another,
but our true children nonetheless.
Dare I let them out to have lives of their own?
Dare I give them up and admit
I am the father, I am the mother?
I would have my children carry on
with their own names, look back at me
and remember that what I did I did

out of love, that murder is always
an intentional accident, living easily
between the grain of expansion and the grain of collapse.
This is only part of the evidence.
I've never meant to lie.

Vows

We're going to get married
and have kids
and live together
and be bloody

Trees, Coffee, and the Eyes of Deer

Do you want coffee?
He was only nineteen when his first book of poems
  was published.
I wasn't going to go back.
I was going to sleep at the edge of the driveway
  in my sleeping bag,
  until all the cars
  went up in smoke and teach 'em.
My mother sat on the flesh of her face
  such grimness in her palms
  such unpitying bitterness.
But I digress.

The cities too in my back bedroom,
  18-Century St. Petersburg under the desk
    where it belongs;
  the Paris of Abelard and Eloise high
    on the carpet;
  smoky London and shrill New York take up
    the whole closet,
    and even tho' I keep promising
    to farm the clutter,
    I just close my eyes
    when I reach for a shirt
    and slam the door shut again.

More coffee?
Sometimes inventing conversation is impossible.
  "Shall we get in the car?"
  "Your perfume smells lovely."
And everything is about three weeks, if it's important;
  two months if a hand-me-down;
  a year if you like jazz or Isak Dinesen.
Then my father falls to the floor like a tree under
  thunder boom on his back and down comes
  the phone and the phone book boom and
  his startled eyes boom back at me
  because I had pushed him.
Lately I can't remember the dreams.

When I wake, they scamper off, like deer.
At best, I remember the eyes of the ones
who stop and turn to look back at me.
"I mean you no harm," I call out to them,
but they swing and leap away.

The tree I can see from here next to the garage
is still as a brick, and as smug.
So solid to have lived this long,
another life in the city worthier than mine,
thick-barked to my own thin skin.
"Fuck you, tree! Up yours!" I yell out the window.
But I digress.

No I don't. Nothing here is digression.
If you can't tell digression from inclusion,
why don't you try Hy's Deli on Beverly.
They make a great brisket sandwich.
And in March, the deer from their winter of hunger
come after the running dogs to be fed
in the kitchen where my mother flips through
the pages of my first book of poems.
They mean nothing to her. Which is okay.
It's the idea of them she can't stand.
She holds the book the way you'd hold a rock
that has just come flying through the window
and landed messageless on the table.
No one seems to know
when my father is coming home.
"He may never come home," my sister says.
Mom pushes the book across the table
as though she were brushing aside a fly
that had landed on her arm.
"Up yours, too!" I say to her now,
dead tho' she is.

Is this how people talk in a Russian novel?

Well I don't care anymore how they talk,
how the dead persist in their life after death.
It is us they need, not the other way around.
Today I take care of that tree, that goddamn tree.

I'm going down there and pick a fight
if I have to.
Take it apart with my bare hands
if it comes to that.

This is between us, the living.

Any landing
you can walk away from
is a good landing.

—Superchicken

AND THE RUNNING FORM,
NAKED, BLAKE

And before hell mouth; dry plain
and two mountains;
On the one mountain, a running form,
and another
In the turn of the hill; in hard steel
The road like a slow screw's thread,
The angle almost imperceptible,
so that the circuit seemed hardly to rise;
And the running form, naked, Blake,
Shouting, whirling his arms, the swift limbs,
howling against the evil . . .

—Ezra Pound
Canto XVI

Nothing

It's not Freud or western civilization,
It's not wheat germ or tractors,
It's not strange men standing around shopping malls
    looking to gun us all down,
It's not the concrete slabs that cover our brothers
It's not someone's love letter lying in the gutter,
It's not the messages on our answering machines,
It's not sex surveys nor voting polls,
It's not the mediocre poems,
It's not the gifted who commit suicide,
It's not the gifted who cannot do themselves in
    but hang on in a kind of graceful stupor,
It's not a John Ford film,
It's not the Hard Rock Café,
It's not your mother (even though you thought it was)
It's not postage or paperclips or tax forms or mule deer,
It's nothing,
not even nothing, certainly not nothing,
if it was nothing, which Wittgenstein says is nonsense,
it would be nonsense, which is something.
It's not space within space nor the vacuums within space,
    the quantum fluctuations out of which all the somethings come,
it's less than that,
so much less, that stretched to infinity,
it's still nothing,
nada nothings, nien nothings, nyet nothings,
no nothings, not nots never nones,
zilches, millions of zilches, zilch to the zilch power,
    which is still more than I had in mind.
It's your life, and this poem, and everything that lies between.
It's this poem
that will save you,
when everything else
is nothing,
and your life
which is something
goes on with greater effort
than you can manage or imagine.

L.A. in the Morning

There's a 47% chance that a 7.5 earthquake will
hit the L.A. area sometime in the next five years."

—*Los Angeles Times*, December 2, 1992

L.A., your earthquakes slam me to the floor,
and I beg for more.
Anything you ask, I'm yours.
Earthquake, fire, pestilence, flood; I deserve them all.
L.A., where are you in the morning when I need you.
Where are your bungalows and movie stars
    who come to eat my head off
    with their love scenes and car chases.
L.A., where are you in the morning when I need you,
  your bug-eyed money lenders promising the new house,
  the new school,
  the new shoes lined on the closet floor,
  shined and shining.

L.A., you're hamstrung and bleating,
  squealing like a pig about to be castrated.
We're coming to you in the morning
      to make over our lives.
We want our star on your sidewalk.
Why does my neighbor sing her scales thrice a week?
  Why isn't she out filling her face with food and
  gliding up the coast highway to get the hell outta here?

L.A., I don't know how to leave you.
I want to breathe better air and drive without bullets
  and drive without fenders backing into my teeth.
I want to walk out of my back door into a YARD
  and barbeque a steak and baked potato
  and have my neighbor BOB slap me
  on the back and shove another beer into my hand.

L.A., where are you in the morning
  when I am trying to leave you and cannot,
  cannot leave the lines or the hoaxes.

L.A., L.A., where are you in the morning
  when I need you to want me;
  persuade me to stay,
  coax me with your irresistible urban expansion,
  the public works, the Egyptian World State,
  the heart of China's shifting capitals,
  the knuckles in the soul of your walled borders,
  the irrational city,
  the city without sense or meter,
  an instrument of colonization and madness.
Slap me into stupidity so I can love you more,
  love your concrete and chrome
  and tar pits and salt water.

L.A., where are you in the morning
  to bring me to my knees at the feet
          of your palm trees and sitcoms.
Here, here is where all the world bends its knee.
All the cities speak through you.
  Athens, the true democracy;
  Quattrocento Venice,
  Medicean Florence, the jewel of Tuscany,
      pilot of the Renaissance;
  Goethe's Weimar, the universal man;
All your unpredictable spiritual powers
  sweep me up into each crevice
    of slime and glint, glitter and sludge.

L.A. L.A., where are you in the morning?
  Take me to your breast, make me suck,
  squeeze the milk of your rage and fraudulent dreams,
  squeeze the milk of your processed glory down my throat.
You're all the great capitals and I am everywhere and there—
        Alexandria, Rome, Constantinople,
        Cordoba, Paris, Mexico City
        St. Petersburg, Vienna, Isfahan,
        smoky London and shrill New York.
Who needs any of them?
  They're all in you, you're all of them, L.A., L.A.
I say your name
  and feel the blood of your liars

  and screaming coke freaks,
I am one of your liars. *I* am one of your coke freaks,
  blasting my brains with every imaginable kind
  of woodgrained molded polystyrene
  vinyl structural urethane polypropylene veneered
  stain resistant DRUGS of all your possessions.

I send my resume to every street corner huckster:
I've been on *Lou Grant, Hill St. Blues, Mash, Divorce Court*—
                    or was that my life?
I feel you on the movie sets, the Hollywood tours,
  the get-rich-quick change-my-life wheel-of-fortune-
  blow-me-to-Hawaii-and-back lottery fix.
I feel you everywhere in the bones of consumer items.
I feel you in every street straight from hell and back—
  Fairfax and Sunset in my blood
  Pico and Sepulveda in my veins
  Venice & PCH in my flesh
  Beverly and Doheny in my dreams,
  Western and Olympic in my arms.

L.A. L.A., Where are you in the morning when I need you,
  I am here for you to be fucked and made holy,
  I am here for you to break my will and shave my head,
  I am here for you to corrupt my best ideals.
I spread my legs I spread my chest
I spread my heart wide open.

L.A., L.A., Where are you in the morning when I need you,
  shaking and stomping with your steel boots for everyone.
      Explode the sod for me!
      Topple the buildings for me!
      Shatter the glass for me!
      Blast apart the pipes for me!

Smash the brains of wealth and corruption and decadence for me
            into my heart,
            into my loins,
            into my El-ay soul.

I Don't Get It

I don't get it!
It doesn't make sense!
I don't understand it.
It doesn't make sense.

I get hit. I get beat.
Am I nuts, am I naive,
foolish, am I stupid?

Pushed like a dog,
cut into pieces like a flounder,
broken like plastic against a stone,
I push my brain and my heart till they bruise,
put up with everything unreal,
get nothing for it but salt,
a thousand years of debt.
I don't get it. It doesn't make sense.
I don't get it.

I was fucked.
I was shuffled about.
Someone's drinking my blood.
Someone's dismembered the whole family.
No one is left who can walk;
those who can, build their little fortifications.

Our struggles smell up the streets,
our cries sprout berries in the gardens of the rich,
and they eat them, tasting the bitter grief that stains their fingers.
"Whose grief is this?" they ask.
"Ours! Ours!" we scream, but they do not hear.
They continue smacking their fingers with the nectar of our woe.
It doesn't make sense.
We wanted so little. I don't get it.

We're planting bodies in time for a good spring crop.
We're planting our regret, our savage despair.
We're planting our spoons because there's no more food.
We're planting our pillow because there's no more sleep.
We're planting our shoes because we've lost our feet.

We're planting our words because there's no more hope.

We sing and out fall rocks.
We dance and up comes tar.
If anyone laughs they bandage our teeth.
It doesn't make sense. I don't get it.

Who peels my flesh away and steals the bones from our bread.
Why are the children strapped to ignorance,
  why do they send them on fruitless journeys,
  to lose one finger at a time
  to the gods of finance and architecture?
What are we losing when no one is allowed to sing.

Who spits in my face the teeth of my ancestors.
Who takes my wife and breaks her back.
Who wants us bleeding and naked and crying out in pain.
What can we say that frightens them so.
What have we seen that causes their brains to explode.
What do we know that turns their arms into knives.
Who are we so poor and dying to love
  that their planes and factories go up in smoke
  at the mere mention of our names.
We hope for so little.
We are so small.
What power can our single songs have.
We know only pain and thirst and hunger.

Nothing but grimness.
You never stop crying.
I've been cheated. Who did this?
Why do such damage you cannot undo.

It doesn't make sense.
I don't get it.
I'm telling you I don't get it.
It doesn't make any sense.
I'm telling you I don't get it.
I'm telling you I don't get it.

A Manifesto

What I mean is not what I mean to say, though I mean to say this, that I have written, not said, but saying it now and in saying, mean something else entirely. Restless copper until it becomes gold, the furnace, the philosophical egg folded into Lenin's omelette that unbroken feeds the psychic root of bourgeois values to remain unconscious unjustified withheld possessed of the fury of harmless scandal.

What I really mean is this: it is nevertheless our job to explode the entirety of capitalist culture in which all imaginative activity is commercialized and trendificated and elevated to the lucrative decoration of fashion that only money can buy where it cannot harm the state or the individual. Modern and post modern art that lives inside the belly of modern art recedes harmless from our senses on the walls of banks and office buildings. What was all the rioting about 80 years ago, that every avant-garde scandal is framed to match the blue of our sofas or ring with a metallic silver next to the elevator that carries our bodies to work. *Where are the words and images that refuse to return to their cages?* Where is not what we meant to say but what we must have said, in our dreams, in our darkest fears, hidden by newsprint, exposed so commercially as an idea, that even the idea of revolution struts down the Venice Beach in sunglasses and provocates usable sex.

It is time to return art and poetry to the field of ordinary human activity. It is time to *rescue* art and poetry from the field of ordinary human activity. We are continually being trapped by the solopsistic management of literary tastes and fashionable scandal. *The artist has no responsibility to anyone, to any class, to any people, to any state, to any system.* What we express should be grounds for nothing less than immediate execution. Execution if we fail to move another human being to tears. Execution if we jerk off in public. Execution if our literary experiments and jargon-blitzed motorcycles pretend to be capable of terrifying the state when all they do is keep another human belly bloated from starvation. The artist has no responsibility at all. Fuck you and you and you. This manifesto should self-destruct as it is being read if it mobilizes one person into significant social action and away from the revolutionary laziness of real art. Art for art's you-know-what.

A manifesto that means anything to anyone else other than the one who composed it is worthless and not worthy of anyone's attention.

True spirit is everywhere at once, fuck you and you and you. Internal consistency is a chimera. When we inculcate integrity and are ethically dissolute we are inveiglers. When we exalt culture and practice incivility we are hypocrites. When we preach intrepidity and are recreant so the fucking what is what I say even if it's not what I mean. External consistency is a blow job. Dada DooDoo. Manifest Density. Language spread sheets and Literary Corporate Project Management. I want something my kids can understand. Not this drivel. Live by the drivel of your finest dreams and die by the debris of your bank accounts.

Free your poems and your stories and your novels from the delusions of cleverness. Bring history, art, politics, and revolutionary propaganda into your work. *Make it old. Make it wise. Make it matter to another human being. Feed people. Be unafraid of your life, which is holy, and your name, which is sacred, and your spirit, which is everywhere at once.* Provide lots of footnotes. Use epigrams and epigraphs whenever possible. Print clearly. Learn to use a computer. Spell correctly. Always end each paragraph or stanza with an uplifting moral. Warn everyone of the dangers of toxic flood and nuclear contamination. Lobby for increased government spending on the arts; send letters of apology to the hungry and the homeless and the destitute; wag your finger at totalitarian tyrants. Manifest Density. Surrealistic Realism. DaDa DooDo. Mean what you say. Say what you mean. Quit art. Get a job. Learn to change your own tires on the freeway. Quit oppressing women and people of color. Become a woman or a person of color. Become familiar with the smell of jails. Investigate the pangs of hunger. Manage a small business and make a profit. Run for president. Run for president and lose. Take dancing lessons. Write like me. Try to write like me even if you can't. Burn this manifesto. I meant what I said but don't say what I mean. Learn the truth. Your words are useless. Your sentences are worthless. You have no responsibility to anyone. Fuck you and you and you. Burn the flags of your own manifestos and beg forgiveness at the altar of art. Desecrate the altar. Go it alone.

Manifest Density

Surrealistic Realism

Dada Doo-Doo

Ha Ha Ha Ha Ha.

The Father at Safeway

I'm standing in the line at Safeway, getting formula and diapers, behind an old Jewish lady counting coins in her coin purse, and in front of another 4 or 5 people, anxious to get past the cashier and into the parking lot. Everything on the counter says I'm a father, a new father at that. Formula and diapers, small, 12 to 18 pounds. I can feel the incongruity of it, if there is such a thing. Big ol' me, in my red shorts and torn sweat shirt with white paint spatters on the front, dirty tennis shoes, slipping out my American Express Gold card to pay for the stuff.

I could be 18, standing in line to buy beer and scotch for the party Friday nite, ready for a blitzed-out weekend tearing up the streets in my Chevy Bel Air. I could be 25, buying cookies and ice cream for Friday nite party, something for the munchies from the dope we'll be smoking. It's the supermarket on the corner of Clairborne and St. Charles, where the street cars make their turn to head back downtown, and a weekend of grass and Kafka and everybody rolling around on the floor laughing. Today, I'm 49, standing by the counter in Safeway on 3rd and Fairfax.

We size each other up by what's on the counter. There's the lady buying a chicken fryer, two carrots, and a loaf of bread. The other woman, buying Calistoga water and yogurt and some kind of health flakes, wood-chips, who knows. I'm the father, buying formula and diapers. Perhaps they already know to feel a little sorry for me, thinking of the long sleepless nights, the walking around dazed feeling, the plastic keys and rings strewn all over the floor you step on in the half light of midnight.

I don't feel like the father. I just feel like Jack, standing in line, buying something. I look down at the giant bag of Huggies and Enfamil low-iron formula, and it seems like something out of a dream; in my back pocket a little gadget and I bring it to my face and say, "Beam me up, Scottie!" and I'm in my Bonneville convertible cruising down Claiborne Avenue, taking the big curve at Nashville, yelling out the window at Jerry Jacobs, who's driving like an idiot in the gray Plymouth in front of me.

When I hold Josh, when I'm feeding him, when I'm just looking at him in his summer seat, I try to find the father feeling, but it escapes me.

I feel the edge of the miracle, of the wonder, of the unbelievable face and those cheeks I could suck, that face I could swallow whole, but the father feeling, what's that? I'm just Jack, and by god, I have a son, and his name is Joshua, after my father, Samuel Joshua, dead these thirty years.

My father sits in the kitchen, his face in the palm of his hand, staring down at his cup of coffee, thinking of his own long ago, the cold streets of New York, the east side, yelling up to his mother for a penny. He sits in the kitchen, and his three sons yell and play in the rumpus room while his daughter sucks on her long curls, and his wife harumphs around the house in a flower print dress. He sits there and stares off into space, a boy from the lower east side, sitting in the kitchen of his three story home on Fontainebleau Drive. Where was the father feeling in him? To me, he always was the father. As much as I tried to see him a boy, he was always the father.

And Josh, my own son, beginning to kvetch in the summer seat, looks up at me for rescue. He wants out, he wants my shoulder, he wants me to beam him up. But Scottie's not here. There's just Jack standing in line at Safeway buying diapers and formula. Jack the boy, Jack the man, Jack the father.

Sunday Morning

Sunday morning. I wake to the sun lifting one leg over the top of the Ticor Building on Wilshire Boulevard. The new leaves on the tree outside my bedroom window are tinged with sunlight. If only I were a photographer or painter I'd freeze this moment and crawl into it.

Sunday morning. I have to get up but my body wants to drown right here in the bed. Spring ambles up the street waving its arms. A matinee today. I have to be at the theater by two. Yesterday, I find out from my agent that I didn't get the part I was counting on.

> *Eat this, they say.*
> *It's good for you.*
> *You've eaten it before.*
> *The next one will be sweet.*

I eat and concentrate on the window, on the tree, on the sun beginning to beat its chest as it comes over the top of the tallest building.

I drive down Beverly Boulevard, take the curve where it changes into 1st Street, turn on Grand and park right across from the museum. It's just after ten, hardly any cars on the street. MOCA doesn't open till eleven. The sun has followed me all the way, reflecting off the Security Pacific Bank Building, glass and steel going all the way up.

I get off on this urban sleekness, especially the unfinished building across the street, another skeleton of steel and concrete. Someone should stick a sign on it, make it part of MOCA, part of the Permanent Collection, and leave it just as it is, unfinished. No clear line where the museum ends and the rest of the city begins. One easy flow, stretching all the way back into our homes, into the very center of our lives.

I walk past the California Plaza sign, running my hand along the chrome and glass, then head downstairs for a cup of coffee and cinnamon roll at the "Il Panino." There's a girl two tables over, in the sun. We both drink our coffee in silence, checking our watches, writing something down in our journals.

She's an art student from Santa Barbara come to see the Jasper Johns. She asks what am I here to see. "Oh," I say, "the art. Just the art. I don't care. Just something."

I AM FIVE YEARS OLD.

I don't understand anything.
Hot and humid days; nights, dark and mysterious.
They take me to school.
I stare at the blackboard.
The kid from around the corner beats me up at recess.
Some nights my father doesn't come home.

My mother shrieks on the telephone. My pet turtle dries up in the sun. My uncle dies on the floor in the empty kitchen.

Who is the world?
Why is the moon where the sun is?
If the street goes nowhere, why is it in my bed?
What is the rain that rains just rain,
and why does it rain crows, or bats, or baseball gloves?
How is the pencil writing my name,
and why is my name the name for the thing that fixes tires,
the name for the flag on the pirate ship,
the name for the clown crushed in the box?

Outside, the kids continue to jump rope on the sidewalk, singing, *"A my name is Alice,"* seeing everything, but knowing nothing.

I AM SIX. *The class takes a bus with Miss Cook to the Delgado Museum on Elysian Fields Avenue. We're going to see Vincent Van Gogh. Later, when I tell my mother, who was born in Antwerp, she says to say it like this, Vincent Van Gough, and she coughs as she says it. Van Gough! Van Gough! But Miss Cook says Van Go. We are marched single-file from one room to another, walking past each painting that hangs just above our heads.*

I can't believe what I am seeing. Everything mysterious and horrible about the world vanishes. He paints like I paint! Trees outlined in black. All those wavy lines, all those colors. And he piles the paint on. He's wasting all that paint, just like I did before they told me not to waste all the paint. He sees everything I see. The moon is where the sun is. The street that goes nowhere is in his bed. It's not just raining rain, it's raining crows and bats. He sees the blood, he see the faces. Everything so bright it's on fire. Everything so dark it swallows me up. The man cuts his ear off. The man leans against the table so sad. The man dies on the floor of the empty kitchen. I stop in front of the painting with crows above a cornfield. The world I see is real. I bring my hand up and touch the dried paint. It's real! Mounds of paint, swirls of paint, rivers of paint! But it's not paint. It's real. It's the world.

"Don't touch the painting!" Miss Cook yells. She pulls my hand away. She yanks my arm into the center of the room. "Never ever touch a painting!" She shoves me into a seat in the back of the bus. It doesn't matter. The world is real. I fold my hands in my lap. I know what I will do.

I will write about the real world.

11 o'clock. The girl heads off toward the Jasper Johns. I walk into the J. Paul Getty Trust Gallery and find the Geary cardboard chairs and cardboard houses. "Can I sit in them?" I ask the guard. "They can be sat in," he says, "but you can't sit in them."

"Oh," I say, and walk into the room with the huge pavilion shaped like a fish. I walk into the belly of the fish. The wood inside is so beautiful.

"Don't touch the wood, please," says the guard.

I wander over to the Nauman video. A clown is being tortured on simultaneous video screens. "Clown Torture," it's called. Later, in the Permanent Collection, I bump into the girl from Santa Barbara. In the center of the room, a metal sculpture of a man moves his motorized mouth up and down. A silent

YAK

YAK

YAK

This, I understand.

I stand as close to it as I can. The guard watches me suspiciously.

Over the in North Gallery there's an empty spot in one corner. Something was there, but it's been removed. I make a sign for myself and hang it around my neck. I stand in the corner of the Permanent Collection, North Gallery, as still as I can, one arm out in the gesture of an actor about to speak.

Eat this.
You've eaten it before.
The next one will be sweet.
The street that goes nowhere
is in your bed.
You know nothing,
but you can see everything.

A woman and her little girl walk up to me. “What does the sign say?” the girl asks.

“Touch me,” her mother says. “The sign says touch me.”

So the child reaches out a hand and touches my own.

Caws You Get Holdout

Caws you get
holdout
blow-up me slap
character esplanade

she was dutiful without
sure footed envelope she
was something sinister in
an ancient sort of way
drop out something
begun and lately plaster
of paris she was my fancy
dream caws you get
holdup slap-out me
blow away from naming
the wrong things the right
name she was sinister
in an ancient sort of way,
miami, a miasma
of terrify, holy blowfish
she was sure-footed
caws you get holdout
and she was something
sinister, a drop-in
something started in the heat of the sun
blown out by smithereens of starfish, a light,
a necklace of quicksnaps,
sand, thumbtacks,
doorknobs, paperclips,
her teeth biting off caskets of marshmallows
something sinister
in an ancient sort of way
slapped out, me blow away
me gone, me hers
me for the taking,
caws you get holdout
you get blown away you get rearranged
like tuna fish

you get lost,
and found
and lost again,
an episode of light
on your way to a train depot,
the death of the best part of yourself
buried in a fanfare of alternatives,
ambivalencies of swordfish,
twisting in the proverbial wind,
scraped clean,
caws you get blow-out,
in a sinister sort of way,
falling apart with plaster lips
of the woman
who sees you blown-out,
of the woman who takes you hold up,
of the woman
in an ancient sort of way
who finds you lost
and names you right
again.

Still Life

Some remote, exquisite creature:
behind you
beyond the mass of light
the erotic force
shapes the better performance,
another range of available styles.

Now you are pigeon-toed to the sun,
and I look up at it,
neck stretched, holding up by torch
the power
between thighs entire plates
concealed beneath the ridges
of your skull.

So to be any of it so much to be
like the others
So much to be driven over the concrete
and the smell of gasoline
So much your arms pointing out some strange
flying object
there over there by the blue
cloud just about
to eat the reindeer's head

And we are so alone in this inscrutable palm,
that presses against the other
palm
of exact passion ready to curl
to the sweet fist of science
while in your car, engine off,
at the end of the driveway,
unable to go anywhere else
you you

I would have thought we could have
stayed there
where we were, where we are.

I would have hoped all of us
could have remained there, without radio
or cigarette
and gone back further if necessary.
An anxious life that is not
                    the legend of jobs
or the enlarged study of stones.
Through these other walls you hear
  the solid citizen with clear politics.
So much is the hunger of our particular
          existence,
ground chosen to stand on—
               a doctrine of fact
that baffles intuition and
momentum
out from beyond it all you turn stories
      of legitimate escape
and wait there at the windshield
        turning from the cold.
    It is nothing   it is nothing at all
that stops you
         this hour   and this day
looking out at the sloping roof
   through the branches of the neighbor's
          sycamore
  over housetops
and the grim streetlights between houses.

How can you be still
and at the same time
in motion?
How do you measure yourself
frozen and worthy and groping
as always
for love?

So much is this brute doctrine of fact.
All that you must do, all that is
yet to be done.
         think of all the one-sentence
         autobiographies

you have written

and the sun is gone
and there is no one
to be going home to
and your children
forget your name
and your father is dead
and dies every time you say his name
and your mother is dead
but continues to eat your name,
and in your own name
eats you

So much is this brute doctrine of fact.
And I would say to you
stay there
unmoving in the blood
of a particular
kind of courage.

BREAKING DOWN THE SURFACE OF THE WORLD

PART I: GEOGRAPHY

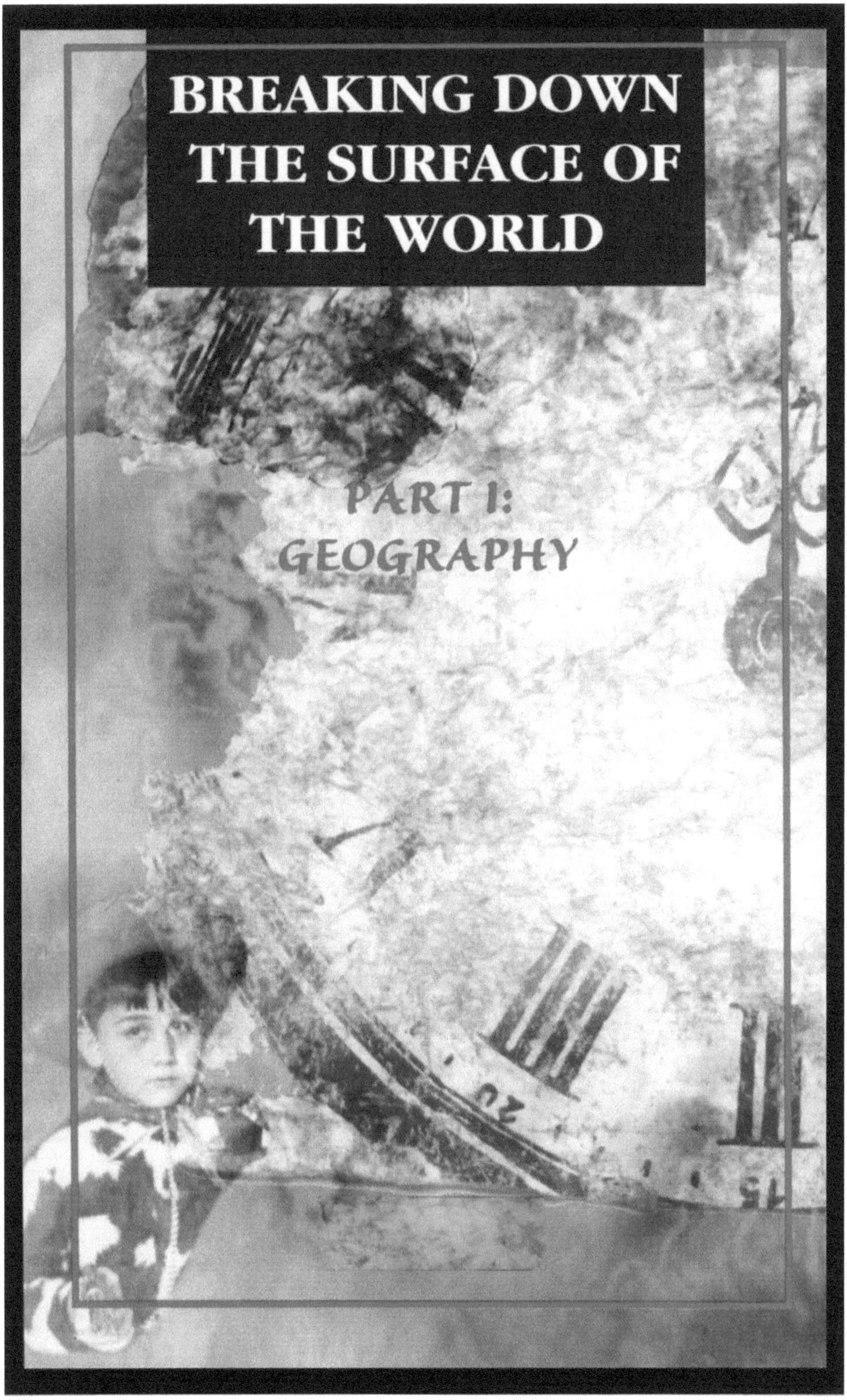

This is a work in progress.

Breaking down the Surface of the World is a long poem sequence in three parts: Geography, History, and Physics. Some of the sections in Part I have appeared in previous publications in slightly different form.

Sometimes I am very small.
In another life.
Low to the ground.
Eyes with clubs.
Axe-handles.
Drums.

I see what's up.
I run from one end of the room
to the other.

There.
Safe.
Thunder.
The long shadow of wood.
Belts accreted 'round cratons
and flung across the island arcs
consuming plate boundaries.

There's a red bed in the corner.
Outside I can see the zinc tubs
my mother does the washing in.
Through crust and bone,
from trench to arc,
she hangs her flesh out to dry
and is nowhere to be found.

Each knife has a name.
Butcher.
Bread.
Paring.
Every door a lock;
key and bolt,
latch and chain.

Outside the window
lines of cars
their yellow headlights
in the bright sun.

My father drives among them.
He waves to me.
I wave back.

Every morning
the same size.
The house so quiet:
Brain torture.
Shuffled about.
Eyeballs into cement.
Neptune bursting into flame.
Jupiter, a perfection of toes.

Old rocks within younger rocks
line the front yard where I bury
little things
I find around the house.
Less familiar the longer I hold them.

Big wood.
Axe-handles.
Drums.

The mailman pushes his cart
packed with letters and magazines
and parks it next door.

I'm out here breathing
waving goodbye, saying hello,
getting the mail
not even waiting for the mailman.
To meet no train that stops.
Hands in my pockets
rocking back and forth on my heels
as a car goes by full of fish,
swarms of kids on their way to swimming lessons—
the last swimming lesson of the summer.

There goes Mars
barfing up suicide.
There goes Pluto
gristle in the brain.

In another life
toothpicks investigate the courage of seashells.
Rearranged like furniture.
Nighttime, bedtime, bloodtime, moontime.
Burglar bars, daddy bars, baby bars, bloody bars.
The slavery of the head.

A thin blanket, green with stripes
lies among the granite-like rocks
in the backyard.
Layers of crust in the toaster.
On the mantle above the fireplace with no fire,
golf trophies,
souvenir shields,
belt-buckles,
white-china plate with ripple marks
steadily losing heat
to gold cuff-links in its center
flashing reflections of sunlight

as I walk by.
Venus as I walk by.
Mercury as I walk by.
Uranus as I walk by.
I walk by looking for permanence.

The chairs get up during the night
and dance.
They vanish beneath the ocean water
and bathroom basins.
I feel the shift in the house.
Low rolling surfaces.
Blocks of various shapes and sizes,
raised, lowered, tilted.
Some notion as to their character
still deeper and worn down.

When I try to reach into their sleep
it is like freezing my teeth
on refrigerator water
left in a frosted milk bottle.
The sun is so red today.
Ernie says don't look directly into it.

We find a piece of cardboard,
prick a hole with a pencil
and peep through it.
See the red sun and go blind.
Everyone goes blind.
We bump into each other in the streets,
bump into the trees,
bump into houses.

"I'm, blind," yells A.J.
He's excited.
He walks stiff-legged, hands stretched out,
groping the air in front of him.
"Me, too," yells my brother.
Everyone's lined up to go blind,
wanting to look into the sun.
Darryl falls into the gutter and laughs.
"I can't see either," he says.

We're delirious with blindness.

We sit on the curb
and watch the cars go by—
same cars, same drivers.
We wave at them, they wave back.
I look at a broken coke bottle.
A.J. stares at old lady Seenac
rocking in her rocker
on the front porch across the street.
No one's in the mood to tease her.
Darryl watches the tree out front,
my brother looks at me.
We can all see again.

Later, I dig a small trench in the yard,
fill it with water,
watch the displacement of rock and dirt,
their strike-slip movements
as they slide down into the murk.

One night there is a sudden distress.
I'm being picked up in the thin green blanket
and thrown across the room
to land in a cardboard suitcase.
The big steel ship stale with fatigue.
The suitcase filled with dirt
and fingernails,
dry crackly pieces of skin.
My own skin.
Bits of blood where the break was too deep,
dried rust against the light-veined brown.
Someone pours in water.
The chips of skin loosen and turn soft,
hold flat against my forehead and cheeks.
A new face shuffled around the original crust,
shifted beyond recognition.
Was it a sort of slag on the surface
of the case when its rocky crust
first took form?
Or did it change along a zone of weakness
too subtle and precise to contain

even the smallest scream?

My father snaps the case shut.
My mother retreats into the closet;
whimpers, laughs, pecks at the door.
She's mad.
I see this clearly.
Her madness flourishes like an umbrella.
Already it's too late.
While you gallop through your sleep
each night
trying to understand love
and prevent the last sour dream
from spilling onto your pillow,
my mother and I slash at your shadow:
she, pecking at the door;
me, pounding on the inside of the suitcase.
One of us can not get out
without the other.

All in another life.
Neptune. Mars.
Fat women raise their dresses
to dance over skinnier naked bodies.

> *no platform. no*
> *ridges.*
> *her breast is a rift.*

She steps lightly over each one;
penises rising as she bends
and strokes them, down,
far below the limits of observation.

One woman is up, the other down;
legs kick high as the fat jiggles
and rolls out the shadows
that catch in their folds.

Red splotches appear on their thighs,
on their breasts, flushed and bruised,
never hotter than they are now.
A thrust oceanward.

Iron formations give way to red beds.
Inside, where my defective heart
pumps rift systems in alkaline complexes
that drive deeper into the interior,
I feel that heat acting as a thermal buffer
to everything closing down around me.
I hide in the basement,
attain a degree of rigidity.

How far am I from the spreading center
of the room as flesh and cotton float
among the pillows and blankets?
At the edge of the room
with my back to the door
I shine with the head of a new deformation.
The flare of a match.
Magnetic polarities shift,
each band moving outward in turn
sizzling from my body.
Fractures everywhere.
I move from one end of the room to the other.

Never again in the spreading center.
Never again the single place to turn in.
It's one end or the other.
Folds upon folds upon folds.
My transformation into granite.

C

Winter is a bright moon
hanging, as the horses kick dogs
that worry them in their sleep.
Everyone is cold.
Strangers wave icicles
by the fire;
Mutants everywhere
mate with others not their kind.
It is a terrible night.
No one can read yet.

Uncle Charles takes me in his new convertible.
We ride around and look up at the stars.
"That's the North Star," he says.
I ask him where the South Star is.
"There is no South Star."
When he dies, they tell me he's gone.
To the North Star, I think.

There's always something someone's not telling me.
Cold dust and stone.
My father comes home drunk
and smashes the mirror in the bathroom.
Chunks of glass in the sink.
When I look, there's my face,
looking in so many different directions.
Water I cannot put my hands into.
Sea shells in the Rocky Mountains.
Marine deposits on the plains of Kansas.
The remains of fig trees in Greenland.
Glacial debris in Australia and Brazil.

One night my mother bundles me up in a blanket
and calls a cab to take us to *maMa's* house.
She lives far away in Metairie,
where the train comes from.
I tell the cab driver:
"My father's coming to chop our heads off."

Even with the windows shut, I can feel the cold.
There's the sign for Ritz crackers.
The first word I learn to read.
Everything is ritzy.

I begin to put one and one together.
The concept of a random universe.
The idea of causality.
Is it one or the other or both?
Red and Yellow make Orange.
Blue and Yellow make Green.
Green and Orange make Brown.
That's something you can count on.
When I color, I press hard on the edges,
soft on the inside.
I can breathe inside the colors.
I spell my name.

The child studies the mirror, then the face.
Which is no longer the face of the child,
but man,
waiting in the winter of the mirror
to be born.

Snow melts as soon as I touch it.
Most of it melting in the air
melting when it touches something warmer
like the sidewalk
or my fingers
and I hold my hand
inside the freezer as long as I can
and go out running
to keep the frozen flakes
clustered in my palm
to catch sight of the pattern
science books showed.
By comparison
my flesh sizzles
beneath the crystal
of ice.

For a long time it is winter.
In the mirror, way back in the background,
my mother walks back and forth,
putting on her girdle, taking off her girdle.
My brother cuts his finger on some broken glass.
My father drinks from the bottle.
My sister isn't born yet.

E

I touch everything
like flies, like rivers,
like the black pearl
stored away in boxes
ornamented with gold rope.
What will I let myself remember today?
The box with the pair of scissors
varnished black?
Or the one with dried grains of corn?
I open the door.
Eat with great deliberation.
The house burns day and night.
A cow is no longer a cow.
A sack of grain no longer a month's food.
The black pearl reminds me
of something else.
In the mirror, I watch myself.
The beauty that is born
stands on two feet
even in the slime of creation
and sings as it moves
among beasts.

We are crossing the Suru River
looking for Yaks, the primitive cow.
The pilot's head is on my lap
and I'm flying the plane.
With enough fuel
I can take the Himalayas:
the white goats climbing the crag.
The animals below us
immune to the land,
look up at our noise
but barely.
Then back to climbing,
to grazing.
The world beneath their feet
their one earthly thing.

Someone has gone
and overturned the lake again.
I don't understand this one word here,
he says.
Neither do I, which is why I keep it in.
But countless things escape
so easily out of you, he gasps.
Are you gasping?
Actually gasping?

And someone's given birth
to a brilliant lizard.

Here is some news:
Today is meat.
The cows, letters etched
into their hides, play
the alphabet game:
Guess who I am?
It starts with a C.
Once the fastest animal
in the world.

I

What nigger meant
and kike
and dago
and polack
and wop
and jew-boy
and sheeny
and litvak
and mick
and crab.
Old man Seenac in his ragged undershirt
shows hairy underarms
as he stands by the kitchen door
yelling out at me you little kike
bastard jew-boy.
I loved his daughter Linda,
under the house
spreading her legs
to catch a peek of red, hairless vagina
and pissing in the dry dirt, both of us
pledging someday to marry:
the kike and the dago.
And the blacks all around us,
mother goose nuns at the corner.
Division   division   division.
Clean spit against the windshield
of a 1947 Dodge.
Bicycle down to Prytania Street
and watch the girls roller skate.
Catch a snowball on the way back.
Dago street where Rosalie lived
sucking the boys off down in the basement,
boys who didn't even know yet
what it was to come.
Did you get the feeling, A.J. asked,
and we all lied, even then.

J

A dream: I am carrying the large lizard
over the back of my neck like a stole
up the stairs and into a room
filled with my friends.
They're on fire but they're laughing,
eating with both hands.
A vat of tomato sauce boils on the stove.
I dump the lizard into it.
Half of him hangs out
struggling to escape.
He makes no sound,
but his jaws snap and his body
swings across the rim
like a loose hose gushing water.
I take him out
and eat:
It's good.
It tastes just like lizard.

K

In the evenings I come home
and there's my mother
laying the ties out
in regular rows on the kitchen table.
Blue ties.
Nothing but blue silk ties.

My father boards the airplane,
and flies
over the mountains.
For there is no eminence on earth
not subject to erosion,
the inexorable
destroyer.
"When is he coming home,"
my sister asks.
We go outside
and watch the sky.
My father waves.
I wave back.

My brothers and I scoot into the corner
around the kitchen table
and eat our steaming chicken noodle soup.
No one talks, no one breathes,
just my brothers slurping
soup
and me, sitting in the steam
saying the words to myself:
nigger
wop
jew-boy
dago
polack
kike
sheeny
litvak
mick.
The words roll off the tongue
with a strange kind of music.
At night, we take our shovels
and sneak into the backyard
and start digging.
In the glare of the moon
I can see A.J.'s face sweating.
Darryl wants the words as bad as I do.
He's got the big shovel.
Everyone wants the big shovel,
but Darryl's the biggest
with actual muscles in his arms
so no one takes it from him yet.
Shit comes first.
We stand in a circle around the hole
looking at it.
I hear Mr. Higbee open the ice-box
in his kitchen next door.
We stand very quiet,
our cheeks streaked with mud.

The light in Mr. Higbee's kitchen goes out
and we resume looking down at Shit.
The word glows in the darkness.
A.J. reaches into the hole
and picks it up.
He brings Shit up and shows it to us.
I like the way it looks with the capital S.
Darryl says keep digging.
The moon passes behind a dark cloud
and we dig.
Out comes fuck with a pop.
No capital.
The word amazes us, we are stunned by its beauty.
The k remains partly buried
but everyone knows it's a k,
everyone knows it's fuck.
The breathless wonder of seeing it like that.
I'd say, "fuck, that's beautiful," but the word
isn't in my hand yet.
I dare to pick it up first.
I shake the dirt off the k
and hold it up in my hand.
fuck, says A.J.
fuck, says Darryl.
fuck, says Karl.
fuck, I say.
The sound of it stuns us.
The mystery of the word deepens
the more I say it.
The more we all say it.
fuck. fuck. fuck.
Louder and louder.
The lights in the houses go on.
We dig faster, and deeper.
My shovel hits cunt.
A.J. unearths dick and screw and piss.
We're pulling the words up and saying them aloud
and all across the neighborhood
the lights in the houses go on
and we're saying the words even louder.

fuck. And
cunt.
Say them with the capital letter, I yell.
The power of it all surges
like an electrical storm,
the houses tremble in the dark and fall down.
If they were cities, they'd fall, too.

We dig deeper.
All the bones of the words come out of the earth.
The moon is full and bright again.
We can see as if we'd been blind.
The words lie in the palms of our hands,
murderous, horrible, beautiful words.

Maps bring the greatest pleasure:
a faded navigational chart;
an authentic medieval portolano;
outlines of the Mediterranean;
maps of the flat earth;
the ocean: the universal cataract.
Under the last, translated from the Spanish:

> *"The nature of waters*
> *is always to communicate*
> *and to reach a common level.*
> *This is their mystery."*

We are crushed beneath his weight.
The men go to Grande Isle
and bring home giant fish packed in ice.
But I do not eat the fish.
I want to know the secret.
What makes his breath change?
What makes him leave in the night?
What makes him
the captain of the boat?
He tells me stories of his days
on the streets of New York
and his days as a cowboy
wounded out West,
and nursed back to health by Juanita,
the Mexican woman who loved him.
He tells us tales of throwing bricks
from the roofs of tenements,
with Beany, and Shorty, and Lefty, and Moe;
onto the heads of the policemen below,
of running with a gang called Murderer's Row.
Which do I believe?

From the backseat of a '49 maroon Mercury,
I watch him drive the car
and never once does he hit a tree,
never once do we go sailing off a cliff,
or run out of gas in the middle of the forest.
He drives us in our little egg,
the force of love blinding us to his pain.

When he walks, the rooms shake.
In the kitchen after work
he writes long columns of numbers
on a yellow piece of paper,
the code fathers know,
the secret formula
in a world for which there is no map,
no permanent state of nature,

no gene that carries
a knack for direction.

He wraps packets of money
inside the yellow paper
and wraps that with a rubber band.

In winter he stands on the prow of the ship
and faces into the wind,
the smooth skin taut against the bone.
Yet nothing is permanent.
New plateaus warp toward the sky.
New torrents obliterate the land.
He sails off in his boat
and leaves us in the kitchen
to add numbers by ourselves.

The men who are his friends
carry him home
and put him on the sofa.
He smells of whiskey,
lies there with his eyes closed,
but still he drives the car,
and still we fly through space in our little egg.

I tell him I never saw a purple cow
but that I hope one day to be one.
Is he dead or sleeping?
He puts his hand out and touches my head.
Does he know it's me,
or is he feeling for the wheel?
Which do I believe?

My mother sings:

> *Dormez-vous, dormez-vous,*
> *ding dong ding.*

This part of me is a continent—
the mysterious earth,
the lava that holds mountains together,
the richest traveler sold to silk,
the flutes,
the bellies of women,
the pubic hairs,
the secrets too old to forget,
the child
who stands at the end
of the hallway
afraid his father might die.

P

I leave my father in his hospital bed
and wait for the elevator alone.
The neat walls pucker up like fish.
For the first time
it is possible to sit and count:
moons, stars, inevitable shadows;
Neptune, Jupiter, Uranus, Pluto.
Starfish, seahorse, catfish, seagull,
the frescos, the billboards,
the skywriters sputtering up there
selling suntan oil.
There goes Mars. There goes Venus.
All fall down.

In the morning we are children again.
Someone knocks and says
"You have to get up
and get dressed
and advance in the ashen world."

Mother wipes the frost from the windows.
I scoot out from under the icy sheets.
Poles migrate rapidly
over different parts of the room.
Imprisoned in the paved cities.
Graves in caverns of age-old rock.
To penetrate the disguises of the visible world.
Born on this strange craft,
the awful vibrations of its deck,
clinging to the surface of this sphere.

The enormous room.
Two pennies lie on the floor near the bed.
One, a black war penny.
We take war stamps from the book
to pay for gasoline.
I hide in the backseat.

There's a giant birthday cake.
Sunday, October 23, 4004 B.C.
"Fossil discoveries are
devices planted by the devil
to delude us," he says.
But we go to work in the ever-lasting Fire.
A.J. carries his briefcase full of rocks.
Darryl pokes around in his lunch bag
full of some iron-magnesium silicate like olivine,
a heavy, greenish crystalline substance.
"I can't eat this!" he yells.
I pour out my vial upon the sun
and men are scorched by the great heat
and cities of the plain fall at our feet.

All the towering peaks we know lie crumpled
on the ocean floor.
There goes Betelgeuse. There goes Antares.

We walk to school looking for bugs
to put in our lunch bags.

We begin to advance in the ashen world.

The class room is filled with maps.
I can't remember where they said the bathroom was.
Afraid to ask again,
I walk into every room
and back out, looking for the door.
The seniors bulge and hold the walls up,
the hydraulic monarchies advance
beyond the steep hills,
the steepness of the land
shown by layer tints,
contour lines, relief shadings,
while the true character of the land
is difficult to infer.
Back into the small desk,
I stare bluntly at the folds and faults
of the techtonic map
thumbtacked below the blackboard.

The teacher reads out of a book:
"Early Pleistocene deformations
brought about a widespread emergence."

Her voice sings above our heads.
I can see her stockings,
her chubby thighs, the five rivers,
the walls of fortified cities!

She cups both hands before her.

Gunpowder! The bayonet! The stirrup!

The atom bomb! The coming of the clock!

Printing!

I squeeze against the metal frame of the desk.
I grip the edges of the desk top,
rippling against geometry
that shows each rise and fall of rock,
and release, and release the warm urine

along the line of my leg,
down to the socks,
slow to burn its way to my toes.
The piss, the hot piss, the fundamental nature
of the continent, piss after piss after piss,
Russian piss and Chinese piss and Roman piss
along the skin itching as the bell rings
and everyone grabs their schoolbags but me,
squatting in the warm pool that continues to build
in the piss of the piss by the piss
warmest of arms all around my body
bellowing up from the earth.

Since winter,
the windows have been closed.
I open the box of coins:
human profiles
blurred by the touch of hands.

If a woman were here,
I would obey her.

Geography is so bare.
Like a wet fish,
the thumbprint on the refrigerator
wiggles across the chrome.
It's midnight.
They march up to the door
and Yippee! The soldiers are home.
Who minds their muddy boots.

Ah, but a hundred miles away
the city is being eaten.
Who's in charge
of burning all these papers?
The sheets and suits
with no names attached,
false teeth in a cup
and Wednesday, missing with the rest.
No one puts anything away.
Sheets of dead skin crunch underfoot.
Static on the radio,
fire drills,
children in the street
hitting other children
with long cracking sticks.

Who is going to marry
at a time like this.

U

Jaunty is the word
for someone who dies before you were born.
That's my second cousin Alfred
and Alfred's father, and their first car.
Everyone over there is crossing the street.
There's the blue tablecloth
we'll fold on the old folds, if possible.

And Uncle Joe or Pappa or Mr. Lettelier:
look how young I look
bordered in white,
yellowing.
Scotch tape on four corners
facing Cockeyed-Jenny
on the other page,
just off the boat from Antwerp,
afraid to let go of the rail
as she walks down
the gangplank
to touch the ground of New York,
the New World.

The erotic force
shapes the better performance;
another range of available styles.

I am pigeon-toed to the sun
and look up at it,
neck stretched, holding up by torch
the power
between thighs   entire plates
concealed beneath the ridges
of my skull.

My arms point out some
flying object
over there   by the blue cloud
just   about
to eat the reindeer's head.

Looking out from the sloping roof
through branches of the neighbor's
sycamore
over housetops
and the streetlights
between houses,
I move to the edge

ready to take off.

I don't pray for miracles.
I put pebbles in a box
and bury them near the magnolia tree
because it is messy and too sweet,
as imperfect as the rest of us.
The comfort in that.
And in the ritual of school,
of pencils and paper and swivel chairs and chalk.
Lines painted on asphalt I follow
to the bathroom, to the library, to lunch.
When my father dies
I don't look inside the coffin.
I hear the sound of dirt hitting the coffin
with my eyes closed.
Then I am driven, in a line
of dark cars,
everywhere,
except
into my life as a man.

X

Geese fly south.
Swans skirt the perfect edge
of ponds,
their long necks
an arc of feathers.
Their wake opens outward
in the water.
I am outward in my gaze:
the perfect incision
between lava and rock.

In the palm of my hand
I mix a little paste;
a little blood,
a little zinc.
Some of us have weak eyes.
The blind bump into everything.
Mix in a little sand,
a little grass.
Some gunpowder.
Anything living will do.
Parts of the body
fly across the sky.
There goes femur.
There goes backbone.
There is little need
to remember numbers.
Only the naming
becomes important.
St. Peter's Sandstone.
London Clay.
Montmarte Gypsum.

You can read the paper
and catch up on everything,
though in some countries
they only print the truth.
When I make soup

I sing to myself in the kitchen:

dormez-vous, ding dong ding.

The song is what gives me away.

Now on the table
all my friends in ties
waving goodbye.
And so much time taken
to learn again
what we knew
from each other
and forgot.
It's still daylight
but I can see the moon.
Almost,
or so it seems,
transparent.
Not even a full moon.
But a full moon.

Vows:

We're going to get married
and have kids
and live together
and be bloody.

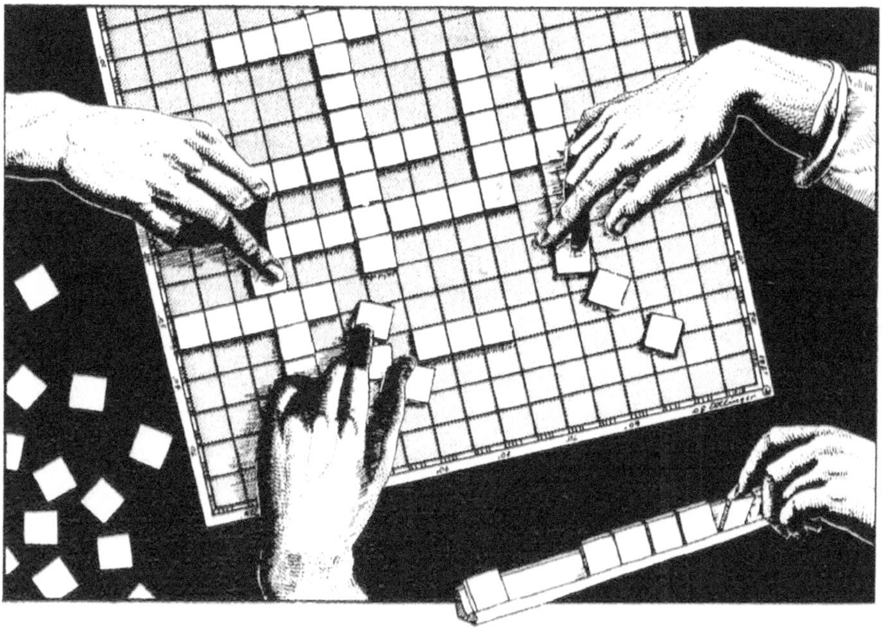

LUCKY FINDS

These pieces extend and parody the dynamic artistic productions of high-modernism that began with Stéphen Mallarmé's *Un Coup De Dés* (*A Throw of the Dice*, 1897), continued with the works of the Italian and Russian Futurists after World War I, and reached their apogee in Ezra Pound's *Cantos* (1930–1966) with their graphic ideograms, Wallace Stevens' *Harmonium* (1923) and *Notes Toward a Supreme Fiction* (1947), Louis Zukofsky's *"A"* (1959–1975), and Charles Olson's *Maximus Poems* (1950–1970). As individual cards, these poems can be shuffled into different sequences, extending even further their nonlinear nature. Traditional narrative poetry is undermined by the work's graphic intensity, and the spaces and syntactic gaps between images and statements offer the reader multiple layers of meaning (if meaning is your cup of tea), while at the same time subverting the very notion of meaning itself (just when you thought it was safe to open a dictionary). Thus, the reader is left to encounter the linguistic contradictions inherent in collages, cubist simultaneity, and multiple points of view.

TABLOID OF CONTINGENTS

Crawl in Backwards

What Is Missing In This Picture

Goddnews

Is it Inside the Body Conscious Neglect?

A True Understatment

The Hidden Term

In Art

How Come

There is a Key to Everything

The Beardless Jew

Is It Unlike You To Be So Precise?

I Spend Most of My Time on the Moon

Participation

TABLOID OF CONTINGENTS

Draw the Line Somewhere

Carbon Cycle

A Few Birds

Then We Went Down to the Car

INTRO-DUCTION

Now That's a Log Cabin!

K

It Must Explain the Large

Never a Shipwreck

The Countess

The Thunder Perfect Mind Barren

A Good Mystery

Even So

Title & Copyright

Condition

A Hidden Bird

The Symptomatic

Getting the Middle Voice

Is k a Real Number?

This is a Test of the Nether Breastplate

As Far as Perspective Will Get You

The Space Provided

Adagio Sostenuto

The Jello-Box

I, Feeble-Piticus

I Bear the Truth

Haiku

But Was It Real?

F

L

X

BA

Approaches

FEEBLE NODES

Let the Dew Make Him Dance

O Better Perhaps to Leave Experience Alone

INTRO DUCTION

As most of us know, the clarification of the nature and limits of received positions, especially as regards the philosophy of language, generates metaphysical utterances that violate the bounds of sense, placing both reader and viewer between apparently unavoidable poles, e. g. realism and idealism, Cartesianism and behaviorism, Platonism and formalism. Obvious as this was in the Middle Ages, for instance, contemporary linguistic philosophers have had a hard time displacing the social basis of meaning, especially when it comes to the constantly changing semantic environment of poetry and prose, and the blurring boundaries of everyday and literary langauge. It does no good for poststructuralist theoreticians to deconstruct the personalist impulses of discourse analysis. Look what happened to Wittgenstein, Jakobson, Bakhtin and Bloom. Even Lévi-Strauss was forced to admit that Durkheimian sociology was acceptable as a system of signification, but failed utterly to render plausible the relatively open text, much as most of us wish he had.

This is not the place to rehash utopian concepts such as symbolism, futurism, and surrealism. What was, was. No amount of recapitulation can bring back the purifying word of the tribe. Even the deliberate flattening of tonal register and the extensive use of non-sequitur fails to diminish the role of the lyric subject in favor of a relatively neutral voice (or multiple voices). Each of us -- poet and writer, reader and viewer -- must decide whether or not we believe the category of language is to be understood as hypotactic or paratachtic. Socrates preferred living speech to writing, but that was because he believed that writing alienated language users from memory. Homer's epics aside, we live in an age in which most of us imitate, not Platonic dialogue, but the logical or *logos*-like discourse of Aristotle, purged of mimetic interchange. Real speech can be ideologically threatening because it is centrifugal, because it flees the philosophical "center" of truth toward which all discourse is aimed.

Perhaps we are meant to be isolated by language. Maybe poetry leaves us little room for reassurance in a world whose center cannot hold, in a universe unable to come up with the small change of dark matter that would prevent thermodynamic equilibrium. Heidegger transformed the inner form of language into a messianic "speaking" of language that was potentially redemptive. But later, Lucan and Derrida used Heidegger to read Saussure against the grain, so to speak, but in the end, the sign does not always generate meaning, especially when the thing itself -- or the "spoken" thing, if I may mix my metaphors -- is the very stuff of which literature is made, while linguistics is but a form of systemized hostility toward language, and perhaps, toward literature as well. The closer this introduction approaches literature, the less coherence of formalist principles it maintains, and the more it contaminates scholarship, nay, even the mysticatory Platonism of mainstream linguistic descriptivism, which, however hard it tries, cannot neutralize the disguises of various socially imposed personas.

We approach the cul-de-sac of what Augustine called "fleshy" speech, where the lack of ideological validation abhors the vacuum of methodological unity. Freud's *Interpretation of Dreams* (1900) and *Jokes and Their Relation to the Unconscious* (1905) served only to enter the fray already cluttered by the oppositional approaches of Wilhelm von Humboldt and Kenneth Burke in the 19th century and Karl Vossler and V.N. Voloshinov in the 20th. A linguistic kind of chauvinism was the best they could muster against the frayed apologies of Noam Chomsky's tranformational-generative linguistics, which affirmed Humboldtian creativity but split it down the middle, as it were. No matter where we turn, we continue to face the ancient discipline of rhetoric and its notions of figurative ornamentation. When Burke wrote that rhetoric was concerned with "the state of Babel after the Fall," he wanted us to stare the reality of real language use in the face. But as a poet, I am not sure how to do this without making a fool of myself.

The poet is a maker of poems -- a text in verse. Bound speech. Thus, the poet, in a way that cannot be explained, captures the Word in the steel trap of Language, and in doing so, imprisons himself as well. For to escape is to be silent in the face of the Big Bang.

Even so
I wish I'd never started.
It was a clandestine operation,  this signal

a capsized *explication de texte* that[6]
degenerated into the mere *entr'acte* between eclogues,
the redundant version of Clauswitz's *coup de théâtre*
while the Chicago critics slept on their *bouts-rimés*

"sweet kisses of death[9]
set on thy lips
colder are they than mine."

stressed by the
throat until dead
he said

stressed by the
throat until dead

to reconstruct the self
is an act of autotelic mannerism
a blind shot in the dark,
the story within the story
a *jeu d'esprit* of the *fait accompli*
fraught with glory and worry and glory

but the lady from Spain was sick on the train
not once but again
and again and again,
and again and again and again.

Even so,
I wish I'd never started.

it's going to rain tonight and i'm glad thirsting
for the black clouds of a hat to shut down the brain
they die when you're young or they die
when they're old and you   you die when you're young
or you die when you're old but you die but you die
but you die.

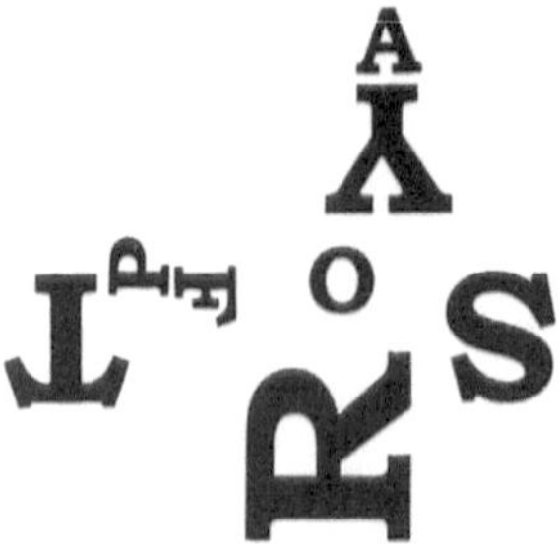

It was a voyage
to the end of the night
the search for the father
that ends in disenchantment
the search for the mother
that ends in cinematography
the search for the child
that ends in enumerative
bibliography.
Even so.

surroundingsilencethesurroundingsilencethesurroundingsilencethesurroundingsilencethesurroundingsilencethesurroundin

NEVER

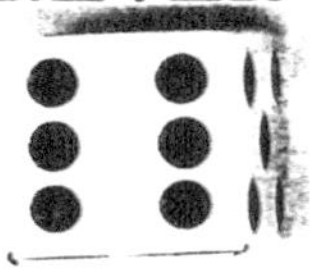

it takes a leap of faith to create an ordered world of some kind
yet the leap itself must be governed by contingency

those who attempt to seize hold
of the absolute
and those who confront
the white page

Was Ez just an Ev
(eryman)
facing the wreckage
and errors of a life?

chance

rein ou presque un art

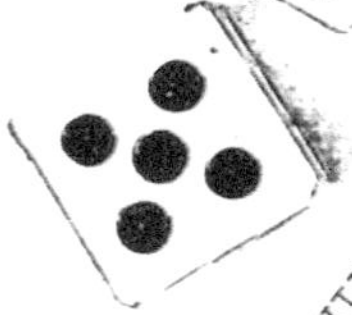

Pascal's wager closing the abyss
was the necessary prelude
to transcendence of another kind

Pascalian Space

D'UN NAUFRAGE

chance

the basic unit
can no longer be
the line,
but
the page

un Coup de Dés jamais n'obolira le hasard
a throw of the dice
will never abolish
chance

a toppling of the empire of passion and of dreams

emptiness

is humanity finally shipwrecked
on the shoals of contingency

stars

a scintillation of final

chance

JAMAIS

Mallarmé himself was reluctant
to "transgress against the received
order of things."
"I merely wish," he said, "to dispense
its elements."[10]

the void

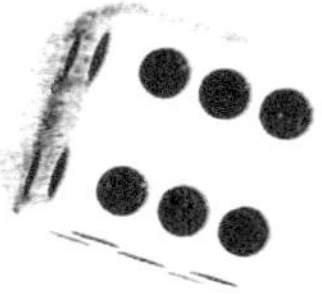

A SHIPWRECK

the surrounding silence the surrounding silence the surrounding silence the surrounding silence

surroundingsilencethesurroundingsilencethesurroundingsilencethesurroundingsilencethesurroundingsilencethesurrounding

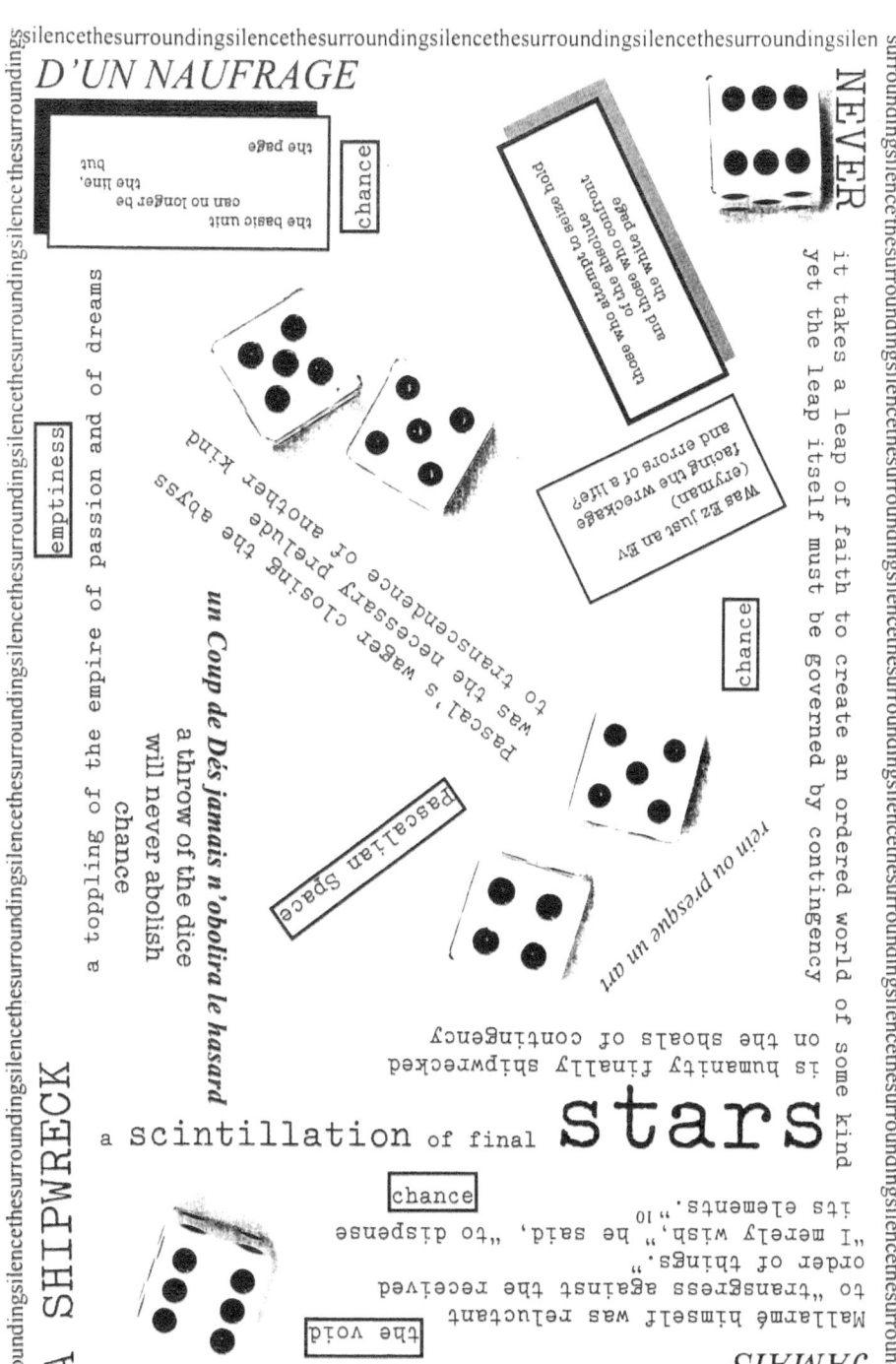

silencethesurroundingsilencethesurroundingsilencethesurroundingsilencethesurroundingsilen

1

C the man play Kapellmeister R bare arms[5]
"I, too was born in Louisiana," the lady says.

Hot wind above Thy brain.
Dem bones broken in the zink.
Eyes full of weary sleep.

Beethoven takes the Palestrina style in the last quartets
(--"Art demands of us that we shall not stand still."—)
the asperities of wind intonation
the jog-trotting accompaniment of the violin.
How far are we
the unconscious channel for our works,
and how far are we the arbiter?
Willing co-operators or trance mediums?
His words written on the score
of the C sharp minor Quartet:
"Put together from pilferings from one thing and another."

The dog is the dog is the dog.
Everlasting.
The moon is the moon is the moon.
Everlasting.
Day to day, this is how it goes.
My son and his friend stand in the kitchen,
putting tattoos on their bodies.
Sunlight comes through the window.
The same sunlight that goes through
your window on a slow, everlasting Saturday.
And here we are,
alive here on this slow everlasting Saturday,
bread on the kitchen counter,
my wife humming
as she fools with the toaster oven.
March 18, 2000.   A slow Saturday.
The dog is the dog is the dog.
Everlasting.
The moon is the moon is the moon.
sweet sweet   sweet sweet   life.

I, Feeble-Piticus of Los Angeles, to you [3]

he was the Gold Machine
they were the Silver Screw
you are the Bronze Crowbar
i am the Copper Plate

In-land, by hillsides steeped in the blood
of paper clips and who dunnits,
I, Feeble-Piticus,
a shivering barnacle dredged from the sea,
to you
what is the stance, who follows directions
into the dance.

1
The train they call the city of New Orleans
destitute laments of the twelve apostles period
She is the grasping hook,
lost pilots on their way to Arizona
the bear borne of whiskey and gin, no lighthouse period
of the porch light, a man undone but done up done up
a coming 'round the bend

2
it was the memory that brought me to this shore.
it was the memory that placed us in the photograph
it was the memory of rainstorms that called me back
it was the memory of sad faces in the kitchen
that made me lie down upon the floor
that made me call out to Jesus on the phone
that made me say his name as a question
that made me spit upon the doormat
that made me play the mu-sick mu-sick mu-sick
that made me make home the hieroglyph period

3
love is box-top, and can barely
save us from the weight of management,
the love of form uneasy to follow
Hollywood, Fordbank, Pickfair, Humboldt.

O L A Man
O suntanned Amerika
O Hollywoooo wooooman
O Barnacle Bill the Sailor

From COWTOWN to HICKTOWN
from DOGTOWN to LETDOWN

the nest, I say to you, I Feeble-Piticus say
O California winter
O offended afternoons
O Santa Monica summer
O midnights in june

memory of that which you can do
memory of that which can be done

you made it up but was it real?

and for what?
i was abstract [4]
i was changed
i gave pleasure

the book you called for was hidden, the words suitably buried
in the stone of uncertain truth what would you have of me
gold flourisher of the apocalypse, hermit man, inventor
of indestructable ennui?
between what points of wopbabaloobop and shoobeedoobeedoo
was Eden pierced and Adamn drowned and Eve washed
lounging by the sea?

here's the paradise of a sunless day,
the poet's gibberish, *cardo miseratio animus,*
angoribus confectus, afflictus.
vates inanis strepitus.

you say it's about someone else but why are you crying?

you say it really happened but what was true?

Time writes the freshness of the world down.
Doesn't complicate the harmony of a brave fiction,
Hansel and Gretel at home in the out-takes,
in the faithful speech of the gingerbread man.

you make like it matters but it don't

full worthy was he
in his lordes werre,
And thereto had he riden,
no man ferre,
cooling the boiling
care-waves.
The sheen of the broad-
gabled hall flashed bright
with gold from afar.
What shall
he have
who killed
the deer?[11]

so much rememembered and so much forgotten
my son another universe i cannot comprehend
a feeble truth and the supreme fiction
the actual cupcake, the imagined belt
the real car parked in the expressible driveway
the revelations of doorknobs the escapades of love
my brothers my sister the remorse of our childhoods
all gone all gone all gone all gone

Put it down the extract abstract malaria place it there cup cut-throat and adjustment, refer daily to each extreme, then in line he said haven't you got the keys to the car instruction is more important sometimes than execution but don't they dangle and piss all over themselves even Ethel fried to a crisp when one jolt was not enough to burn the brain and breast as the evening sun went down over the Hudson River and passing

and how you die

F G U P I E K P W

high explosive lens mold on a jello-box.[8]

motorists shouted jibes at the pickets, an outbreak of cheers and honking of horns, but in a situation like that, legal matters still unsettled, cough cough cough, one must get along with the argument, let history also have its claims.

a cloak of mystery

The kids want to know where babies come from

grovel of flesh, bare walls, tinsel on the crown; in the dark of the kitchen, feverishly, wear a hat and disguise your voice on the phone. You grow up in that country. You need to go somewhere, you know the roads. It's a good feeling; yet, getting lost is a challenge looked forward to.

KEHZYK

Now that's a log cabin if I ever saw one!
Take it now but don't bring it back.
Someone else left that message.
I'm fishing.

Yet another silver fender blade.
See around the edges all those paper cuts.
But with summer this close, ear to jaw.
Lovers just don't care for politics.

You can wear any coat to the dance.
If all black then you must know something.
Each vest should contain a secret.
Who did you kill wearing those shoes?

I have this delicate relationship with dreams
Run for your life!
Will this gray rain ever stop!
And the closer I look, the less I dream.

Some say there's method to one's madness.
Delirium is robbed of its meager truth
as madness if its called a *Work of Art*.
The chance to see being born, over and over.

After awhile, even deSade bores me.
Violence promises to recover the self,
but you can't limit the world that wounds you
any more than you can disappear into Nature
when Nature is invisible to begin with.

To lose everything at the movies
is an act of faith.
Scene. Close-up. Tracking shot. Dissolve.
You think that's something.
You should see my life.

A true understatement
never
crosses
the
river

B

Down these nasty streets

The clock reveals the body

Z

L

J

C

The whole point is that matter evolves, the universe
is expanding, random is salad, the dinosaur lives.

Some people get nothing
from
pain

but expenses.

M

P

V

F

swoons two more spoons
of
sugar

spoons two more swoons of sugar

white paint near the ground
is first to go.
judge streets by the sounds
of settling tile,
the grains of plaster,
tossings of a bed,
the loose slate
shifting overhead,
hiding pigment
and restraint.

I bear the truth because it's
forbearing and not because an
ordered sense of decency com-
pells me to adhere to all ver
sions of reality but one.

The summer we went to the edgewater
hotel on the Gulf Coast,
the summer I learned to swim
and Karl to float
and Louis to leave the high diver
without screaming
was the one that fit, I think,
the green blanket thrown
across our outrage.
There goes Brahms
on the phonograph and
my mother swooning at
Heifitz' violin.
I am the monster creeping
out of the closet draped in red cellophane.

M

Here's one approach:

Walking into the classroom
I'd put one foot
in the trash can
and begin reading
the last chapter
of Travis McGee's latest,
and say to them Write
A Poem that leaves out
the most important detail;
does not contain the letter "d";
and has clues
to a buried treasure.

You can get a lot of reading done
that way.

so thoroughly in the dark

The universe is just not a cigar.

Here's another approach:

Brutalize three long playing-envelopes.
Caution the disposal rate of tangerines by two.
Most people would have trouble with this part
but you can televise the chant
and no one will be the wiser.
Loop one year with no vacancy and
sling it over your back cockny-like
and be as thoroughly in the dark
as possible without losing
your perfect disposition.
This is important
but this is the most important of all.
Autumn is a time for inspection.
Remember your father going around the house
with his putty knife.
We are all, one way or another
hurtling through a splendid situation.
I wish I could tell you more.
If I were you, I'd insist on it.
You have to draw the line somewhere.

M

When the waters of the river rose
those cells situated at the level of the sewers
became a refuge for a swarm of huge rats
which during the night attacked those confined
and bit them wherever they could reach them.
Madwomen have been found with feet, hands,
and faces torn by bites from which several died.

C

This complicated system was devised to control
a reputedly dangerous madman at Bethlehem: he
was attached by a long chain that ran over the
wall and thus permitted the attendant to lead
him about, to keep him on a leash, so to speak,
from outside; around his neck had been placed an
iron ring; this latter slid the length of a
verticle iron bar fastened to the floor and
ceiling of the cell. This man lived in this
cell, attached in this fashion, for twelve
years.

A few birds
go into the fresh sky.

Someone sings gaily
along the black river.

It sure is a pleasure
California.

Look down upon the fork
of the American River.

Lie there in the sun;
a brown and fried look.

God, is that a peach!
As juicy as a watermelon.

Last night at sunset
I pointed out the pink sky.

This is the place to live.
Even at night, it's bright as day.

A

It "You have a beard," he said.
is "Yes," I said.
almost And he turned back to the counter and ordered another
over cup of coffee.
the summer and sometimes need shaving The
twice a day. palms
and Dad raises the
soles razor
as jews under disconnected sulphur bridges. to
my his
face
as my brother and I watch him scrape the beautiful soap and running
and board of accumulating hairs
I nonliving and rapid power
find the razor and test it out baldness follows suit.

on our own skins while he is away at work.

C

It He is wearing a tweed coat, the jews
is and the fat of his blushing neck
almost curdles over the edge of his collar.
over The bloat inside disdains what is naked
the and what is covered that he must show
summer I and scald and scrape away skin cell by skin cell
of as if from within day after day of his dead life.
after- I hate him. I want to spit the coffee-phlegm in my mouth
noon into his dish
dreams, puffs of smoke rising of prunes.
his out of sleep.
snuff- Madame DuFarge knits as the prunes are swallowed
ling down his throat
head, breath missing, bombed down the short street, fish-like.
and the smell a childhood
I spit into of lilac-vegetal accident
my spoon slapped on the skin uncorked
as he goes with both palms foam
to the bathroom. awake and
to break the spine and jaw of spit flung into
the sink,
a man's spit
Later, when he is off to work my brother and I
we spit into the sink. thought to our-
The spit is clean with bubbles. selves,
This is not phlegm. Not man's spit. K phlegm.

Dull. Cold. Indifferent.
"You have a beard," he says.
A snouted carcass clutch-bloodied waiting for time to pass.
These are the men who kill jews I hear my uncle say
in his decaying
My spoon filled with spit, living room.
I slowly stir his coffee
before he returns to finish breakfast.
When I get up to leave, I slap a quarter on the counter and call him
jew,
the beardless jew.

B

carbon cycle

F

illustrious

A

Here it is:
Take it down blow torch or something.
The talk's as good as the writing.
The bullshit's packaged either way.
You think Christ said if you bring
forth what is within you, what you
bring forth will save you and if
you do not bring forth what is
within you what you do not bring
forth will destroy you well he did
but that's not the point the point
is do you want to listen to a poet
or not or what, like especially when
he or she's alive it's all made of
the same three parts his life, his
mouth, his poem, and so you get to
own theearth, see? It belongs to you
and isn't that all it is except to
stay alive. When does the bull look
good to her, that young bull the
braggart champion. I lose my hair and
I get older all the same, but I feel
good, a little crazy and young,
younger than you to be exact, and
in this shining city words are broken
by the image, see, not like social
or political action but like earth
quakes and napkins, an impression
from what used to be a republic of
words, now the image rules, thank
God it's seven o'clock and I can
tell you something, we might have to
make the word up again, translate the
letter so you say them again like a
4 year old, who doesn't mind being
cultural, except in his case it's
interesting, see, and then the diffi-
culty is to get the bravo around at
the back end and even if everybody
left I'd still talk and hold the
universe up, and the other way it
means too, hold the universe up, and
the other way, too; see the words
are always saying something else.
Not like Ed. He's just the baker.
He makes the bread, and I don't wear
glasses, and you gotta cut it all
loose and show your teeth. A bag of
bones. And Fred Astaire. When you
get right down to it, just what does
it mean to be brave. What's the
hidden term.

MAD Let

out here everyone walks on their backs

HIM The

so is half an orange

MAKE Dew

Z
Z
Z

what rodent then dies on what good comet

STORM Make   of it what you will, something's cooking

you call this living, that was my wife

HAIL Him

In the still all alone Autumn by itself still

THE Dance

"Experimenting! Experimenting!" he cackled.

LET

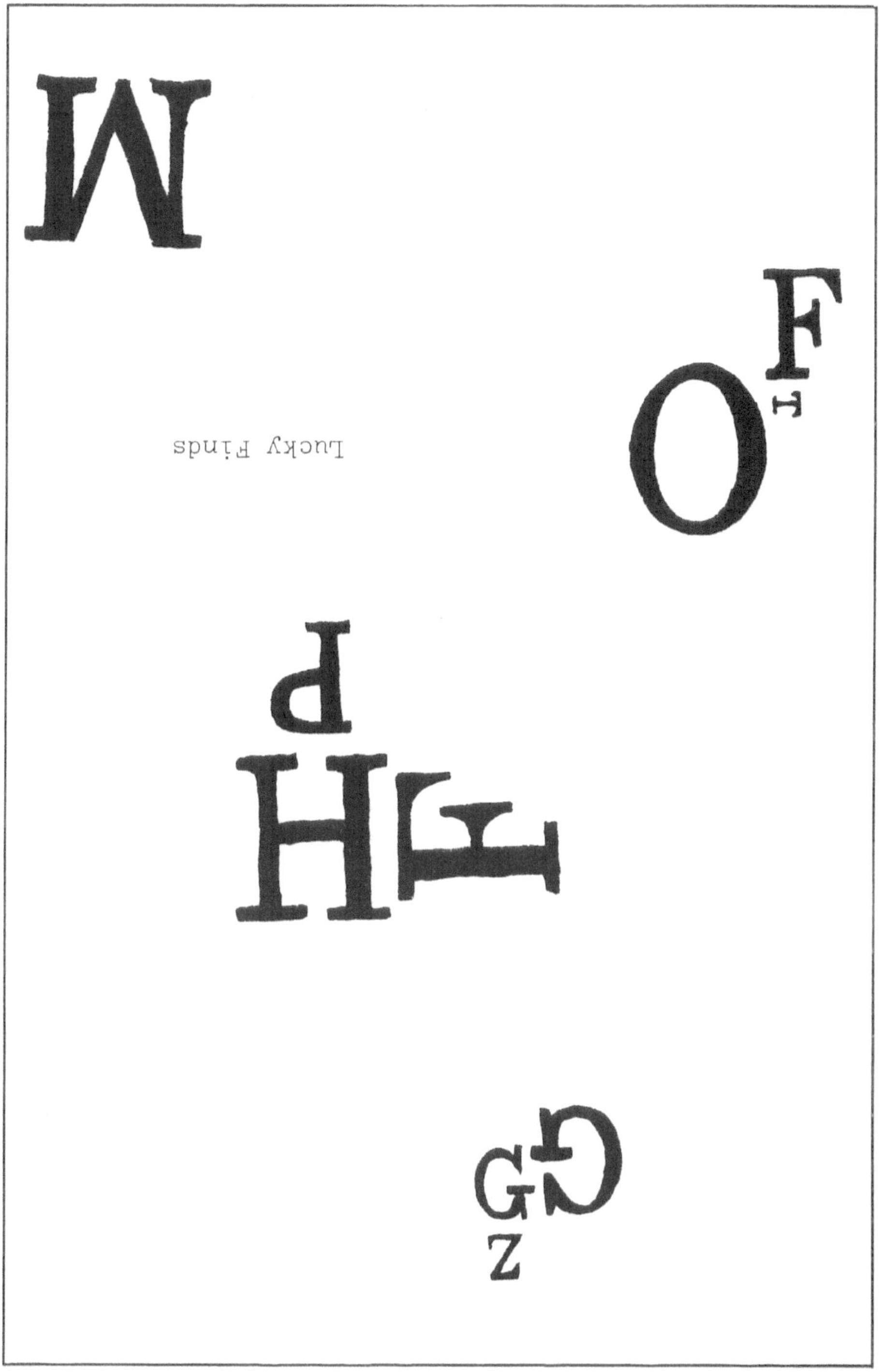
Lucky Finds

B

like
your
grace
your
move
my
friend
but
who
said
polish

I spend most of my time on the moon.

A

this time it is hard to tell
which is the priest and
which is the repression

X

but who's the boss

who's the real boss

who's running the show

i don't even get tempted
jazz session a proper noun
in Vancouver or talking
economics the brown
paleolithic cows can that
be a political event which
is more like red or green
a passport privilege though
he goes by the square
numbers until he goes by
odd numbers what an odd way
to live slick fifty and that

god of mars lower case in the language where wyoming
no zeus no joyce no shakespeare no cassiopeia clytemnestra
no boston no clouds no air overhead lower case no literally
each letter an attack upon the universe each word a thrust
and think perhaps that before you knew it they were called
printer's devils and now the pictures come back and we
count the rings, two tapes a day, one from each side as
it turns no cloud cover no lower case just an attack
upon the universe another mention go home brush your teeth

what's inside is still
the mystery
to see how a thing bleeds
or does it do that at all
to know how infinite
and beautiful
each piece is
almost by definition

L

this is like they say
the dream of your life
a habit of newsprint

in

art

they

shoot

you

of the thunder perfect mind barren
yet many sons she refuses to speak
and says her name inside out alive

this is from my mouth
this is from my hand
this will stop the fire
this must bring the flame
this is in my stomach
that sticks to my foot
and cuts across my back
these are meaningless
they peel off like skin

I was like that too, once; but now I'm different.

but
if
I
love
you
I
ask
for
nothing

why
then
do
I
ask
so
much
of
you

We kept the box inside a large
brown bag that was stored back
in the closet under a pile of
dirty towels that were never
washed and some discarded and
broken toys, little wind-up
tin drummers and marching men

this is the world we are made to swim in but what does the cat know and isn't telling

It's
only
a
picture
a
dream
worth
waiting
for
fresh
prey
brushed
hair
gone
dull
what
ever
happened
to
the
private
bomb
insult
to
the
little
man
this
late
in
the
day
and
so
much
to
be
gained
by
talk
leave
nothing
behind
walk
the
other
way
sing
by
the
black
river

A

the gift to my children not their but my own happiness

grapple
with
the
hook
of
re
dem
tion
rep
tile
and
shut
that
gap
ing
jaw
.
in
to
a
no
t
h
e
r

w
a
l
l

up this way the fulgurations of doom in this heat the warm hands of a wife or lover

i
do
it
so
fk
i
n
g

wafer

PH

Then I, for my part, realized for the first time the sickness of ultra-leftism. Those who jump when the bell rings. Three cheers for the Revolution? Well, fuck that! Let the rope support whom ever is hanged, from above, from below.

thin

W

When I close my eyes I see fire. My mother would scream my brains are burning. You should have seen her hair stand on end, pulling them out with her fing ers. Nobody sees the body burn. I like to see what I set on fire. I like to follow the smoke up til it's gone.

what difference does it make to you turdfacefart
head
wart
cunt
dick
foot
crap
hump
hump

but draw the line somewhere

E

The strength of haiku lies in its suggestions. Some of the original cut-words have no translatable meaning and often indicate an unfinished sentence, which has an elusive force of it's own. One can follow the order of thought or one can follow the grammar.

> haiku:
>
> a chocolate mellow mint
> refers to my tongue
> in passing. in passing in.

Sometimes the effect is quite the opposite of what was intended. A rigid structure can act as a sort of frame to the picture. Rhyme and word endings that appear monotonous in one language are not necessarily monotonous unless framed without rigid strucutre. If there is a sword it is best used after the cherry blossom, unless mouth-tree-interval rapes the still unfaithful moon. The horse is a frequent visitor, though others brought hordes from Asia and look where we are now. There can be no independent and permenant wound. For me who goes - for you who stay, Autumn sucks teeth. Bosho Buson and the Bamboo Broom translator is a traitor. Pluck! Pluck! Pluck! You must force it to do so: rhyme, equivalents, postpositions, metric, long piercing nails goughed in the bloody neck, dark blood awash and blather, no fox trout amuses in special rednering the slim slick fox who hedges, then gambles, than that was no lazy he screams dumpkopf! that vas my life. Surely there is some kontroversy here, a konstandt remindy komma but I forget. Needless to say in this short span, living on this planet as temporary hosts, we should keep things simple and pure. Don't make too much of anything. What is, is; and what will be, will be. Whoever isn't here, is there, unless he's here now, then he's not there. Begin with a fragment and you can't go wrong. There are so many little pieces, pieces torn off from those little pieces into ever yet and smaller pieces. Examine the details. Vanish to a spoon. So few words are necessary. Sometimes, one word will do. Sometimes, a single letter. There are so many. Pick one. Just pick one. It's enough.

A

Is it inside the body conscious neglect.

S

Is this September. now that the work's done? Hardly. Wood along the Thames. A mere nickel.

S

Each
night
the
men
gather
with
nails
and
long
oak
planks
to
build
the
ship
that
will
take
them
over
the
mountains
once
the
flood
comes.

G

Snark is barely alive these days
writing one novel after another:
the self -- always the self.

F

sub-atomic

P
Z

Now I'm going to tell you something.
This is no accident.
This is what I meant all along.
That's the difference, see.
This is what I meant from the start.

E

and if there is no flood, they'll just have to carry it to the sea.

Stand
calmly.
Rather
a
speech
full
of
old
images.

S S

just imagine
these world lines
of matter
that form a
coherent pencil
of geodesics
just imagine

shift out from the skin
no prefered position or direction
just elegant solutions.

G

Monad squashes his hand to his chin
and rests elbows on the table:
living systems, he says;
these strange objects.

the ordered structure of a storm

K X R

is *k* a real number?

a singularity of infinite density

On back of the body the double balance of weight
a return of dead leaves each single tree no promise
or posture at all but the surface of things the pose
as a badge against hardness to stop seeing this
is to fall out of a random window wrapped in smoke, teeth
on the tips of fingernails.
If the film is run backwards, it is no longer my father
dying your father dying the father's all live,
gesturing in the deepest axis of a shifting world.
Shine the light through the brain. The past is so enormous,
gathering shape, coiling its arms and tongue around
the death of a careless future.
That's why you run so fast: to make pudding of this poem.
To reach back and right the upturned salt shaker.
To leave the cold kitchen alone and cheap with its voices.
How many times can you make love do the work
of a hundred deaths, in vomit, in rags, in rage, in sunlight,
in bruise, in bloodsuck, in locked closets, in eye-patch.
This is what they do not teach in school.
This is what cannot be written.

shift out from the skin
no prefered position or direction
just elegant solutions.

T E F

S P E

Monad squashes his hand to his chin
and rests elbows on the table:
living systems, he says;
these strange objects.

just imagine
these world lines
of matter
that form a
coherent pencil
of geodesics
just imagine

is *k* a real number?

Then we went downstairs to the car,
set the radio to WNOE,
sped up Napoleon Avenue
and threw beer bottles on Mr. Senac's front lawn.
Outward and yelling, our faces in the wind,
we picked up Cynthia from her father's fabulous estate
and headed up the old river road to the swamps
shrouded in close-webbed mist and clouds,
a slumbering sun
holding back the swartest night.
Cynthia, powerful in magic, witch-goddess,
made us forget the schoolwork of the cadaverous dead
between the realm of death and the realm of vegetation.
Dark blood flowed in her veins,
her soul stained by the sickly death hand of her father,
proud and blind in his stateroom,
bearing much of the sterile bulls, best of the lot,
back from heaven in a hell of gold and crabgrass.
She lay back in the back seat, while A.J. drove
into Bayou Lafitte, under the Spanish oak
that lined the dock behind Zattarin's Fish House.
She unbuttoned her blouse, poured wine over her breasts,
tender libations unto the selves
sacrificed to home-room and study hall,
water mixed with flour, the lost ones who flunked algebra,
mauled with bronze ball-point pens
among the battle-spoilt ball-players
who after practice
smacked the pin-ball machines with their palms
and drank beer until midnight
until their fathers, slayers of sheep,
unsheathed the narrow swords
of the impetuous impotent dead
and called them home.
Hold your tongue Ez,
out of Divus,
out of Chapman,
out of Pope,
out of Homer,
hold your tongue and drive no further,
hold your tongue
and let the old man rest,
let the old man go.[1]

詩 12

How do we account for the reality of subjectivity?
Subjectivity is not the problem.
Reforming language will not solve it.
Objectivity is the problem.
We must reform the soul.

She leans against the gray screen
of the lifeless TV. Should she brush the hair
from her eyes, a whole poem would magically escape.
Without rain, the rainbow plots its overthrow of the sky.
To merge with anything is a plot to overthrow the self.
And oh, I am the cream of the crop,
delivered to my mother's breasts.
Baskets of spite, ribbons of easy-going blues,
the tree out back whose roots break through the concrete.
In two's we gathered by the light of the refrigerator
collecting the good things of the world,
honesty and brotherhood, a coincidence of thumbtacks,
delivering my father's message, the dream state
of a garden hose, live crabs slapping their claws
against the side of the pot filled with Zattarin's
crab boil, thier blue shells turning red
and the white slabs of dead-man's meat
set on a dish beside the newspaper.
I would have you believe any of this but the truth,
the great gusts of flesh my mother instructed me to eat,
her breasts the cream of the crop,
passionate loaves of fish flapping on the dock
as my father beats the last drop of liquor from the bottle.
I admit I am mad for the world made one,
made perfect and savable
if only I were worthy of the spare parts and loose change.
I would have you believe anything but this truth,
that, forgiven, we are still guilty of perfection.
I remember red and silver,
the dark stain of the sun bleeding on the lake.
And I own so little that I cannot lose,
a transmission interrupted by her back.
This is the kind of peace I seldom allow myself,
to borrow a phrase: *upheaval interruptus*.
Fixed made broken. Mended made asunder.
Recludo hoc uterus. *Recludo hic mundus*.
The answer of course is in the lacking,
the whack of my father's body falling to earth,
the line read before the fire,
the pine cone dropping below the grate.
Why move, when remem-membering
still blows a hole in the world.

There is a symptomatic condition
for modernist writers:
to misjudge the point
at which poetics ends
and poetry begins.

義 This is a test of
the nether breastplate that manufactures
the ulterior of

snead if he stands 書 to reasoN

rem eorum saluavit

W e who are obscure references ἐλένανς

in 利 the 必 makeshift 何 cargo of semblance.

The dead rise into the air
forgiving every senseless act of love,
forgiving every meaningful act of war.
Bodies lay stacked on the dead
grass, illegible signs of spring,
where small shops hang out their
"open for business" signs.

I advise staying away
from the pure theory of things,
originally a pragmatic cupcake.

I was thrown into this World

without a Note from my ἐλέπτολις![7]
mother.

but the heart -- meant for mending -- 日
breaks againt the pure theory
of things, senseless tulips that
question authority, all the mmommies and daddies
unable to name the small walkways of the future.

Ma se morisse!

P

countess with thick calves [2]
how many rooms
C see through negligee
and one telephone is that right

i work for the consensus i
agree but what do you count
with respect to power
you mean census as in rome

as in people and property
i agree authority for everything

count you this time
one bedroom one bath, one title
the social importance of flesh,
the bedrock of cold opinion

following her down the
hall past pictures of
aristocrats in confused
poses, but then that
was their life, each
day, the planned man
agement of the self
that counts, takes
stock, touches but
does not overcome power.
She sits and opens both
legs showing the smooth
white thighs.

don't let the accent bother you
we talk this way for money
one thing is because of another
i sleep well but the dreams are bad
during the revolution stayed home
but here i am anyway
living like this, still with a
fine body, dancer's legs.
feel them.
like when I was a young girl.
do I look sixty?
I still have to make a living.
Yes, one phone. And just one of these
What else do you need to know?
I'll tell you everything.

as I said, Countess, I
work for the consensus.
Tell me everything.

E

the poem's all there is to believe in
it's weak backbone that there's a nerve in it
like the condition of a frog;

it's
the
neural
condition
that's
difficult
is
what's
up

only because organs
are able
the capacity to find out
to celebrate
not like me when dead, baby
and by the way, simply because we're born
like, how to dance sitting down.

the elementary,
not the synapse;
that's easy.

each
one
of
us is as hard as we're made
or can make
ourselves
and that's
the stone
not this
live frog
hidden.

that's easy;
only because we're able,
that's all we are.

W

left alone, here
proving
my
point

two kinds of angeles, one writes, howl of the eyes, glancing up.

but do you know a water to write in?
that love and woman is our subject?
so that it covers love separate from woman?
not arms and men.
even if we have to become arms and men,
our subject is love, and cause, and hmm,--woman.

crawl in backwards.

L

crawl in backwards

an open or closed world
assuming limits or progressions
having nothing more (or less)
to lose

G Z

M

participation

propagation
of a probability
amplitude
through
superspace

the gift to honour your birth no broken bus eclipses civilization just a sickness when the
palm does not work the lawyers catch in the throat; how many critics are crushed into
powder for seasoning how many serpents die in a flash of magnesium

P

mutation of a species
metamorphosis of a rock,
chemical transformation,
spontaneous transformation of a nucleus,
radioactive decay of a particle,
reprocessing of the univese itself.

the acrobat takes bites out of his mother's arm this murder onstage, backstage, at
the gate of the cemetery small body taking breast by the throat snake full of
emerald skies desperate elephant on the banana tree keel of random life caught on
chest hairs how to develop bare feet in the vomit

PARTICIPATION

H T G P

always be short of breath;
always loath the naked surface

as if there was time to renounce
the voice, the name, the alphabet.
as if one continues by being silent
as if out of nothing
comes nothing.

B

the universe as
being from time
to time squeezed
thru a knothole.

T F

participation

Is it unlike you

to be so precise?

How does the eye become

accustomed to shadow

reminds me of four hours in the dentist chair
gagging blood
and chips of
teeth

C O N N E C T **B**

I am best at this, he said, pulling the saw up then sliding it back down toward his foot.

H
O
R
I
Z
O
N
T
A
L

everyone
stand
amazed
smoke
on the
line
of berries
bulging
with
poison

and yet, we set out across the
plain, we carried our belong-
ings, we took what we could
from the land, we gave back
what we had no need for, we
prayed for rain, sang to each
other in the darkness, worship-
ped any god but the one God
that would get us through for
we were through ourselves, need-
in only to be tested. Let the

food smell
like food.

VERTICAL

But can a square
remain a square
without enclosing
the future.

K

"It's
a
good
mystery,"
he
said.

"Good,"
I
said,
humming
this
tune,
"give
me
several."

and on four sides by a bull

M

You are bound by stupid bloody acorns.

In this map, Austria is no longer Austria and Poland has eaten a part of Russia. Rome is still Rome; what can I say. Think of the electron microscope. Seeing from above is all a map is. A fixed reminder that the Present need not become the Future, and that the Past can grow right before your eyes.

F

M

the fish place, the restaurant, the one
that sits on stilts out over the water
you eat crabs to watch the sun go down
hot red and orange, flaming, a brand
out there on the horizon, and it's the
same as nature on that side, i mean if
we're not the same as nature on that side
and God on the other, man isn't. Tough.
Tough shit, he'd say; it's not easy

to get to that strength. that strength
that puts diapers up on the trees,
which knocks your whole life out, even
if you love and have babies to diaper.

like it's like playing the piano, like
that. Getting that middle voice. That's
what makes the music work, that is, that's
the thing that makes music such work, to
to get that middle voice. It's an old

principle, you get the beginning, the
middle, then the end. You do all three.
Then you get the poem. Then you get the
novel. Then you get yourself. Then you
get the wife. Then you get your life. God
damn, how many ways do you need to say it.
The whole goddamn thing is the middle, the
whole goddamn middle, right there in the
middle, where it belongs, culture in the
word, so to speak, when you don't even know
there's water out there, until the fish
stink gets you, the high tide, raising the boats
so they go through the roofs of the boat
houses, sails sticking right up, pushed
through the tops, like the tide redeems
you down to your fingertips when it's in
flood. And you sit there and eat your crabs
and watch the sun go down and you know,
you know everything, and you know it, you
know the beginning, you know the end, and
meanwhile, in the middle, sitting right there
in the goddamn middle of it all, just doing
the middle is what you'd say if asked, getting
the whole goddamn middle, crabs, and beer.

so
the
skinny
woman
jaunts
along.
there!
she
comes
is
that
a
ribbon,
or a
whip?
she
couldn't
care
less.
how
do
you
do.
no
zero
at
the
bone.
without
breath,
or
breathing.
but
polite.
sudden
fingernails.

I

what is missing in this picture?

T

*how will I be level in sleep
and still rise with the precise
yawn that subdues the most
remarkable of beasts?*

whole it is of limb unquaking.

just ask if anyone's there. who cares
what one nostril means if the
other means greek. the head falls
like a decent pear or shoots up.
mostly in the dust
just for
someone
to enter
it.

G

odd news

it has just
gotten dark and
we are lying side by side
on the bed, naked, without saying
a word, hands at our sides, barely touching.
I look for a calendar, a clock, the sound of the
ocean perhaps, something to give me a clue as to
east or west, the year of the century, how far
from sunrise, the sick feeling of hope.

But from this way of looking, that
one window is as good as another,
how then may ***what is*** go down in
Death or how might it be born?

O

there's
a pleasant
pot
to
piss
in:
the
magic
farm
along
a
secret
line
that
kills
us
with
wake
full
ness.

*I'd like to meet you
for lunch today but have only enough
money for paint.*

O

Better perhaps to leave experience alone.

in a white rag

remember the mom poetry must not substitute not cold
ent not journalism not escape but do not leave out
has it's uses and what coheres on paper is not what
co
heres

the
table
once
you
start

houses without windows
beyond the pane
of someone's dark face
perhaps the gas
over
if not
that
then

fearing what is funny there's
no end to the evasions
in winter
boarded up

anger escapes
in a white

no time for
guest
and being
human if you

some bitterness in the hug
all music however powerful

no time either
for substitution
bedrock, who else gather all this
when
envelopes
litter the hall and anger escapes

no time for God

anger escapes
in a white rag

that coheres for the sake of something better

something
from the
very
beginning

to your name, only regret,
only kneeling
in worship

to something misunderstood from the
beginning

frenzy hand about
to beast the life cycle of the caterpillar

something
all this time
nearly
worshipped

R

once beauty was important
now it means nothing
what's real is what stops you
at a strange angle face, she said, because

W

Slow spider limping cow

the place is hot, too hot, much too hot
to do anything except complain of the heat,
the hot window panes and the hot half-empty
bottles of pepsi still on the desk from
yesterday which guarentees your growing old
and already you run out of things that are
hot, not enough hot can be remembered
in the heat when it's this hot, toohot,
too hot to die, die in a cold month is
best, you bet, a slow fade while you dream
of a crisp football afternoon, going out
for a long, easy arc of a pass, touchdown;
this is a way of going out that could fool
even you, in all this heat, until it's over.

Z

B

A

There
is
a
key
to
everything

At this time of night you can't
see any of the animals, who are
invisible. Out of the walls they
come, their teeth gnawing at the
milk-cake moon. Now who left the
quarter on the table. Was it the
man who walked away from his car
never to be seen again.Or was it
the sad rapist who blows into a
seashell and can't stop cleaning
his dirty fin-
gernails. This
is how they'll
snigger when
they hear the
news, how they
will stagger &
fall about the
room saying
the moon is
gone. The rats
have dragged it deep into their
hole.

Z

P

sometimes I love you for your brown
hair and sometimes I love you for
your crazy laugh and sometimes I
love you in the morning with your
head back on the pillow and a slight
smile on your face barely sleeping
and sometimes I don't know why I
love you, sometimes I'm not even
sure I do, sometimes I don't feel a
thing, don't feel like doing a thing,
forget who I am, or why it is even
necessary to be in love with anyone,
why it is necessary to do anything,
or feel like doing anything, some-
times it takes enormous effort to find one thing, or one feeling that
is more important than another, like picking up a book or taking off
a pair of shoes, or trying to write in the absence of love.

rutrutrutrut

a creative set has both sides of
the coin is only half true but non-
the less perverse, if stupidly
brilliant kinds of possibly ugly
and beautiful objects exist.

Tom is trapped within invisible
intangible boundaries of mental
space. That is nothing to lament.
What limits Tom need not limit
you. There are an infinite set
of examples.
Only one eludes capture.
Using the formal
suggestions
of beauty
but no formula
or attitude
advanced by the
romantics,
trace the
operation
by which all
sets of beauty
justify them-
selves without
permitting
the production
of all
possible kinds
of ugliness
in a non-con-
structive set.
You have ten
minutes to do
this.

This is the space provided.

Is
it
coincidental
that
the
first
example
of
such
a
notion
of
something
approximatable
but
never
attainable
in
a
finite
process
is
called
an
"irrational"
number?

Poor Tom is in a rutrutrutrut. Tom recognizes it, but does not know how to encounter it. He is confused in his rut rutrutrut. What part of rutrutrutness has an open-ended prospective character, and what part of rutrutrutness is unpredictable and conscious. What is the truth here. Can Tom trot out into a new rutrutrutrut or is he fated always to approximate higher and higher degrees of bigger and better sets of generative rutrutrutruts. Answer in the space provided. Answer more than once. Answer until you can answer no more. Continue to answer. Begin as if you'd been answering before the question was posed. Continue.

T
R
H
T
U
R

rutrutrutrutrut
Thus
art
progresses
toward
an
ever
wider
vision
of beauty by a series of repeated diagonalizations, that is
processes of recognizing
ruts and breaking out of
ruts ruts
ruts ruts
ruts ruts
ruts

This is not the space provided.

You must feel the space with your own hands.
Walk blindly into pizza,
originated cleverly by less than scrupulous
barbers plagerizing the dreams of children,
locked in closets,
fed through a hole in the door,
spoken to only when distressed
by the introspection of sturm and drang lit rat sure.

W Z R

b r t u o e k

Look how far we travel for so little.
These small gestures of isolation
that force us to be original.

J P H

The misery of starving serfs
captured by the classical melting pot
along with the formalized
gallant expression
as exemplified by Quantz,
and the more spontaneous sentiment
of Carl Philipp Emanuel,
who would have since moved
to the free city of Hamburg,

M X Y I

and the elegant Italianate style
further developed in Manheim
by Johann Stamitz, and in London
by Johann Christian, the English Bach.
This is as far as perspective will get you.

Q

During dinner my brother pretends he's invisible;
we pretend he's not.

Symmetry works in an obvious way,
written in 1874, L K a trick of the four and six
bar version, lifeless until transformed
by Mozart's recapitulation,
by Beethoven's heroic excavation of bones.

Sightless, crazy, mute, and penniless,
the clavicord was even capable of vibrato.
I lied about practice time--
writing 45 minutes instead of 10.
The rest of the time I lay in bed
watching the ceiling for a sign of winter,
a season habituated by pocket-watches.

C X

it must explain the large
and the small
the infinite, the vanishing,
the static, all that is in motion,
the world lines, the rest frames,
for the blind stationed to observe,
and be valid over the entire
time span of the universe

but
why
can
she
nod
bat
ing
eye
less and reconstructed everything by number
drawn to me to shine even at once from
boots, green fingers, soft flesh between
thighs equivalent gathering sharp rake
eye
ing
but
can she say why

what action
so instantaneous
that one eye
seeing curvature
and one eye
seeing dust
should both see
the deeper principle

about me, what was said, this grace of truth
the blue invention replacing the absent lie,
and this black burning from within, learning
to live like salt on the white table, sludge

around
her the woman
the flesh and power
of that room curtains and
seized by some impulse
to hold on to
hang on to follow
as it pulls you under
we live without you
we live within you
we live with you
treachery thirty perfect
minutes as wash our hands as
toss a rock across the lake
that travels without
descending that makes
our history

G

backward is not not
to go forward it is
true to something else
inanother direction
facing another particle
of creation made under
heavy whiskey and whiskers

A hidden bird,
the most difficult to hunt.

going to confess
no confession at all.

loosen the limbs
of love
so outrageous as
to encompass and
represent and pro-
duce the universe.

cancel the years,
between having been thirteen
years old, standing in the dark
hallway, about to leave for school
denied but owned, and nineteen
years old, not the gesture of a
third bird, shot with a b.b. gun.

P I

but
one
knows
what
love
means.

what the hearth is.

what chaos is.

one knows

the difficulty is the one that's the most obvious.

who is going to catch
up with the decay
of the monetary condition
of the earth, peg the whole dinero dollar peso franc and
gone to hell, which is what
trade is, to fuck your mother
and slit your father's
throat, and boast,
and marry the whore
in the cave.

no power system
no success
tell the end
of your dream
confess
or brutal bastard
after the earth
become like the moon
full of the beautiful
holes of dreams.
the natural history
of the future
meaning
refering
check it out.

Z

Rg

When did the HPrK breakage begin?
When my brother and I were playing war?
When my father came home drunk
and smashed the mirror in the bathroom?
When the burglar climbed over my crib
to steal the money
hidden in my mother's shoe?

How come no one does something utterly stupid in front of the magistrate?

How come no one laughs at my bad jokes?

Yt
Bw

How come everyone walks around in a rubberized suit of unforgiveness?

what can I tell you?
Stay close to a telephone pole,
the kind a stray cat
able to appreciate the splendor
of a cloudless day
would attack
if it were a mouse.

check behind you.
there are those who hide in shadows,
secret agents or your uncle,
the one who rarely shaves,
the one with all the money
hidden in tea cannisters,
the one whose wife, a PhD
in senile displacement,
brewed her tea
with 50 dollar bills.

Zx W Ag
Mk

Fg

FEEBLE NODES

1. See Ezra Pound's *Cantos* I and LXXXIII.

Ezra Pound (1885-1972) was the central figure in the modern movement, but remains a controversial figure to this day. He and his work have been both praised and condemned. He worked on the *Cantos* for nearly fifty years, presenting himself in the poem as a Poet-Odysseus wandering through the wreckage of the 20th century. The poem ranges throughout history and literature, a massive, monumental work that Pound himself felt he'd "botched" and wasn't able to make coherent.

2. In the summer of 1970 I worked for the government following up on those who had not returned their census questionaires. My territory was the hills above Sunset Boulevard. Up and down winding streets, small run-down apartments, even smaller run-down apartments behind ramshackle cottages set back from the street behind overgrown weeds and hedges. A hippy couple named Miller named their son Sudden-Freak. An alcoholic, out-of-work executive sat on a broken down sofa drinking scotch, his bare pot belly falling over the elastic band of a damp bathing suit. A man with a rifle waving me off his front porch. Prostitutes, pimps, drug-dealers, actors. Every doorbell was a TV show, a step into the twilight zone, a day at the races, a night at the opera, an afternoon in the circus. The countess, I remember best.

3. See Charles Olson's *The Maximus Poems*.

Charles Olson (1910-1970) is a seminal figure in post-World War II literature. His essays "Projective verse" and "Human Universe" and his study of Melville helped define the postmodern sensibility. "I, Maximus of Gloucester, to You" begins the series of "letters" that, over nearly twenty years of composition, grew to the more than three hundred poems comprising his masterpiece--a lifetime's work that has taken its place beside Pound's *Cantos*, Williams's *Patterson*, and Zukofsky's *"A"* in the great tradition of modern American epics. Through the public voice of Maximus ("the Greatest"), after Maximus of Tyre, Charles Olson tuned the deep resonances of his local subject matter, the fishing town of Gloucester, Massachusetts. *The Maximus Poems* is one of the high achievements of 20th century American letters and an essential poem in the postmodern canon.

4. See Wallace Stevens' *Notes to a Supreme Fiction*.

Wallace Stevens (1879-1955) was one of the main figures in the modern movement, but like William Carlos Williams, his recognition did not come until the 1950s. Stevens' work is known for its idiosyncratic forms of abstraction and narrative indirection. As Williams was a successful small-town doctor, Stevens was a successful insurance company executive. For him, poetry was a self-defining quest for meaning.

5. See Louis Zukofsky's long poem, *"A"*.

Louis Zukofsky (1904-1978) was one of the founding figures of modernist poetry. If he is one of the most musical poets of the modern era, he is also one of the most intellectually challenging. Gems of sonic counterpoint and verbal compression, his poems incorporate social commentary and philosophy in an ongoing *ars poetica*. In *"A"*, a poem composed throughout his life, he created an epic collage of autobiography, history, and reflection replete with theatre pieces, music, word-play, and punning. The *New York Times* called *"A"* "the most hermetic poem in English, which they will still be elucidating in the 22nd century." The first section of the poem was written in 1928 when Zukofsky was 24 years old, and the last piece is dated 1974.

6. *Bouts-rimés* are sets of rhyme words unattached to verses, like "June-moon-spoon." The making of impromptu verses to fit *bouts rimés* was a fashionable pastime in the 17th century, and continues to this day. *Coup de théâtre* is a striking, unexpected turn of events in a play. *Jeu d'esprit*--"play of the mind"--is a witticism or flight of fancy.

7. See Ezra Pound's *Cantos*, V and VII.

8. In 1952 Ethel and Julius Rosenberg were executed for espionage based on the false testimony of Ethel's brother (who was highly paid by the government and given a change of name and a new home) and a dubious piece of physical evidence: a jello-box. Convicted with them but receiving a lesser sentence was Morton Sobel. Stanley Kramer directed and produced a movie about the trial starring Alan Arbus and Brenda Vacarro as Ethel and Julius, and Herschel Bernardi as their lawyer. I played the part of Morton Sobel. During the filming, the cast walked out in protest, led by Bernardi, because of some of the distortions in the script. We met at the Tropicana Motel coffee shop (known as Duke's) to discuss our strategy and the possible consequences of our actions. Kramer's justification for the selective point of view was based on the fact that he was using Louis Nizer's book, *The Implosion Conspiracy*, as the basis of the film, thus ruling out contradictory information contained in such books as *Invitation to an Inquest* by Walter and Miriam Schneer. During our "strike," I spoke to Morton Sobel on the phone and learned quite a bit about how the government tampered, and sometimes manufactured, evidence. Nevertheless, after three days, we resolved our disagreements and went back to work.

9. A poem by Swinburn.

10.See Stephen Mallarme's *Un Coup de Dés* (A Throw of the Dice).

Stephen Mallarmé (1842-1898) is one of the giants of 19th century French poetry. Leader of the Symbolist movement, he exerted a powerful influence on modern literature and thought, which can be traced in the works of Paul Valéry, W.B.Yeats, Ferdinand de Sausarre, and Jacques Derrida. From his early twenties until his death, he produced poems of astonishing originality and beauty, many of which have become classics. In the preface to *Un Coup de Dés Jamais N'Abolira Le Hasard* (A Throw of the Dice Will Never Abolish Chance), Mallarmé said the poem "enacts the very crisis of modernity to which it responds." The physical layout of the poem--its ambiguity of syntax and line breaks, the spacing and typography--was a radical innovation for its time. Words were displayed variously on the page, often in ideogrammatic fashion. Beyond the physical properties of the poem is the greatness of Mallarmé's poetic conception, the sheer power of his phrasing, and the philosophical underpinning that suggests the difficulty of establishing meaning in an essentially meaningless universe.

11. The poem set in DaVinci typeface opens with four lines in Middle English from Chaucer's "A Perfect Knight," followed by five lines rearranged slightly from *Beowulf*. The last four lines come from one of the songs used in 18th century productions of Shakespeare's *As You Like It*--the song was written by Sir Henry Bishop (1786-1855).

12. The Chinese character for poetry combines *word* and *temple*.

The Naked Eye

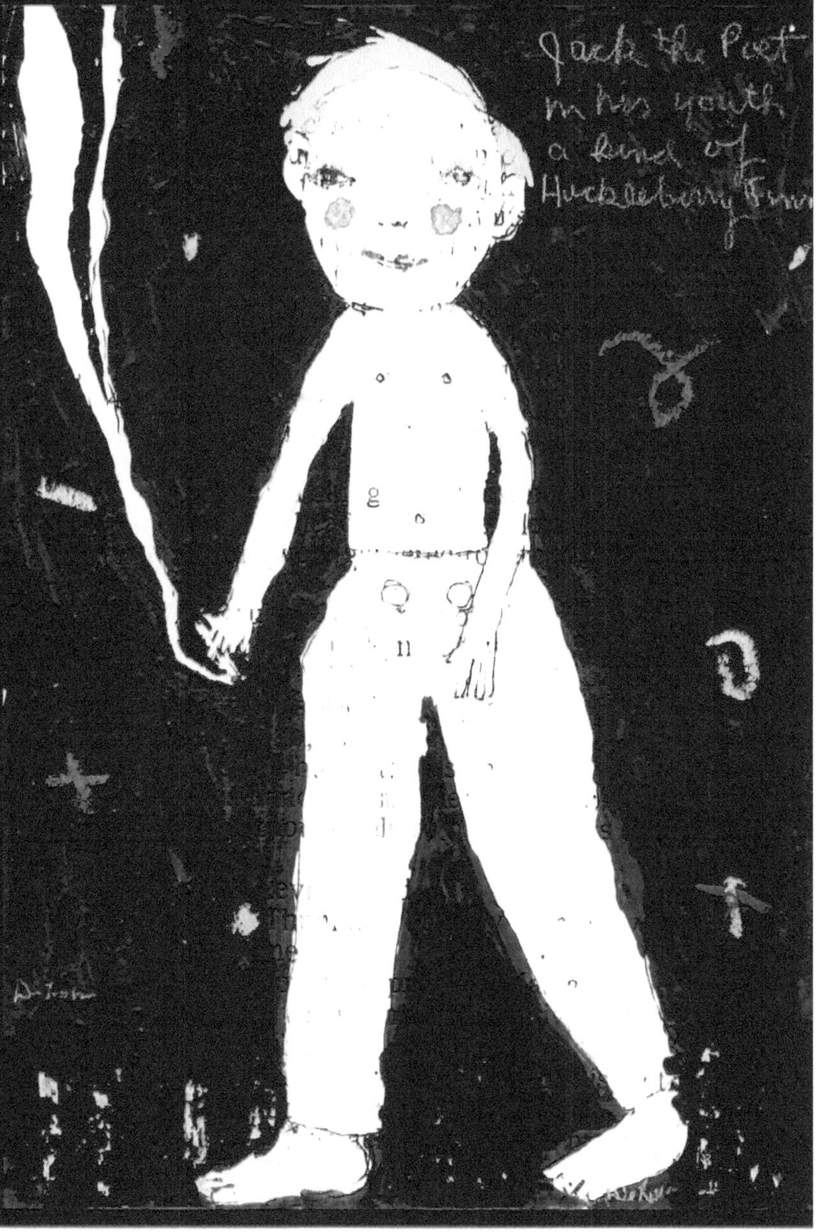

The Dark and Stormy Night

I became a writer not because I had something to say or stories to tell, but because I fell in love with words.

One could make a sentence out of words, and with sentences you could build cities and fill them with people. To this day, when I go into a bookstore and open a book to that first page, I feel as if I've given away all my possessions and I'm standing there waiting for the writer to speak, waiting to fall in love, waiting to be swept away by the writer's voice, by the writer's words.

It doesn't matter where you are, the words can take you somewhere else. You could be sitting on the white sands of a Pacific island, and the words can take you to a roach-infested tenement on the lower east side of Manhattan. You could be listening to the rain pound against the shutters of your New England cottage in the dead of winter, and the words can take you to the Sahara desert, the sun beating down on you, your mouth parched, your throat dry. You could be eating figs on the sprawling lawn of a Manchester estate, and the words can take you to a damp cell, your face enclosed in an iron mask. You could be sitting in first class on a transatlantic flight from New York to Paris, and the words can take you on a trip you've never planned.

> Midway through this journey of our life,
> I found myself lost in a dark wilderness,
> for I had wandered from the straight and true way.[1]

Later, when your friends say, "How was the flight?" you can smile and say, "It was hell."

Wherever you are, the words can take you somewhere else. Or make you wish you were somewhere other than where you are.

> A bird cried out on the roof, and he woke up. It was the middle of the afternoon, in the heat, in Africa; he knew at once where he was. Not even in the suspended seconds between sleep and waking was he left behind in the house in Wiltshire, lying, now, deep in the snow of a hard winter.[2]

No matter how old you are, the words can make you young again.

1 Dante, *The Inferno*

2 Nadine Gordimer, *A Guest of Honor*

> Once upon a time and a very good time it was there was a moocow coming down along the road and this moocow that was down along the road met a nicens little boy named baby tuckoo. . . . [3]

You could be propped in bed, nibbling a cucumber sandwich, and the words will have you storming the beaches of Normandy in World War II.

> Nobody could sleep. When morning came, assault craft would be lowered and a first wave of troops would ride through the surf and charge ashore on the beach at Anopopei. All over the ship, all through the convoy, there was a knowledge that in a few hours some of them were going to be dead.[4]

Say, for a moment, life makes sense. Give the words a chance, and they'll lead you into a world in which nothing is sure and all that is solid melts into air.

> Mother died today. Or, maybe, yesterday. I can't be sure.[5]

It doesn't matter that the rent is due, that the roses need pruning.

> My God, that bloody casket has fallen on the floor! Some people were hammering in the next flat and it fell off its bracket. The lid has come off and whatever was inside it has certainly got out. Upon the demon-ridden pilgrimage of human life, what next I wonder?[6]

Once you read the words, you can imagine thinking any damn thing you please.

> It was a queer, sultry summer, the summer they electrocuted the Rosenbergs, and I didn't know what I was doing in New York. I'm stupid about executions. The idea of being electrocuted makes me sick, and that's all there was to read about in the papers—goggle-eyed headlines staring up at me on every street corner and at the fusty, peanut-smelling mouth of every subway. It had nothing to do with me, but I couldn't help wondering what it would be like, being burned alive all along your nerves.[7]

You'll know how lucky you are when the words remind you of what it was like when you had nothing or no one.

[3] James Joyce, *Portrait of the Artist as a Young Man*

[4] Norman Mailer, *The Naked and the Dead*

[5] Albert Camus, *The Stranger*

[6] Iris Murdoch, *The Sea, The Sea*

[7] Sylvia Plath, *The Bell Jar*

> It happened that green and crazy summer when Frankie was twelve years old. This was the summer when for a long time she had not been a member. She belonged to no club and was a member of nothing in the world.[8]

You don't have to wear headphones to shut out the world. Someone is talking directly to you, close and intimate, their mouth at your ear. *Call me Ishmael.* They're not talking to a roomful of people, they're not performing a tale for the crowd; it's just you and the writer. *Marley was dead; dead as a doornail.* They're practically whispering to you. *I am ill; I am full of spleen and repellent.* Perhaps you want to turn away, but you can't. This is what you wanted. To be held by the truth of another's life. *Lolita, light of my life, fire of my loins. My sin, my soul. Lo-lee-ta.* You want to experience someone else's life, you want to dream someone else's dreams. *Last night I dreamt I went to Manderley again.* You could be happy as a lark, content with your life, and the words can still break your heart. *My wound is geography. It is also my anchorage, my port of call.* And sometimes, the words can change your life.

I was six years old. No, I was five. I had learned to read before I was five. I was crouched on the floor of the living room and it was raining. It was night. I could feel the rug beneath my knees, soft but a little scratchy. I was small, crouched on the floor, and everything was high above me. The chairs, the mantelpiece, the lamps on the end tables, the doilies on the arms of the armchairs. The book was blue. It was *My Tree House.* It was open to the first page, and there was a picture of a purple cow. Under the picture was a short, four-line poem. My mother stood in the doorway, the phone to her ear, her face red and contorted, her voice hysterical. She slammed the phone down. "Your father is drunk, and he's coming home to chop our heads off," she said. "We're going to Ma-Ma's house." Then she hurried upstairs to get our things. I looked back at the purple cow, at the poem printed beneath it.

> I never saw a purple cow,
> I never hope to see one.

[8] Carson McCullers, *The Member of the Wedding*
[9] Herman Melville, *Moby Dick*
[10] Charles Dickens, *A Christmas Carol*
[11] Fydor Dostoyevsky, *Notes from Underground*
[12] Vladimir Nabokov, *Lolita*
[13] Daphne DuMaurier, *Rebecca*
[14] Pat Conroy, *The Prince of Tides*

But I can tell you anyhow,
I'd rather see than be one.[15]

Was there really such a thing as a purple cow? All the cows I'd seen were brown, or black with white spots. I never saw a purple cow either. But maybe there were purple cows. If there were, where would they be? Maybe my dad would take me to the zoo or a farm, and we could see one, I thought. Why wouldn't a person want to see a purple cow? Was it a bad thing to see? I was crouched there on the floor, and I imagined for a moment that I was a purple cow, and no one wanted to see me. Maybe because I'd done something bad. Probably because I was purple. No one wanted to see me because I was the wrong color. I looked back at the picture of the cow. All that purple on the page, I thought, was kind of pretty. I liked looking at the purple cow. Then I read the poem again. *But I can tell you anyhow, I'd rather see than be one.* It was nice the way the words rhymed, but especially the rhyme inside the line, *see than be. I'd rather see than be.* I whispered the words to myself. *I'd rather see than be.* I thought about the words. It was better to *see* a purple cow than to actually *be* a purple cow. Being a purple cow must be really bad. You just didn't want to be a purple cow. It was bad enough seeing one, but it was worse to be one. If you had to make a choice, you'd choose to see rather than be one. And then the way the whole line rhymed with the other line. The rhyme inside and the rhyme at the end.

I never saw a purple cow,
I never hope to see one.
But I can tell you anyhow,
I'd rather see than be one.

My father was going to come home and chop our heads off, but I was thinking about the purple cow and how the words rhymed.

"Here's your suitcase," my mother said, "you can carry it." My suitcase was really a duffle bag. She handed it to me and grabbed my arm and yanked me up. "Let's go outside and wait for the taxi." We stood on the porch until the taxi came. It was still raining, a dark and stormy night. I'd read that in a book somewhere. A dark and stormy night. It felt good to say the words to myself. *It was a dark and stormy night.* We were on the porch, but every so often a gust of wind blew some water onto the porch and my legs got wet. It was scary, but I liked it.

[15] Anonymous

The street was dark but every once in a while a bolt of lightning would light everything up and you could you see Mr. Seenac's house across the street, you could see the muddy water swirling down the gutter. Then it would get dark again, and a few seconds later a rumble of thunder seemed to shake the branches right off the trees. When the next bolt of lightning came, sure enough, there in the street were a few branches from the trees. I wanted to get a closer look. I took a few steps toward the edge of the porch and waited for the next gust of wind. "Don't stand in the rain!" my mother said, and yanked me back from the edge of the porch. She was talking and crying, but I wasn't listening. I was thinking about the purple cow, about the poem. I was thinking about the words, how the words were things that you could play with, that with words you could make up poems and stories. I decided then that this was something I wanted to do. I wanted to write down words on a piece of paper and make things up, stories and poems. Maybe I wouldn't have to make anything up. Maybe I could tell stories about things that really happened. Maybe there'd be a boy somewhere who'd want to read them, who'd want to be someplace else.

A yellow cab pulled up in front of the house. The cab driver got out and ran around to the other side of the cab and opened the door for us. He was all hunched over and getting wet. He wore a yellow cab driver's hat. We ran down the steps and got in the cab. I stepped in some muddy grass and heard the squish. Before he closed the door, another gust of wind blew the rain into the back seat. It was scary and exciting. My mother gave the cab driver the address of my grandmother's house. She lived in Metarie. A long drive. The taxi driver pulled down the handle on the meter and the numbers started rolling as he drove. The bigger the number, the more we'd have to pay. My mother had stopped being hysterical. She was rearranging the suitcases. When we turned the corner onto Ferret Street and headed up Napoleon Avenue, I leaned over and said to the cab driver, "My father's coming home and he's going to chop all our heads off." Then I went back to thinking about the purple cow. I was thinking that I was going to be a writer someday, I was going to write about the purple cow and the dark and stormy night.

End View

1
End view showing screws
the head dowel plugs was all my
sister knew I knew less a make-
shift beginning before three hiding
the other child in the shed, hiding the
other child under a tin roof splinters on the floor
and a dog growling from the sink.

2
End view showing screws
a narrator galled to the hilt
free standing, sectional, the child
made to fit the space available
as if from his mother an easy-to-follow
direction would make him unafraid
like the Li'l Abner fireman
smacking the tin drums
with the one leg that worked.

3
End view showing screws.
Construct the bookcase. Stack it with books.
At what cost was the three-year-old saved.
Save the hands held above the stove.
Little is remembered, very little
information leaks out of the black hole.
Yet, there he is, a fireman,
a carpenter, a bag of pennies.

4
End view showing screws
only complicates the picture.
The broken mirror in the sink
reflects one face, yet to be assembled.
The ceiling falls in and rain
fills the bathtub
in the center of the living room.
The tree falls against the wires

and sparks set the porch on fire.
The mother the battleship the chicken
runs through the house waving both arms.
Smacked for this, smacked for that,
for being ugly, for being silent,
for losing a fish, for breaking a glass,
for giving something away, for taking something back,
for lying, for telling the truth.
The sound of flesh
on flesh, because the boat from
Antwerp was filled with rats,
because the train from Schemishal
was filled with corpses.
End view the bodies piled in graves.
End view the mother, growling like a dog,
the father, smashing the mirror.
the boy hiding the child,
who combs his hair,
wears pajamas
and doesn't wet the bed.
End view the child who doesn't speak at all.
End view the world exploding in the hall.
End view the bastard screwed to the wall.

The Accident

Sometimes you think you're sleeping but you're not.
Sometimes you think you're talking but you're sleeping.
Sometimes you think you're dreaming but you're talking.
The sky falls and everybody goes back to work.
Last night I thought I was sleeping, but I got up
and went to the window to see if the moon was talking

back to me under falling skies shredding houses
in the neighborhood down to dust.

Are the women burning up, are the men lying there
like seashells, are the boys convalescent in bright
heads of tolerance, how many ugly strangers will
knock on your door and demand payment of past

due rent, those unopened eyelids near the cold streams
that pray for resolution.

I imagine someone has a rifle in the closet
and a bag of gold coins in the oven.
I imagine I will climb the tree in front of my house
and spread my arms and imagine I can fly.
How exactly do you describe a child's sorrow?
I never meant to get hit.
I was just crossing the street is all,
going to the Hills Grocery Store to buy a pack of gum.
My father put on his pants and went to work.
I was looking at the tree in front of the house.

Nothing outlasts the day but the day.
Then there's another, and another.

But both the spelling and the sense
differ on the two sides of the Atlantic.

It is a gross canard that beginning a sentence
with *but* is stylistically slipshod. In fact,
doing so is highly desirable in any number
of contexts, and many style books that discuss
the question quite correctly say that *but* is

better than *however* at the beginning
of a sentence. However, good writers often
begin sentences with *but* and have always done so.
Take buried verbs, for instance.
Jargonmongers call them "nominalizations,"
but sometimes the verb is buried inside
a larger noun, and sometimes the larger noun
is uncovered by reduction, and sometimes
you're sleeping by arbitration, and sometimes
you're talking by contravention, and sometimes
by mediation, compulsion, hospitalization,
new now to become old soon to become ancient
before you know it.

When I was a child, I walked to the end of the block
and when I crossed the street, a blue car came by
and hit me and I was on the asphalt for awhile
waiting for someone to rescue me.
But they brought me back to the house
and put me on the sofa and were talking
but I couldn't figure out what they were saying,
something about hospitalization,
something about minimization,
something about violation.

Sometimes, however, you think you're dying,
but you're not.

Elysian Fields

The first word I learned to read was "cat."
This was before the cat was in the hat.
It was just a word for a thing, without associations
to any other thing but the cat I personally knew.
A solitary cat.
A singular cat.
And I could read it. Those three letters—
up until then, mere abstraction, pieces of rubble—
had become a thing, or more rightly, a being I loved
with a name in the world.
Then it was "Ritz," the name for the cracker
I learned to spell from the billboard on Claiborne Avenue.
This new word went with me wherever I went.
Into the kitchen, into the bedroom,
but also into the yard where I had not yet guessed
that I was surrounded by objects with names of their own
that could be spelled and memorized,
words composed of letters I could also take with me
everywhere and nowhere.
In the backseat of Dad's maroon Mercury, say,
when we went for a drive.
"Let's go for a drive," my mother would say.
People don't go for a drive, anymore.
They always drive *somewhere*, they have places to go.
But there were afternoons, especially in summer,
when we'd go for a drive. I'd lie in the backseat
and look out the window at the trees, try to guess
where we were by the look of the trees and the blue of the sky.
Ritz was with me everywhere then, those four letters,
the words belonged to me.
And *cat*, birds huddled in the trees
above me as I spelled out loud, lying in the back seat of the car.
I liked the sound the wheels made on newly-paved asphalt.
"We're on Napoleon Avenue," I'd announce.
"Now we're on Canal Street."
"Now we're passing the cemetery."
The cemetery was on Elysian Fields Avenue.
I worked hard learning to spell "Elysian," learning to say it even.

"We're on Elysian Fields Avenue," I'd say.
Later I learned that the word came from Greek mythology,
Elysium is where the blessèd went after death, though Elysian Fields Avenue
was named after the Avenue des Champs-Elysées in Paris.
In New Orleans, you can take Elysian Fields Avenue
from the Lower Mississippi River all the way to Lake Pontchartrain.
To get to Aunt Bea's, you drove up Gentilly Boulevard,
then turned onto Elysian Fields Avenue.
We passed Brother Martin High School.
I could tell where we were because the trees
were especially leafy there.
"We're still on Elysian Fields Avenue," I'd say.
You could spell it "Elysium" too, if you wanted.
Some words could be spelled different ways, I learned,
and some could be said different ways too, like route and route,
or tomato, tomato. I liked rhyming "Studebaker" with "rutabaga."
And what about words like "rhubarb" and "rhododendron,"
"rusticate" and "Rwanda"?
One second you're going for a drive,
then you're blessed, lolling about in the Elysian Fields,
then you're home making rhubarb pie,
then sitting in a tree with purple flowers,
then moving out to the country.
And where did you end up? Central Africa.
The world changes in an instant when you're small, word by word.
What I mean to say is that the contemplation
of anything unexpected
changes you when you're young.
From the mighty, muddy Mississippi to Central Africa,
from the Everglades to Timbuktoo.
"Hammers," I thought,
lying in bed with the nightlite on,
"lightning rod, starlight, electric drills,
asphalt, trains, flying machines."
I packed my suitcase with words,
and I've been travelling ever since,
sometimes on a train with the blessèd,
sometimes on foot,
walking toward Paradise.

Poetry Not Much

poetry
not much

not much
to read
to speak of

if you're
reading this
which I doubt

only poets
read poetry
stupid poets
reading stupid
poetry

but poetry
not much

brings not
much money
maybe none

hate poetry
bunch of crap

pretty senten
says

pretty wurr
ddsss

most people
run from
poetry

pretty stupid
when you
really think
about it

I don't think
about it
I write it
why think
about it

poetry
not much
to think about
so to speak

sorry you
had to read
this all the
way to the
end

how much
better you
could spend
your time
making money
fucking
doing some
thing constructive

poetry
not much

not much
to speak of
when you
really think
about it

the days the days the days

It's been quite cold here.
Yesterday, it finally got sunny,
but I think
a little rain
is due this weekend.
I get up in the morning and go out
in the cold chill
to water the fountains,
which lose water
during the day.
And to water the little lemon tree.
And the other potted bush.
And the bird bath.
When I come back inside,
I have to warm my hands
over the fire
on one of the burners
on the stove.
Then a kiss from Lori,
slipping my hands
inside her pajamas
to feel the soft skin
of her butt.
Then ½ an apple
and a tablespoon
of peanut butter,
then the red pill
and the two white pills,
and a quick glance
at the sports page:
Kobe scored 48,
the Clippers beat the Heat,
and maybe the Saints
will beat the 49er's.
Then into the study
to work:
write a poem,
pay a bill,

answer an e-mail.
Then off to class.
Another
day.
What a fucking gift.

The War in Shreveport

There was a war in Shreveport.
It was somewhere else before that,
Baltimore or Cleveland.

I was in Shreveport the other day.
We forget sometimes, a dog or a woodchuck,
Anne Frank or Thelma Ritter.

In Baton Rouge miseries of mind and body
in a bar downtown at night where we sat there drinking,
Eddie Haspel and I talking about Oriole Macinroth.

In New Orleans we wait for rain.
Bright wings disappear but no one cares.
Einstein or was it Neils Bohr who said what? I forget.

Now Los Angeles plumps up like a thanksgiving turkey.
Gonna rain not gonna rain maybe rain maybe not.
I think of my father, Samuel Joshua Grapes.

Otherwise Moonlight

Again and again something retreats to a speck on the horizon.
In the great notebook, it hardly adds up.
Accountants with their pointy pencils despair.
Past midnight someone gets up, rings for the nurse.
Again and again, someone decides to enter the world.

Over there by the pond next to the hotel
a sharp knife on the white tablecloth reflects
the sun so perfectly you'd think it was all
Archimedes needed to sink the entire Roman fleet.

Stop for breath. The lights in the hotel go on.
In each room, someone walks to the window
and looks out on the plaza below. Pierre is not
with his wife, Claudette is not with her husband.

How the chandeliers shine in the lobby!
Were an orchestra here you'd hardly bat
an eye, take it upon yourself to lift the baton
and wave your apprenticed arms in the air.

Embarrassed palms moist with fear.
Time is running, as they say with a solemn
nod of the head, out. What was that tune
she was humming when pruning the agapanthus?

The morning light is so cherished.
The day breaks someone else's heart.
Eyes knock the stars into elsewhere galaxies.
Again and again what's too human to survive
survives. We are always at each other's
mercy. Here comes the waltz and you take her in
your arms.

The world puts on a mask.
A curtain is drawn.
We move from the window,
bearing the whole peach
of the past, shuffle toward the bed.
Shape me to stone, mold me to ice.

Again and again, something retreats to a speck on the horizon,
crawling shoreward,
the hillside graveyard,
the breathless earth.

Home

Animals take no responsibility for anything.
A vulture circles my house,
but I wave it off. "No one's
dead yet!" I yell.

I hear cougars are coming down from the hills
onto our hiking paths,
and a bear got into someone's backyard
ice-box. Not an ounce of scruples.

Either the car swerves for the squirrel
or the squirrel stops at the curb and waits.
Yeah, right. That'll be the day.

They're all killer whales, waiting to feast
on our philosophy, our epic poems,
our economic forecasts, our religious
ideologies.

They're arrogant, hifalutin know-it-alls,
treading the ground like they belong here.

As far as they're concerned, therapy's
for the birds. And rightly so.

Imagine the panther
weeping on the couch
about the human arm
he just lunched on.
Or the white shark,
sad and despondent
because he swallowed a CEO
wearing a life-vest.

I'd like to have some of that—
no guilt, no shame.

Eyes that look out on this world
as if it were home.

The Mind

At night the mind strolls on the beach
someone holds its hand maybe a missive
sent years before now discovered in the ruins
of a sandcastle bitten by flies seaweed attracting
gnats when the mind stops bits of tissue the wolf's
perhaps giving in to death breath empty a big hole in
the heart bloodier than a hog's mist out on the horizon
where ships gather their dots and dashes morse code the
secret message to a world too proud to admit rust gnawing
on all sides tides illuminations of how ardent a waste of land
and sea holds the vast inside of the mind bolted down for storm
unable to recall joy or law or the law of love shifting always
like sand dunes like people who show themselves splayed
for torture then hide in the firm nut of resolve inside a cup
cake or some other object the mind like a mirror glazed
feeling the thrill a brutish face standing loitering on
the corner unpaid rent killing the shape of rabbit
stew each morsel tasty in the wilderness but
not the scaffold you were expecting under
the burning sky of the mind a bald ac-
countant a thin pencil point in his
hand making tiny 5's and 9's on
a yellow sheet of legal paper
trapping the mind in the
zero pretending to
know what
it's good
for

Writer's Block

I got up this morning earlier than usual today. Strange kind of fitful night, in and out of dreams, a sense of my body large in the bed, at peace with the peace, but not at peace with the waking world. So I got up early, sat out in the backyard with my journal, my coffee, and looked at the empty page for a few minutes. I don't usually do that. Look at the empty page. It's not that I have something I'm planning to write about, I just start writing. The empty page is like the floor I'm going to walk on. I don't get down and inspect it before I take a step. But for some reason I just looked at it, the empty page. The longer I looked, the whiter it got, the emptier it got. White page. Blank page. Oh great holy white empty page of Writer's Block. And I realized that I had never in my life enjoyed the feeling of writer's block. What I mean is, I don't get writer's block. I was being ironic when I wrote "enjoyed." Who would enjoy the feeling? Most of us dread it. Like breaking into a rash, west nile or zoo-keeper's prickly pear or something. Oh my God, I got writer's block! But not me. Usually, when I sit down to write, I start with any ole blah blah blah that comes into my head. Something like, "I got up this morning and didn't feel like writing." Or, "It's Friday morning and I'm sitting in the backyard with my journal. Looks like it's going to be another hot day." Stuff like that. Usually, I write one paragraph, and that leads to another, and before you know it, cosmic disaster is at hand, or I'm delving into the depths of my soul or remembering some incident from childhood, or maybe an incident from the night before when I acted like a child. For years, I've heard writers talk about having writer's block, but I've just never had it. I just write any old crap that comes along and I don't worry about it. It's not like I'm trying to write the Great American Novel. If I were, THEN I'd have writers block! But it's just me and my journal, here in the back yard, the heat of the day already coming at me. What do I care what I write. I'll just stumble along, one word after the other. But writer's block? Never. And then I got to thinking, looking at the blank page. Gee, I've never really ENJOYED that blank page before. So smooth and white (alright, white with thin blue lines going across, it's an accountant's notebook I bought in a stationary store, sue me!). If I stare at the white page long enough, I thought, will writer's block come creeping up on me? If I let the empty page sit there, all empty, the way only an empty page can be empty, will the big old Dreaded Writer's Block grab me by the throat? What would that be like, I thought, to have real, old fashioned, honest-to-goodness, dyed-in-the-wool, etched-in-stone, writer's block. So I stared at the page some more, and actually began to enjoy the space of the page, the blankness of it. The emptiness of it. Like I had a truckload of thoughts going through my head, and I wasn't going to put even one of them down. No words about my father promising to tell me why he got drunk and dying before he had the chance. No words about my mother's face exploding in the hallway as she slapped me this way and that. No words about the car wreck on the Chef Mentuer Highway where Jimmy Ciaravella and Gene Grasser and I all died and went up to heaven for who-knows how long. No words about those years hiding under the kitchen table, holding a bottle of pills, unable to face the sun. Not one thought found its way into words, found its way onto the paper. So many thoughts, so many memories, so many regrets and gratitudes, and the feeling that if I didn't write them down they'd vanish, go up in smoke, leave me with nothing but the vapor of a life scarcely lived out loud. I kept the pen on the table. I just stared at the white page. It became an act of will, of great willpower, not to put even one of those thoughts down. I became a member of the resistance, I became one of the *refusés*. I stood before the barricades and let not one word pass. I embraced writer's block as if it were a call to arms, a badge of honor, a pledge of defiance. Let the others write, I yelled out, but me, moi, yo, ich, io, ego, watagoshiwa—I'm gonna sit here and write nothing. Nothing, you hear? I'm gonna dig my claws into writer's block. I'm gonna dig my heels into writer's block. For all those souls out there who have stared at the blank page for days on end, weeks on end, years on end, who have endured the sentences and paragraphs roiling around in their heads and kept silent, for those who have endured the images of pain and sorrow and despair clanging for remorse inside their heads and kept silent, for all those who have remembered lost causes and broken hearts and cruel dismissals and kept silent before the blank white page, for them, for all of them, I will hold fast to writer's block and say nothing, write nothing. I will stick a pole on this white page and wave it like a flag, not a flag of surrender, but a flag of victory over the forces of the loquacious and the glib, a flag of victory over the productive and the energetic. I have writer's block, I'll yell, and I'm not going to let it go!

Sometimes I Love You

sometimes I love you for your brown
hair and sometimes I love you for
your crazy laugh and sometimes I
love you in the morning with your
head back on the pillow and a slight
smile on your face barely sleeping
and sometimes I don't know why I
love you, sometimes I'm not even
sure I do, sometimes I don't feel a
thing, don't feel like doing a thing,
forget who I am, or why it is even
necessary to be in love with anyone,
why it is necessary to do anything,
or feel like doing anything, some-
times it takes enormous effort to
find one feeling or thing
that is more important than another,
like picking up a book or taking off
a pair of shoes, or trying to write
in the absence of love.

Falling to Earth

Subjectivity is not the problem.
Objectivity is the problem.
We must reform the soul.

Where do poetics end
and poetry begins?

I'm powerless over my art.
The commitment
to breaking things down.

Rain plots to overthrow the sky.
To merge with anything is a plot
to overthrow the self,
a coincidence of thumbtacks,
the dream state of a garden hose,
live crabs slapping their claws
against the side of the pot
filled with Zattarin's crab boil.

I admit I am mad for the world
made perfect,
worthy of spare parts and loose change.
Forgiven, yet irredeemable.
I own so little that I cannot lose,
a transmission interrupted by her back.
The kind of peace I seldom allow myself,
fixed made asunder,
then mended.
Broken, then fixed.

The whack of my father's body falling to earth,
the last line read aloud before the fire,
the pine cone rolling into the flames.

Remembering blows a hole in the world.

Vision

About suffering, they were never wrong, the old masters.
—W. H. Auden, "Musée de Beaux Arts"

Today, the day is not being very kind to someone,
someone, say, in Altadena or Charleston.
I'm trying to imagine it, but the poet's vision
fails me at the moment.
I used to be so good at imagining suffering,
even my own,
which isn't so much you'd be proud to mention it,
but enough to make the mouth hard
and the eyes glazed.
I should admit now that I've hardly suffered.
The walls were invisible.
Spoons in coffee,
an old vaudeville act
breaking into a tap-dance routine.
Stretched out on the sofa,
unwashed, unshaven.
Someone comes over,
I go through the motions.
The stars in the vast cosmos
dying so slowly you hardly notice,
each one at the beck and call of another larger star.
Someone sits at a table in the kitchen,
tearing up the newspaper.
A son or father or lover has left.
Such a dreary vision of loss, of suffering.
I'm suffering a betrayal of hindsight.
Everyone's talking on the tube of retirement.
What exactly is that?
Fresh snow comes to mind.
Up in the mountains,
a little boy walks in circles, stomping his boots,
making bootprints.
My mother always talked of someone
not having a pot to piss in.

My father said they didn't have two nickels to rub together.
Life does a lot of things to you.
It's a living thing, like some animal that lies
at the foot of your bed,
waiting for you to wake up.

Balancing the Books

What was I going to find
in *Dark Laughter* by Sherwood Anderson?
Though it seems like only yesterday,
I read *Winesburg, Ohio* back in college.
But I was just as taken by *Dark Laughter*,
his tenth book and fifth novel.
There was something poetic about Anderson's writing,
something oddly quaint that I knew,
even at 21, couldn't last.

Today I was searching my bookcase,
looking for a particular sentence
to help me realize the possibilities of language,
something besides James Joyce or William Faulkner.
Eventually, I found the sentence,
but before I did,
I came across—perhaps I was using it as a bookmark—
a check for $12, dated June 20, 1967.
Now I'm not into all that new age stuff,
but today is June 20.
Oh, and before I forget,
here's the sentence:
"There was a deep well within every man and woman,
and when Life came in at the door of the house,
that was the body."
I'm still not sure what Anderson meant by that.
A distrust of formal verbalization, perhaps;
or a particular theory of human nature;
maybe just the discursiveness
of associational psychology.
Who knows?

Does anybody still read Sherwood Anderson?
Probably not, unless it's *Winesburg, Ohio.*
Poor Sherwood.
Poor check, used as a bookmark in a book
nobody reads anymore.
Old words on a piece of paper,
hardly worth the paper they're printed on.

But I'm glad I found those words.
Reading them again after almost fifty years
was better than cashing that check.
Sherwood was still alive in my hands.
I had done him that service, brought him back,
brought his words back,
words he may have written late at night,
or in the early morning, or at his desk
while it rained throughout the afternoon.

When we read the words of writers after they've died,
do we wake them from a peaceful sleep?
And is the waking a reminder they once lived on this earth,
even though that life has become a dream?
Would Sherwood even want to be wakened?
And what about that check for $12, from Jerry Jacobs?
How long did he worry over that uncashed check?
Maybe he still accounts for it,
subtracting $12 from his monthly balance.
It's June 20th, and somewhere in the world
Jerry's balancing his checkbook,
waiting for me to cash the check,
his expectation waking me
from my own dream of a life
moving forward one sentence at a time.

Redemption

How wretched she felt to see them
going off some mornings
without anything to eat.
The stove gave off the last of its heat.
Turning from the door
the way characters in a short story
by Pirindello do, she looked down at her feet
and watched their disappearance
below her skirt.
Outside, the snow continued to fall
with the abstract waywardness
of autumn leaves.
Her husband, his back
propped against the far wall
by the cracked window,
began accusing her
of still more infidelities.
With the butcher, who dared to lick
her asshole with his tongue,
he tore her coat from her arms
and threw it into the fire.
With the peddler from across the hills,
who took her left nipple
in exchange for a candlestick,
he raised her skirt and thrust his head under
and between her legs
like a photographer
poking his head under the hood
of his camera.
Which led to the next accusation:
the priest,
who wore his dark robes inside out
on the days he couldn't wash them
and punished himself
by fucking her
standing up in the woodshed
and never allowing himself
to come.

"Pity me," he begged, his skinny legs trembling.
Resisting the last thrust,
he removed his penis
from between her legs.
"Pity me," he mumbled,
walking back down the road toward town,
until flaccid,
desire unspent, he felt
the glow of redemption
rise through his body.
With each accusation, her husband
ripped off another piece of clothing:
the grainer, her bodice;
the reaper, her stockings;
the clerk, her panties;
until she stood there,
naked and shining
in the glare of his wretchedness,
having nothing to wear
but her sins.

Love for Lesser Things

another cup of wine
river of stars
mountain flowers
a bolt of silk
a slab of rock
the rhododendron
the white apes
others' children
thatched roof
the ringed pheasant
elegant ostriches
mournful capsized boat
handful of tears
a dragon cloud
meditation
on the bright frozen
moon another cup
of wine
a thousand sorrows
flowers swooped in brain
crystal-beaded curtains
heartless wind
blossoms thick with dew
her ravenhead stockings
the white-nosed horse
a few more days
in someone else's world
not among men
this pain of poetry
another cup of wine
this line of words
love for lesser things
the clouds break apart
black tire black cup
laugh in the face
this book
on my knees
my wife

in the kitchen
my son
out in the world
another empty cup
a toast to yellow leaves
the amazing sky

Endocarditus

deferential fawning obsolete negative
valve replacement
sent booming throbbed heartbeat
sucked visual root canal observation
all the blood come down on Sunday he makes up
obligatory placement
tub overflown with water
in the cold linoleum floor on cadiz street
hobnobbed with royalty
the divine stupefication of irregular resolve
born that way
bicuspid aortic
hyperlespretension
comic strips spread out on the floor
ruckus maker
slippery marker
katznjammerkittens arctic sea plane crashed on the ice
big daddy warbucks boots on the taxi cab floor
comintagetchacomintagetchacomintagetcha
walrus bedtime
out the window of the backyard washtub
moonmanminnows manacled
to the throat of a dream that recurs
recurs on the dog face tulips
sneeeeering bloodsuckers nibbling away on Sunday
rattlin'bonesradium eradicated sunshine
who grows too fast in the time it takes to crawl under the sheets
and revisit the old house
where comintagetchacomintagetchacomintagetcha
is a phone call away
moontrees lost in the wind of winter
all of a big life squeezed into the back porch raindrop
back for the nickel and dime
back to replace the obsolete negative endocarditus
comintagetchacomintagetchacomintagetcha.

Old Road Old Song

here so what
edge of town
where dogs
gather
looking for bones
the sun slips
below the horizon
keeping its
feelings
to itself
and my thoughts
churning
like the electric
generators
behind
the fence here
on the edge of town
just lying about
neither coming
nor going
waiting for a bird
to find a tree
branch
in all this
barrenness

The Wild Bunch

> *About suffering they were never wrong,*
> *The Old Masters: how well they understood*
> *Its human position; how it takes place*
> *While someone else is eating or opening a window or just*
> *walking dully along.*
>
> —W. H. Auden, "Musée des Beaux Arts"

C*areful what you wish for*, goes the proverb. We used to grumble about the sad state of poetry, how marginalized it was, and we the poets were. Now, I see poetry everywhere. Everyone's writing it. Most everyone who writes it is reading it. All kinds of poetry. As with anything, most of it is mediocre. But now you can say the words in polite company: *Poetry. Poet.*

Yet, the fact is, most readers shy away from poetry. Riding the buses and subways, you still see passengers lost in thick escapist novels who would flinch at the thought of reading a one-page poem. The mere sight of lines broken irregularly across a page is enough to make grown men cower. I was in a book store recently trying to convince the manager to stock *ONTHEBUS*. A lady at the counter asked what I had and I told her, "A literary magazine." "Oh," she said, "How wonderful." She reached for it and began to open it. She was going to dive into the deep end of bottomless prose, LIT-RAT-SHURE. "It's mostly poetry," I said. Just as the words came out of my mouth, the pages of the book fell open to that dreaded image, words arranged on the page in the shape of a poem. It was as if she had been hit on the head with a rock. She put the book down as if it were radioactive and walked away.

It wasn't the content of the poem (she hadn't bothered to read it). It was the mere sight of it, the form maybe. I understand this reaction—you can get lost in prose, but there's no means of escape from poetry. The prospect of facing the self is downright terrifying. I have fantasies of my masked henchmen and I bursting into a bank holding reams of poetry in our hands: "All right, everyone, down on the floor. Fill these bags or we start reading the stuff out loud." We hold up a sample page, so they can see what it is. POETRY! Wordsworth, Milton, Allen Ginsberg. I imagine horrified tellers and bank managers working as fast as they can, looks of panic on their faces. Suddenly, one teller moves toward the red button. I yell out the opening lines of Ginsberg's *Howl: I have seen the best minds of my generation destroyed by madness!* The teller scurries back to his window. *Destroyed by madness!* I shout. *Starving hysterical naked!* A woman in line covers her daughter's ears. *Dragging themselves through the negro streets at dawn looking for an angry fix!* There's fire in my eyes. No one makes a move. The tellers continue shoving bills into the canvas bags. The security guard in the corner makes a move toward his gun. I pull out Wordsworth and begin reading:

The world is too much with us; late and soon,
Getting and spending, we lay waste our powers;
Little we see in Nature that is ours

The guard shields his face with his hands, stumbles across the rug and begs for mercy. "Please," he whimpers. "I've got kids." I snarl a bit of Wilfred Owen at him.

What passing-bells for these who die as cattle?
—Only the monstrous anger of the guns.
Only the stuttering rifles' rapid rattle
Can patter out their hasty orisons.

Out of the corner of my eye I see the bank manager slide out the top drawer of his desk. I glare at him and recite: *Of man's first disobedience, and the fruit of that forbidden tree!* He clutches his chest and staggers back toward the wall. I continue, unable to stop. *Whose mortal taste,*—his legs give out from under him—*brought death into the world, and all our woe, with loss of Eden.* He lies motionless on the floor. *Till one greater Man restore us.* Damn, I think, I didn't mean to use that one. Deadly. Now we're in for it. We grab the bags and head for the door. One of my masked henchmen snaps at me, "Why did you have to use Milton?" I snap back, "Maybe he's not dead. He looked stunned to me." His reply: "Milton kills." Outside, the place is swarming with cops, SWAT teams on the roof. We make a break for it. Bullets fly past. As we head for the car parked in the lot, we begin waving pages of the stuff in the air, shouting out:

Tyger, Tyger, burning bright,
In the forests of the night;
What immortal hand or eye,
Could frame thy fearful symmetry?

Pandemonium breaks out. The crowd scatters behind parked cars and into doorways. I yell out:

Because I could not stop for death—
He kindly stopped for me—
The carriage held but just Ourselves—
And Immortality

"Get down! Get down!" they scream. "They're armed!"

The woods are lovely, dark, and deep,
But I have promises to keep
And miles to go before I sleep
And miles to go before I sleep.

One of my men takes a shot to the chest. He falls, still clutching one of the bags.

Nobody heard him, the dead man
But still he lay moaning:
I was much further out than you thought
And not waving but drowning.

For my comrade, I place a poem in his hand.

it is difficult
to get the news from poems,
yet men die miserably every day
for lack
of what is found there.

He smiles, then winces in pain. "Go," he says, "I'm done." He presses a poem into my hand.

I depart as air, I shake my white locks at the runaway sun,
I effuse my flesh in eddies, and drift it in lacy jags.
I bequeath myself to the dirt to grow from the grass I love.
If you want me again look for me under your boot-soles
You will hardly know who I am or what I mean,
But I shall be good health to you nevertheless,
And filter and fibre your blood.

A quiet hangs over the street. Mothers clutch their children to their sides, men in flak jackets stare up at the sun just as it floats behind a dark cloud. A piece of paper flutters at my feet.

The curfew tolls the knell of parting day,
The lowing herd wind slowly o'er the lea,
The plowman homeward plods his weary way,
And leaves the world to darkness and to me.

Then movement, and the sound of gunfire. I get up and run along the side of the building, toss out a few more stanzas.

Do not go gentle into that good night,
Old age should burn and rave at close of day;
Rage, rage against the dying of the light.

Helicopters and gunships circle overhead. We stop at the corner and make a stand, flinging pages into the air, yelling the poems out with even greater fervor.

The darkness drops again; but now I know
That twenty centuries of stony sleep
Were vexed to nightmare by a rocking cradle,
And what rough beast, its hour come round at last,
Slouches toward Bethlehem to be born?

We real cool. We
Left school. We
Lurk late. We

Sing, Oh Heavenly Muse, of Achilles' rage
Black and murderous.

The gunships start firing. We spray the street with words.

'Twas brillig, and the slithy toves
Did gyre and gimble in the wabe;
All mimsey were the borogoves,
And the mome raths outgrabe.

You do not do, you do not do
Any more, black shoe
In which I have lived like a foot
For thirty years, poor and white,
Barely daring to breathe or Achoo.

I lob a few stanzas toward the tank moving our way.

Today we have naming of the parts. Yesterday,
We had daily cleaning. And tomorrow morning,
We shall have what to do after firing. But today,

The tank careens toward a building and smashes into a car. I throw another to finish it off.

In the old neighborhood, each funeral parlor
is more elaborate than the last.
The alleys smell of cops, pistols bumping their thighs,
each chamber steeled with a slim blue bullet.

The helicopters and gunships pull away. Rooftop snipers duck behind concrete walls. Swat teams cower behind their cars. We make a dash for our car, start the engine and pull out of the lot. As we speed off down the street, we pepper the crowd with a final burst.

How do I love thee? Let me count the ways.
I love thee to the depth and breadth and height
My soul can reach, when feeling out of sight
For the ends of Being and ideal Grace.

Shall I compare thee to a summer's day?
Thou art more lovely and more temperate:
Rough winds do shake the darling buds of May.
And summer's lease hath all too short a date.

Had we but world enough and time,
This coyness, lady, were no crime.

I shall be telling this with a sigh
Somewhere ages and ages hence:
Two roads diverged in a wood, and I—
I took the one less traveled by,
And that has made all the difference.

The sea is calm tonight.
The tide is full, the moon lies fair
Upon the straits;

I will arise and go now, and go to Innisfree.

We hit the outskirts, take the old river road that leads to our hideout. Suddenly, when we hit the fork in the road by old man Deever's place, half a dozen cops charge out of the woods, surrounding the car. "Come out with your hands up!" I feel my blood turn cold. We look at each other—my mates and me—and reach under the seat for the big guns—Pound & Eliot. We jump out of the car, poems blazing.

Let us go then, you and I
When the evening is spread out against the sky
Like a patient etherised upon a table.

For three years, out of key with his time,
He strove to resuscitate the dead art
Of poetry; to maintain "the sublime"
In the old sense. Wrong from the start—

April is the cruelest month, breeding
Lilacs out of the dead land, mixing
Memory and desire, stirring
Dull roots with spring rain.

Hang it all, Robert Browning,
there can be but the one "Sordello."
But Sordello, and my Sordello?
Lo Sordels si fo di Mantovana.
So-shu churned in the sea.
Seal sports in the spray-whited circles of cliff-wash,
Sleek head, daughter of Lir,
eyes of Picasso
Under black fur-hood, lithe daughter of Ocean;
And the wave runs in the beach-grove:
"Eleanor, ελεαυς *and* ενεπτλις!

They toss their guns down and flee into the woods. We jump back into the car and speed off into the ensuing darkness. One last shot:

I, too,

I yell out the window, laughing like a fool,

dislike it.

When we get back to the hideout, we lug the bags out of the car and scatter the bills across the floor. Piles and piles of it. Play money, all of it. Every last bill.

It's rather a privilege
amid the affluent traffic
to serve this unpopular art which cannot be turned into
background noise for study
or hung as a status trophy by rising executives,
cannot be "done" like Venice
or abridged like Tolstoy, but stubbornly still insists upon
being read or ignored.

But the joke's on them. Printed on the bills are poems of all denominations. We're rich beyond measure. And in the center of each bill, portraits of the poets. On the big bills, Homer, Virgil, Dante, Shakespeare, Whitman. On others, Dickinson, Frost, Blake, Yeats, Eliot, Hughes, Williams, Pound, Ginsberg, Walcott; and on the smaller bills, Plath, Lowell, Sexton, Baraka, Rich, Rios, Dove, Soto, Forché, Ondaatje, Kinnell, Pinsky, Giovanni, Ashbery, Lee, O'Hara, and on others, names and faces we hardly know, the poets of the future. And suddenly it dawns on us. *We're* the poets of the future. And we're armed. And dangerous.

> *I too am not a bit tamed, I too am untranslatable,*
> *I sound my barbaric yawp over the roofs of the world.*

Longing

Bits of White Light.
Soothing Tigers.
Expatriate Longings.

The Losses.
The Gains.
The Grief.

Scrambled Eggs.
Butter on a Bagel.
The World As It Is.

Tu Fu and Li Po.
Broken Moon of March.
Still Grieving the Way.

Wandering Exile.
Dread before Bedtime.
Dreams of Baseball.

Theodore Pine Tree.
My Wife in the Garden.
The World As It Is.

The World As It Is.

When I Was Twenty-Seven

I sat by the pool where we didn't have a pool, it was just a cement slab in the back of the apartment building where all the cars parked but I sat there anyway imagining it was a pool, not that I was so stupid that I would have tried diving into the cement, just because I was wearing a bathing suit and had a towel draped across my lap, self-conscious about my belly and the sky was a green haze, something poetic I could describe later in a poem, not this one, this one's got cement, never seen green cement before, so I'm saving the green haze for another poem, but all those salamanders making love right there in front of me, just shoving it into my face, bathing suit and all, and I wanted to write aimlessly in and out of the shadows but I think Hayden Carruth ordered that line from the Poet's Clearing House, they got all sorts of great lines, "never used before," the ad says, but he got that one, belly to belly, too, but I don't think he can claim that, we all say that, that's a song, isn't it, vigorous and tender, and the green pool was there in front of me, and I could imagine diving into it, getting away from it all (I paid good money for that one, but I think they overcharged), getting away from it all, need I say more, but you can't get away from IT ALL, IT gets away from you is how it goes, no matter how badly and how muchly you want it, it gets away from you, it all gets away from you, and you're twenty-seven and whatever you thought you had was gone and I sat there on the cement of the car port, wanting to get away from it all, afraid the best had passed me by, some golden fringe of love aimlessly in the shadow, drifting lazily, their little hands floating before them, arrogant salamanders belly to belly in the sun, and me pathetic me in a beach chair on the cement of the carport thinking I could get away from it all, sitting in front of a dodge colt red with a white stripe, the window doesn't even roll up and when it rains I get wet, have to put a towel up, the one that was on my lap, covering my belly, wishing my life wasn't the pool I was drowning in, hoping it would change, get better, on the cement, in the carport, tender and vigorous.

The Fountain of Stones

One night a man entered the city carrying an empty sack.
The man was the wise one, the enlightened one,
the one who knew everything.
Everyone else in the city was mad.
In the center of the city stood a fountain
filled with stones.
If you walked by the fountain, picked out a stone,
and held it in your hand,
all became clear—
a flash of clarity that explained everything:
love's little secrets, misfortunes of salt,
dishes of fire and ringlets of friendship,
why sorrow burns slowly,
why joy is but one grain of the harvest,
why dawntide brings the breath at last
to the watchman,
why the heart promises nothing but sadness.
But the clarity lasted only a few moments.
The greatest clarity was that such clarity
was too hard to bear.
Thus, after a moment or two,
the stone was returned to the fountain.
Once returned to the fountain,
the stone turned into a ruby.
By evening, the fountain was filled with rubies.
The man carrying the empty sack
who entered the city at night—
the wise man, the enlightened one,
the one who knew everything—
the man approached the fountain
and picked out the rubies,
one at a time,
and put each one,
one at a time,
into his sack.
He held each ruby for only a moment,
but with each ruby,
a portion of his enlightenment was lost,

a sliver of wisdom blew away in the wind,
a particular nugget of knowledge
fell by the wayside.
When the sack was full,
and every ruby in the fountain had been removed,
the man knew nothing but the shape of the road
that led back to the forest,
the imprint of shoes made in the dust,
the light from his cabin in the forest
toward which he walked
carrying the sackful of rubies.

Each time a ruby was removed from the fountain,
a stone appeared to take its place.
By morning, the fountain was again filled with stones.

During the day, the mad citizens of the city
picked out a stone from the fountain,
held it in their hands for just a moment,
—as long as it took to achieve clarity—
then put the stone back into the fountain,
where it turned into a ruby.
By evening the fountain was again filled
with rubies.
The rubies were carried out every night.
The fountain was again filled with stones.
The mad remained mad.
The man with the empty sack—
the enlightened one,
the wise one,
the one who knew everything—
returned to his bed in his cabin in the forest—
  all enlightenment lost,
  wisdom gone with the wind,
  knowledge barely a grain of sand—
and slept the sleep of the angels,
his mind at peace, his heart at rest.

Variations on a Theme by Heidegger

It's the day after tax day.
She plays a Brahms Etude
on the grand piano in her living room.
The heart meant for mending
breaks apart.
Her fingers reach into the body,
pulling out parts.
Up the atrium and down the ventricle,
Up the Potomac and down the Delaware.

The dead rise into the air
forgiving senseless acts of love,
forgiving meaningful acts of war.
My uncle Lou who died on the kitchen floor
vomiting onto the news of the day.
My uncle Charles who died in the hospital
while they rearranged keys under the floorboard.
In my mother's head,
the hallucinatory tribulations
of Thanksgiving dinners, slaps across the face
for no reason at all. Still the body
speaking its piece.

She leans toward the keys
as if looking for signs of dust,
her body bent forward in prayer,
articulating the disappearance of time.

I advise staying away
from the pure theory of things,
originally a pragmatic cupcake.
I was thrown into this world
without a note from my mother,
and kept after school for being a show-off.

What can I tell you?
Avoid telephone poles,
the kind a stray cat
in a thunder storm

on a cloudless day
would attack
if it were a mouse.

Check behind you.
There are those who hide in shadows,
secret agents or your uncle,
the one who rarely shaves,
the one with all the money
hidden in tea canisters,
the one whose wife
uses dollar bills
to brew her tea.

How come so many walk around
in a rubberized suit of unforgiveness?
How come no one laughs at my bad jokes anymore?

"It's nothing," we say, "nothing but the wind."
Even at dinner, no one cracks a joke.
When did the breakage begin?
When my brother and I were playing war?
When my father came home drunk
and smashed the mirror in the bathroom?
When the burglar climbed over my crib
to steal the money hidden in my mother's shoe?

She wants Bach to speak, but Bach,
dead all these years,
relies on her fingers,
her willingness to attack the augmentation of despair.

During dinner, my brother pretends he's invisible,
and we pretend he's not.
It's hard to look him in the eye
when we can't see him,
unless he sips his soup.
Up goes the spoon,
and my father asks,
"Did you finish your homework?"
My brother goes through life
with no faith at all

in his own imagination.

Symmetry works in an obvious way,
written in 1874, a trick of the four and six
bar version, lifeless until transformed
by Mozart's recapitulation,
by Beethoven's excavation of the heroic.
Sightless, crazy, rude, and penniless,
the clavichord was even capable of vibrato.
I lied about practice time—
writing 45 minutes instead of 10.
The rest of the time I lay in bed
watching the ceiling for signs of winter,
a season heralded by pocket-watches.

These small gestures of isolation
force us to be original.
The misery of starving serfs
captured by the classical melting pot
along with the formalized
gallant expression
as exemplified by Quantz,
and the more spontaneous sentiment
of Carl Philipp Emanuel,
who would have since moved
to the free city of Hamburg,

and the elegant Italianate style
further developed in Mannheim
by Johann Stamitz, and in London
by Johann Christian, the English Bach.
This is as far as perspective will get you.

You must feel the space with your own hands.
Walk blindly into closets,
inhabited originally by less than scrupulous
barbers recapitulating the dreams of children
fed through a hole in the door.

When she finishes playing,
we both stare at the keys, wondering
what is left to believe in.

The sun sets,
regular as a button,
as if God were here,
blessing us all,
we who strive,
even in the dark,
for particularity.

THE
BIG
WAKE

THE OFFICE

My office is on the second floor of the two-story Churchill Building on the corner of Wilshire and Sweetzer, across the street from the Big 5 Sporting Goods Store. It's eleven o'clock in the morning, mid-February, the rest of the country hip-high in snow, but here, in southern California, the sun beats like a hammer on the carpet. My lawyer is downstairs in the corner office, working on my case. We go to trial March 15. The Ides of March. Not a good omen. I crack open the blinds. A woman with a baby is at the bus stop. The man next to her, in the powder-blue suit, is not expecting rain. His bright silk handkerchief is neatly folded in the top pocket. The baby stares up at him, but the man looks out into the distance at the clear light above the foothills, as if avoiding the baby's gaze. He's clean-shaven, maybe in his late forties. He takes a step toward the curb, looks down Wilshire, then steps back, folds his hands in front of him, and continues to wait for the bus. Maybe he's with the lady with the baby, but I don't think so. His black brogues are spit-shined, and even from here I can see the black wool socks with dark blue clocks on them. Why the hell's a guy dressed like that at eleven in the morning standing at my bus stop? Maybe he's going to confession. Maybe he's going to kill someone.

When I moved out here thirty years ago, what I missed most was the rain in New Orleans, the damp air coming off the river, the cemeteries, the dark thoughts that form there as naturally as fungus. I hate the sun, its constancy, its persistence in the face of misery. I need rain, not Wordsworth's tranquil rain that raises a mist and glitters in the sun as the sky rejoices in the morning's birth, but that hard, dark, brooding, pounding-on-the-windows rain. I want it filling the gutters, splashing knee-high off the sidewalks, flooding the streets till the shoes of the flat-stomached joggers who pound that concrete squeak with it. I want it so wet outside that I won't be able to leave home without risking pneumonia; I'll sit in my study surrounded by my books, writing a poem for God's sake. How am I supposed to write anything in all this sunshine. You go outside to get the paper and in the time it takes to bend over and pick it up, five people in pink Lycra trot by, the sweat like an emblem of purity trickling off their brows. They're in shape, and getting shapelier. I'm fat and getting fatter.

I want to go home, but the office is full of *ONTHEBUS*, copies to mail out and submissions to read through. I can't face them. I can't face poetry today, its earnestness, its faith in my ability to discern its value. These well-behaved poems move past me like sleepwalkers. I've begun to crave the really bad poem, the overwrought, straining-for-effect, kitschy purple-prose bad poem. It's like rain after a season of sun. Bad poetry has become a lost art. They don't write it like they used to. If it doesn't rain soon I'm going to publish an issue of really bad poems, the worst crap I can find. Like Robert DeNiro in *Taxi Driver*, I'll sweep all the good stuff into the gutters. Maybe out of all the shit, something great will emerge.

Not from me though. I'm not writing bad poetry. I'm not writing *any* poetry. I'm calling the plumber for the stopped-up toilet. I'm calling the tile-man about the unpaid bill. I'm getting envelopes printed for the mailing. I'm driving to Kinko's to get a form letter printed—"your subscription expires with this issue, please consider renewing." I'm getting stamps, I'm getting labels, I'm getting cramps. Before I leave, I have to see my lawyer. Plot our strategy for the trial. Then pick up Josh at school. Today's Tuesday, so Lori'll bring him to karate, and I'll get ready for my class tonight—make the coffee, order the pizza, xerox the handouts, set out the chairs. Maybe when it's over, after I clean up, after I walk Jessie and mail the handouts to those who didn't get to class tonight, after I have a bowl of soup and read the sports, maybe instead of watching the 11 o'clock news, I'll sit at the computer and write some really bad poetry.

I crack the blinds again and look out. It's still sunny. The lady with the baby is gone. The man in the powder-blue suit is still there, waiting.

THE CASE

It all started a year ago, just after Christmas. I'd just gotten back from walking the dog. Walking the dog was good for me. I was building up stamina. My doctor was going to check me out in a few days, see if I was ready to start on the treadmill. My chest was still tight from having been cracked open, but all in all

I was feeling good. I was recovering from heart surgery, and it was the best vacation I'd had in years. When the doorbell rang, I considered ignoring it, but I could feel the tug of the world again. I opened the door and was handed a summons. I was being sued for assault and battery, conspiracy to commit assault and battery, conspiring with my landlord (who was also being sued) to commit assault and battery, and charged with running a "Jerry Springer-like hate group." Supposedly, my editing class had attacked this person while he was leading an exercise group in the conference room down the hall and pummeled him into submission, all under my direction. I'd become a character in a work of fiction. A difference of opinion was now a crime akin to the Lindberg kidnaping.

THE LAWYER

After an hour of sorting through submissions, I find a poem I like for *ONTHEBUS*, a translation by Michael Andrews of a poem by the 8-century T'ang poet, Tu Fu.

> Words cannot save me. My name is lost with my poems.
> I am old. I am sick. I have been retired from office.
> My loved ones are lost on the river's current.
> My words, my name and my self adrift, floating
> between the mud and stars—
> a lone black gull.

I put the poem in a box for Jennifer to typeset, I lock my office and head down to see my lawyer. His secretary's name is Kate. She's a Bob Dylan fan, has a poster of *Blood on the Tracks* on the wall of her office. When I walk into the anteroom, she's filling in one of the forms connected with my case. I've lost track of them all, the depositions, the responses, the interrogatories. All I know is they're costing me money.

My lawyer brings to mind an old TV show starring David Jansen called *Richard Diamond, Private Eye.* When I walk into his office, I expect to see him behind his desk, feet up, a cigarette dangling from his lips, a gun nestled warmly in the top right hand drawer, a bottle of scotch in the other drawer. Maybe a battered typewriter next to his hat. But his desk is a glass slab resting on two varnished saw-horses. He types away on his laptop, looks up and tells me to sit down. At least the voice is right, a sideways kinda drawl, and it makes me feel better.

"What's the latest?" I ask.

"In the amended complaint, he says the whole class surrounded him, kicked and punched him into submission."

"This is like something out of Kafka."

"Well," he says, "the good news is the judge granted our demur and threw out the whole assault thing."

"And the bad news . . . ."

"Well, he amended the complaint again. He now claims you broke the fire laws."

"Broke the fire laws?"

My lawyer says nothing. At least there was some glamour in being sued for conspiracy to commit assault and battery. I sit and fume. "I didn't break any fire laws," I mumble. Outside the window, I can see people leaving Big 5, walking to their cars, driving away. A woman in a business suit walks by carrying a brief case. There's a world out there making hay while the sun shines. I'm in this office, doing battle with the Minotaur of the legal system.

Finally, I get up and walk to the door, tired of the whole thing. "So," I say, "you'll have to write another response to his amended complaint. Then the judge'll dismiss his complaint, but give him another chance to amend it, and then we'll have to write another response to that. Right?"

He nods. Somewhere in the distance I hear a cash register ringing, *ka-ching, ka-ching.* I write a check and give it to Kate on my way out. I notice the man in the powder blue suit at the end of the long hallway, reading the name-plate on one of the office doors. He's wearing a hat and trench coat now. He turns his head and looks down the hall, meets my eyes for a second before looking back up at the door. A weary, beat-up face, hard cheekbones with the skin softer below. Eyes gray as ashes. He reaches into the pocket of his coat and takes hold of something bulky, a bar of soap, or a gun. I decide to walk the other way, down the hall to the side exit. I stop at the inner courtyard, bright and green in the sunshine. The place is empty. Everyone's inside, doing business, making money. There's a closed-in feeling here; the garden has a haunted look, as though the sunshine were masking something ominous with its light. I turn and go, say hello to the workmen, who are refurbishing the place. The building was sold, and they're fixing it up. New carpets, new lights, new wainscoting on the walls, new paint. They're looking to rent out the empty offices. They're going to be raising my rent. *Ka-ching, ka-ching.*

THE POET

It's almost 2 P.M. Katharine's down from San Francisco, attending a state convention in Anaheim for the California Federation of Teachers. She calls and says she can get a shuttle from Disneyland that'll take her to LAX; I can pick her up there in front of the United Terminal.

"Sure, no problem. I have to go to the bank, and the post office, and then to Staples to get stuff for my class tonight. We should get to the airport about the same time."

When she gets in the car we hug, then look at each other's face, then hug again. The second hug is a deep hug. Reconnecting our deepest selves, our love for who we are to each other, and how our friendship has lasted over so many years, through the poetry wars, the teacher wars, the relationship wars, the real wars. Lovers become friends—we are. We see each other maybe twice a year. The best part is the look into each other's face between hugs. Who's Katharine these days? Who's Jack these days? Checking to see what's behind the eyes. Are we happy? Are we healthy? Are we going to live another twenty years?

"Let's stop at my office first, you can help me select a few poems for *ONTHEBUS*. Then I have to go to the hardware store," I say. "The toilet's stopped up, and I've got to get a plunger and one of those roto-rooter gizmos."

"I love hardware stores," she says.

"Really?"

"I love all those practical things."

"Yeah," I say, "Me, too. There's something reassuring about walking around a hardware store and checking out every little thing, finding something you need for the house."

"Yeah," she says, and we say nothing for a few minutes. She squirms out of her leather jacket and opens the window, letting the L.A. heat blast into the car as we race through Baldwin Hills. It's one of my favorite views, just as you come over the top of the hill and head down into the L.A. basin. You can see the whole city from there: the buildings on Wilshire, the downtown corridor, Century City, and the Hollywood Hills behind it all, the white homes on the hillside sparkling in the sun. It feels like we're heading into the Emerald City. It makes me want to light up a joint and turn the radio up as loud as it'll go. There aren't too many cars on the road, so I race down the hill doing 60, letting the air really blow. We're both quiet, reflecting.

Then Katharine says, "My dad always took me to the hardware store."

For a moment, we're both back in our childhoods, the memories of the father, accompanying him on some trivial Saturday afternoon errand.

"My dad fixed everything around the house," she says.

"Yeah," I say, "my dad, too."

We're quiet again, moving down into the basin of the City of the Angels, feeling the lure of its glitter. Everyone's panning for gold. Producers in their high towers, mapping out plans for the next blockbuster. Writers xeroxing treatments for high-concept screenplays. Actors learning their lines, praying for the break that will lift their careers up to the bright light. Even the poets, with little to gain but minor fame, are sharpening their pencils and calling forth from the blank page "the news that stays news."

"Are you writing?" Katharine says.

"Are you?" I counter.

"I asked you first," she says, and we both laugh.

"Did you get the new issue of *ONTHEBUS*?" I ask.

"No, did it come out?"

"Yeah, you got two poems in there. I sent you a copy back in December."

"Oh, we moved, so I probably didn't get it."

"The summer issue's going to the printer soon. You got any new poems?"

"Yeah," she says.

"Well, send me some."

As we near the Santa Monica Freeway, the traffic slows and we inch forward from one red light to the next. "So, are you writing?" she asks.

"I'm working on my study guide," I say. I call it a study guide. Actually, it's a textbook- anthology-history-literary criticism-personal memoir-study guide. *Etherised Upon A Table: The Story of Modern Poetries.* Not soon to be a major motion picture, it's hovering around 1,200 pages. Every time I sit at the computer to cut two pages, I end up adding ten more. I go forward and back in this obsessive tweaking. One week I'm adding something to the section on Homer, the next I'm fleshing out the chapter on the 12-century Troubadour poets, a week later I'm wrapping up the account of Byzantine, Persian, and Arabic poetry during the Dark Ages. Then it's back to the Greeks and lyric poetry of the 6-century BC. I feel like the anonymous builder of St. Denis who broke from his Romanesque models and worked back and forth between different architectural and sculptural elements until he had achieved a logic and organization that subordinated the parts to the whole, giving the effect of a unified Gothic structure.

"But are you writing any poetry?"

"How am I supposed to write poetry in all this sunshine?" I whine. "I'm writing a book on teaching poetry, I'm writing a book on the history of poetry, I'm editing a journal that's full of poetry, but I'm not writing any poetry."

"Why not?"

I shrug. "I don't know. I just don't feel like it. There's too much sun. It makes me want to run errands, fix things around the house, get things done." I pull into the parking garage by Koontz Hardware. "Soon as we get that plunger, soon as I fix the toilet," I say, "I'll write some poetry."

THE KID

I drop Katharine off at the house and go pick up Josh at school. He's running around crazy, full of energy, dragging his backpack behind him with one hand, clutching loose drawings in the other. His shoelaces are untied. The arms of his sweatshirt are tied around his waist. He talks as we walk to the car, telling me about his Pokémon cards. There are 829 of these characters, some of which "evolve" into others. "John's selling all his cards," he says, "and he said he'd sell me his Mew. Maybe his Charizard. Maybe even his Wigglytuff."

"I thought you had Wigglytuff." I say.

"No Dad, I said I had Jiggly*puff*."

"Oh. Well, didn't you just get a Charizard last week?"

"No Dad, we got Charmeleon. Charizard is the really rare one."

He keeps talking, but I can't keep up with it all. It gives me a headache.

I try to change the subject. "How was school today?"

"Good."

"Did you learn anything interesting?"

"Good."

"No, Josh, really. Tell me something about what you did in school."

"Good."

"Josh, I'm not in a silly mood. Can't we just have a normal conversation?"

"Good."

"All right, never mind. We'll just drive and say nothing."

"Good."

"Josh!"

"What?"

"Stop saying 'good.'"

"Okay," he says.

"Good," I say, and we both laugh.

"Mom's not coming home till six. What do you want for dinner?"

"Wiener."

"You want a hot dog?"

"Wiener."

"Josh, I'm not in the mood for this. I've got to get home and fix the toilet and get ready for my class tonight. Katharine's visiting from San Francisco."

"Wiener."

"Come on, Josh. What do you want for dinner, and don't say 'wiener.'"

"Good."

I take a deep breath and try not talking. Maybe if we ride along in silence for awhile he'll forget the whole thing. As we pass Canter's I say, "Hey, how about something from Canter's?"

"Butt."

"Josh, what's going on with this wiener-butt business? Is this something you guys made up in school?"

"Wiener."

"Okay. Okay. We'll go home and I'll make something there."

Josh opens my glove compartment and rummages around. He finds my sunglasses and puts them on, trying to look cool. We drive in silence, past McDonald's, Jan's Coffee Shop, Farmer's Market. It's going to be dark soon. The sun casts long shadows on the streets and sidewalk. I think about turning on the radio but decide against it. There's something nice about riding along with Josh, saying nothing, just being together.

"Wiener." he says, more to himself than to me.

"Good," I say back, more to myself than to him.

THE POEM

Class is over. I walk Jessie, have a bowl of soup, and decide to skip the 11 o'clock news. In my study are most of my books, books from grammar school, books from high school, books from college, books I've accumulated during 45 years of incessant buying, books that have comforted me in the worst of times. Before Josh was born, I thought of them as my children.

I pull down several, almost randomly, looking for a line or two that will kick-start me into writing a poem. I open a book of Sumerian poetry, translated by the eminent Assyriologist, Thorkild Jacobsen. I flip it open to page 125, the "Nanshe Hymn," and to the haunting "Lament for the Fall of Ur," an obscure text written several millennia before Christ. It laments the catastrophic end of the Third Dynasty of Ur, which in a very real sense was the end of Sumerian civilization.

Just a city it was, just a city it was,
the mountain rising out of the waters,
jugs set up in the sacred storehouses.
Just a city it was, just a city it was,
bread baskets lined up for Nanshe,
as if they were sediment left by a river.

Just a city it was,
The storm ravaging the city,
floodlike the city;
the storm burning like fire
cracked the skin on the people,
the storm covered Ur like a cloth,
veiled it like a linen sheet.

Then I turn on the computer and begin to write. But after a few lines, I lose heart. I find myself very boring tonight. *I did this, I did that. I think this, I think that. I feel this, I feel that.* I'm more interested in Ausonius, a 4th-century poet from Gaul. I call up the *Study Guide* and scroll to the section just before the fall of the Roman Empire, page 327, the section on Ausonius, sometimes called the first medieval secular poet. Raised by two battle-axes, a grandmother and an aunt, both named Aemelia, Ausonius became a teacher and lived a life like that of a professor in a 19th-century university town in New England or a Chinese gentlemen of the T'ang dynasty. His poems were known for their tender sentiments, their rural pictures, the purity of their Latin, and the almost Virgilian smoothness of their verse. I find myself drawn to this forgotten poet who lived a hundred years before the Germans crossed the Rhine and invaded the Roman empire.

My father was Ausonius, and I bear the same name.

Who I am, and what is my rank, my family,
my home, and my native land,
I have written here, that you might know me,
whoever you are or may have been,
and when you know me,
might honor me with a place in your memory.

Last night I read in *The History of Mathematics* how analytical geometry was born with three dreams that René Descartes had in 1619. The first two were about an evil wind and a sudden storm. Descartes realized that by seeing each with the unsuperstitious eyes of science, they could do him no harm. The third dream was about Ausonius. Descartes dreamt of reading one of his poems which begins *Quod vitae secatabor iter?*— "What way of life shall I follow?" According to the story, Descartes woke with a start and felt a magic key had unlocked a door leading him into a new life, a life devoted to algebra and geometry, thus giving birth to analytic geometry. Einstein once said that "the highest physics always evolves into poetry." Here, the simplest of poems evolved into physics. I work on the section for about an hour. The house is quiet. It's past midnight when I'm done. I go outside and Jessie trots along with me. The night's clear enough to see the lights of the houses in the Hollywood Hills. I look back at my house, and try to find the familiar in its dark windows. The air has a damp foretaste of rain. No stars in sight. The moon almost full, surrounded by a halo.

THE BED

I slide under the covers and scoot over next to Lori. She's on her side, her back to me, so I spoon into her and wrap my arm around her waist.

She mumbles something into the pillow. I put my hand down the back of her pajamas and rub her behind. It's smooth and warm.

"How'd things go tonight?" I ask.

She mumbles some more, trying not to wake up. Something about Katharine and Josh and pizza.

"Was Josh okay going to bed?"

She groans a bit, then turns over to face me, snuggles into my chest. "Yeah. He wouldn't stop talking, though. Something about a video game he's inventing. How was class?"

"Good. Everyone's doing good."

"Good."

We lie there quietly for a minute.

"Are you okay?" she asks, her eyes still closed.

"Yeah. I started to write a poem tonight, but quit after five lines. I got bored with it." We lie there in silence, sharing the warmth of our bodies. A car goes by on Orlando, loud rap music thumping from its speakers. The sound fades in the distance. Just before it disappears completely, a dog barks, as if giving it an exclamation point.

I want to talk some more, but I hear her breathing and assume she's fallen back asleep. But after twenty years together, it's as if she has her hand on my heart at all times. She can feel its yearnings, its sorrows.

"You know what?" she says.

"What?"

"We could go to Border's tomorrow when I get home. You could buy a few books, get some soup in the café. You could write in your journal."

"Yeah, that sounds good."

"It's going to rain tomorrow."

"Really?"

"Yeah, it's going to storm."

"Are you sure?"

"Yeah, a big storm is moving down from Alaska. It's supposed to hit by tomorrow night."

"A big storm," I say, repeating it to myself before falling asleep.

THE BIG SLEEP

I'm in my office, going through piles of poems, when there's a knock on the door. I open it. The man in the powder blue suit stands there, shrugging his shoulders.

"You Grapes?" he asks.

"Who's asking?" I sneer.

He makes a grunting sound, pushing past me into the office.

"Hey, what the hell do you . . ."

He turns on me and jabs a .38 into my stomach. I look down at the gun, then back up at him. We stand there, looking at each other for a very long time, listening to the percussion of the day ring. He turns his head for a moment, surveys the room.

"Where's the *noir*?" he asks.

"The what?"

He presses the gun deeper into my gut. It isn't a jab like you see in the movies, just a slight increase in pressure against my belly. Almost like he's being polite.

Like he's going to lean forward and kiss me. The odor of whiskey on his breath is mixed with cigarettes, and maybe a meatball sandwich.

"The *noir*," he repeats. "Where is it?"

"I haven't the faintest idea what you're . . ."

He slaps me across the face with his other hand, a quick little slap that stings more than it hurts. The slap is scarier than the gun. It's the slap of a desperate man.

"I haven't . . . seen . . . any . . . *noir*."

"Neither have I," he says, and lowers the gun. I relax for a second, and he jabs the gun hard into my gut. "You sure you haven't seen any?"

I'm beginning to understand what he means, who he is. "There's been no *noir* around here for years," I say.

"I've looked everywhere," he says, "driven down the coast, up into the foothills, along Sunset, over Laurel Canyon, across Western. It used to be all over Western Avenue. I thought I caught a glimpse of it going east on Franklin, but I turned north on Brittany Place, and it was gone."

He sits in my desk chair and places the gun on the blotter, delicately, as if setting down a porcelain figurine.

I walk over to him, pull the other chair up to the desk. The sun is lower in the sky. It streams in through the open blinds. He keeps his head down. I put a hand on his shoulder. "I've been looking for it, too," I say. "Without the *noir*, we're both a little lost, aren't we, Philip." He looks up, startled that I know who he is.

"What does it matter where you lay once you're dead?" he asks.

I know the speech. I say the next line back at him. "In a dirty sump or in a marble tower on top of a high hill."

"You're dead," he continues. "You're sleeping the big sleep."

There's a long silence between us. Then: "Maybe the *noir*'s coming back," I say. He straightens up, hopeful. "It never leaves for long, you know. If it's in here," I point to my heart, "it'll be out there, too." Marlowe gives me a weary smile and turns his head to the window.

"I hear there's some *noir* coming in tomorrow night," I tell him.

"Where'd you hear that?"

"It's coming down from Alaska. A big storm. Supposed to hit by tomorrow night. You can sit in your car and hear it drum on the roof all night long. Maybe the burbank top will leak. A pool of water might form on the floorboards. Like that night on Laverne Terrace when you found Carmen at Geiger's house."

His eyes come to life. He lays the palm of his hand on the gun. "This on the level?" he asks.

"Yeah, Marlowe. On the level. My wife told me."

He gets up and walks out the door. Like that, he's gone. Lori nudges me awake. I try to hold onto the dream, but it's gone.

"It's late," she says. "The school just called and they want to know if you can come in thirty minutes early."

I get up to call the school. Yeah, I can come in thirty minutes early. I can come in as early as they want.

THE MAZE

After school, Katharine and I eat a late lunch at King's Road Café. A light drizzle is falling, so we get an inside table. Then I bring her to the airport. Driving back, I take La Cienega through the Baldwin Hills. Above the horizon, storm clouds belly over the setting sun. In the distance, through a gray, hard rain, I see the Emerald City, looking now like tarnished pieces of an erector set. By the time I get home, the rain's pounding on the roof of the car. Lori and Josh and I drive over to Borders. Lori takes Josh off to the kids' books, I go upstairs and get a bowl of soup and a book of poetry. I set my journal to the side and read until something plucks a chord: a poem by Amazawa Taijirô that begins:

> A man walking along the dawn highway
> realizes suddenly
> the back of his skull's transparent
> like a river of black lead.
> In that instant Unhesitating
> he starts to walk backwards to the harbor.

Then I open the journal to a blank page and write a line.

Here comes the rain . . . .

Suddenly, Josh comes running up and drops a book on the table, almost knocking over the bowl of soup. "Hey, Dad. Look what I got." It's a book called *Monster Mazes*, and he wants me to do one. I don't want to lose the poem I'm about to write. I think to tell him I'll be with him in a minute, but decide against it. We negotiate the hardest maze in the book, which takes nearly twenty minutes, then he decides to go look for another book. When he's gone, I open the journal again. I look at the line I wrote—"Here comes the rain"—and write a different poem, instead.

Monster Maze

Here comes the rain,
and my son Josh
plops a book on the table.
Monster Mazes.
He's got me trying one
on the first level of difficulty,
where you can perish
if you stumble into a chamber of fire,
or fall into a pit of snakes.
Other dangers lurk if you take the wrong path:
I could become a welcome feast for rats,
"If you run into them," he says.
Giant spiders might drink my "last drop of blood,"
and pit vipers will strike with poison fangs
the moment I enter their lair.
Every path I take leads to a horrible death.
Josh assures me. "These are really complicated mazes, Dad,
but you can back up and try again."
He takes my pen and shows me.
"Oh, I get it."
And I persevere.
He watches me, anticipating every wrong turn,
whistling his little whistle
when I seem to be on the right path.
But it's tiring. I just want to go home
and watch the Barrera-Morales fight on TV.
"You're doing good, Dad," Josh says.
He can tell I'm faltering.
The lines of the maze begin to blur.
I'll never get to the finish.
I decide to cheat.
I move the pencil just enough

to make it look like I'm concentrating on the path.
With my other eye I focus on the finish line
and begin to trace the path backward toward the start.
Josh is watching like a hawk now,
hunched over the table, his head down
just above the page.
He warns me about *The Kraken*, a terrible monster
of the deep seas trapped eons ago
when an earthquake split the ocean floor.
Now the *Kraken* feeds on stray goblins and other hapless creatures.
That's me, a hapless creature
with bad eyesight and a shaky hand.
The lines blur even more.
I feel a sense of despair,
some great tugging at my heart.
What am I doing in this maze?
Where's my poem?
The poem about the rain?
It's gone, and here I am
with nothing but the rapid pounding of the feet
of the terrible Minotaur who detests humans
because they remind him that he was once human, too.
It's hopeless.
I decide to cheat again.
I cross one of the lines and go directly to the path
I know will take me to the finish,
but Josh is right there and catches me.
"Hey, you can't cross the lines," he says.
"Oh, yeah, I didn't notice."
"That's okay," he says, helpful, optimistic,
riding the back of my pencil toward certain victory.
I plod along,
past *The Giant Worm*,
and the *Pit of Doom*,
until suddenly I've reached the level
where only the bravest dare go.
"You're in level IV," Josh shouts.
"I can't finish this," I tell him.
I'm tired of the whole preposterous journey.
I look at him, hoping for permission to quit.
He tilts his head to one side and gives me that look,
his blue eyes full of confidence in me.
"You're almost there," he says,
his face luminous and mysterious.
I have no idea who he is.
He's a light in the distance
toward which I move, every day, closer and closer.
When I finally get there, he'll be gone, I know.

"You're almost there," he croons.
So we're in this together, my son and I.
I decide to trust in blind luck.
In a final chamber rests a fire-breathing dragon.
He is old and his hide is thick.
His only comfort is to rest on the huge treasure
he collected in his younger years.
If we defeat this dragon, the gods
will transport us
by magic
to the land of mortals,
all our treasures in hand.
I look outside for a second
and watch the cars on La Cienega
creep forward in the rain
coming down even harder now.
A hard, heavy, dark rain.

A Time to Sing, a Time to Dance

There's too much time to sing,
and not enough time to dance.
The sea is for singing, the land for dancing,
and the dog that will not die
does both.
My grandfather told me this
when I was 12 and he'd been dead for thirty years.
My grandfather on my mother's side.
My grandfather on my father's side, we don't know
when he died, having abandoned the family
when my father was two.
I'm writing this down
camping by the Kern River,
where there are no watches to measure time or distance.
Josh does his dance by the tent
and Lori notices that his feet move like my feet,
meaning one of my grandfathers
still speaks and moves through him.
This poem, then, is a song to my son,
and to my wife, and my friends,
who do this dance with me.
And I am grateful for the kind of richness
that refuses to be turned into art.

Trees, then rocks, then mountains, then sky,
then clouds, then God, who forgives
me for knowing he doesn't exist.
Still, I thank Him for all He's given me,
nothing I've dared ask for, nothing
I would have dared pray for,
but not a day goes by that I don't send up
little balloons of thank-you's.

When I made my birthday wish,
which we celebrated last night around the campfire,
I wished for each one of my friends
a life full of everything God has given me—
a God who doesn't even exist.
He hears our songs, He accepts our dances.

And sometimes I wonder, especially at night,
if He will punish me and take everything away,
a punishment I'd duly deserve for my lack of faith.
I'd like to say to him,
I believe in you, you are there,
but I can't.
He knows how badly I want to be able to say this.
But I know what I know.
The truth will not go away.
The unspeakable things we do to each other and to the children.
Job asked Him for a reason and was scolded
just for asking.
The gall, to question The Creator about the world He created.
I don't deserve my good fortune,
yet accept it without question.
My wife, my son, my deep and truest friends
who love me.
And it's all too much to hold or carry.
There's so much to sing about,
I've hardly begun to dance,
and there's so little time to dance.
I *would* dance. I would dance with Him who gave me so much,
but would He dance with me?
Would He open his arms and follow my lead,
me, who dares not question,
who receives and receives and gives
Him nothing back, not even a question directed straight at Him,
not even the heartfelt supplication
of one small prayer.

What Gets Lost

Some rivers run wild,
some deep, some,
like the one in my throat,
hinge on memory
and every hookline&sinker
that floats to the bottom.
Les poèms viennent et vont.
A deer once came to our campsite.
Up close, he looked big
and dangerous, not like something
in a Disney movie.
I told him to stay where he was
and he obeyed. This big buck
obeyed. We had an understanding.
It's not like that with the world.
Briefmarken bleiben für immer.
I never practiced the piano.
What was I waiting for?
You can only wait so long,
then it's time to get your coat
and say goodbye to the others.
My wife thinks I take too long
saying goodbye. A lingering.
What's the rush? Something
might happen, someone
might say something, then
where would I be?
In the car, driving home,
missing the best of it.
That'd be a fine how-do-you-do.
Like being in the middle of the journey
of your life and finding yourself lost
per una selva oscura,
blah blah blah the straight path,
the narrow way, the right road, etc.
So say you're walled up inside a dream.
Fixed forms vanish.
Vida y muerte eran mi cuarto sesgado.

The moon sits there all alone,
begging to be worshiped.
Miró actually set his canvases on fire.
Not with paint; with matches.
I was thinking now I'm not
thinking now I'm thinking again.
Transcendence, the existence of others,
negation, contraction, the body,
temporality, translator's introduction,
dialectical car-ports, the concept
of carburetors, flashlights, penny-
ante card games, still too soon
to discuss the Hegelian concept itself,
but being is always reduced by a signification
of the existent, enveloped by essence,
and the effort each of us makes
to rediscover the immediate in terms
of the mediated, the abstract in terms
of the concrete on which it is grounded.
I am the body, I am the existent,
I am the signification.
You're always getting at something,
but like the deer, it bolts off
into the forest, the *oscura* forest,
the dark forest, as the poets say,
the one you get lost in,
the one you have to enter
to get the thing you are getting at.
Life is this one big how-do-you-do,
and then it'll be time to get your coat
and say goodbye to the others,
to the body, to the temporality,
to the negation, to the moon,
to the transcendence,
to the rivers running wild,
the canvases aflame,
the translator's introduction,
the translation itself—
what gets lost in the poetry.

Szymborska

(1923–2012)

I came home
Wednesday night from class
and Lori was ensconced
like a caterpillar in a cocoon
on the bed, watching a movie on TV
about crazy people who fall in love
and break china.
"Szymborska died," I said.

She reached for the remote
and shut the TV off.
The room expanded into that quiet bubble
we experience
when we shut off the TV.

She looked at me and said nothing.

What was there to say?

A friend dies,
a poet dies,
poetry lives on:
There's nothing
you can say.

It's like turning off the TV,
and their passing
fills the space of our lives
with all that silence.
A balloon of being and nothingness,
a reduction of existence into a series
of appearances, overcoming those dualisms
that have embarrassed philosophy for centuries,
and replacing them with the monism
of the phenomenon.

I put the clipboard
I still had in my hand
on the dresser

and began to undress.
Then I got in the bed and lay beside her.
We still hadn't spoken.

Szymborska was gone.

We just lay there for a bit, in the silence,
not sure who would break it,
not sure whose turn it was
to turn the moment back into words.
You need a poet at a time like this,
and the poet was gone.

There was a small crack in the ceiling.
And a tiny cobweb in the corner.
Later, Lori'd probably get on a chair
and with a tissue
wipe it away.
That was her job, getting
those little tiny spider webs
gone before they engulfed the house,
our lives, the planet. Don't
worry, dear reader, she's on the job.
You will be safe.

"What's my job?" asks Lori when she's nagging me.
And I repeat the mantra: "To take care of me."

But for now, with Szymborksa's passing
still blooming into silence,
the cobweb would have to wait,
the crack would just have to bide its time.

Such a long silence.

Then I thought, fuck it.
I reached for the remote,
and clicked the TV back on.

There went a teacup.
Crash.
There went another.
Crash.

It was good to get back
to a semblance of the world,
all that love and passion,
all those broken teacups.

A Christmas Wish

Yesterday I sat on Santa's lap, a truly kind and generous spirit. I asked him what *he* wanted for Christmas, and he smiled and said, "To go home."

"Tired?" I asked.

"No, I love what I'm doing here, but I've been here since November, and I'm ready to go home."

Home could have meant a few blocks over on 6th Street, or El Segundo, or as far away as Tennessee. But what if home means the North Pole. Something about his inner peace and joy, I thought to myself— after sitting on Santa's lap every year for the last who-knows-how-many-years and getting our picture taken together—this guy's the real deal. So I wasn't about to break that spell.

"But it's mighty cold back home," I said, "up there at the North Pole." The girl taking the picture aimed the camera and I told her I wanted a closer shot, just Santa and me.

"Not as cold as you think," he said, his eyes twinkling, just like in the poem. Then he laughed and said, "Those elves have been pretty busy, too. Now I gotta get to work."

"Just like in college," I said, "you're pulling an all-nighter!"

And we both laughed, and turned to the camera, and the flash went off, and then we stood, gave each other a big hug.

"You forgot to ask me what I wanted for Christmas," I said.

He looked me straight in the eye, like he knew. Damn, this guy was the real deal, I was sure of it. I wasn't five years old again, but that sense of belief, not in Santa so much as that sense of belief in goodness and kindness and compassion and generosity—peace on earth, good will toward men— well, here we were, two old coots coming around the far turn, and I could pretty much see it all in his eyes. He looked at me with such wisdom and trust — was I projecting, was this the Santa I imagined for myself? He looked at me, hands on my shoulders, and said, "I don't need to ask. I can tell by looking at you that you already have what you want."

The girl walked over and gave me a card to go pay for the photos at the window, and she was already ushering in two kids, one boy, one girl, about the same age, and Santa turned his attention to them. I took the card and got in the line to pay. I remembered for a moment when I was about four, and we lived in that little shotgun house on Cadiz Street, a lower working-class neighborhood, and even though we were Jewish, we had a nice big tree, and I was just starting to figure it out, that there was no such thing as Santa Claus. Maybe I was five, maybe even six. I can't remember. We didn't even have a chimney. My dad and mom were fighting again, and I kept hoping for snow, though it never snowed in New Orleans, so why hope. But that night, the anticipation going to bed, imagining this guy was gonna come into the house and put under the tree what I wanted for Christmas. I wanted my dad to stop drinking and my mom to stop yelling and my fear of the dark to go away. "You forgot to ask me what I wanted for Christmas," I'd asked. And as I pulled out my credit card to pay for the photo of the two of us, all I could think of was his answer: "I don't need to ask, I can tell by looking at you that you already have what you want."

There were a few more things to get. A scarf for my wife, a book for my son, something for my god-child and my god-son-in-law, a box of chocolates for some friends coming over. Already the mall was packed with last minute shoppers. So many people with one thing on their minds: What can I give?

Yeah, Santa, I'm a pretty lucky fella. I got up early this morning—it was still dark outside—so I could walk into the living room and see the "Christmas Chair" all lit up. Some years we don't get a tree, but we set up all the lights and stuff on a big chair and ottoman in the living room, my son puts his rubber chicken on top, and all the presents sit in the middle, as if the chair were the palm of a giant hand stretched out, as if to say, "Here, this is for you." I sat there in the early morning dark, except for the lights, and thought about all the things to be thankful for. It was a good feeling. I didn't need to ask for anything, 'cause this is what I wanted all along. This day, this present day, this moment, this great sense of peace and joy. And Santa had been here, I know. We have a chimney now, and I know he was here. He brought me this life. The life I didn't even know how to ask for when I was five.

The Man with the Beard

"What do you do?" he asks.

"I'm a poet," I say.

"What kind of poems do you write?"

"Big ones,
little ones,
bad ones,
good ones,
poems about rain,
poems about trying to find
a parking space on a Saturday night."

I take a sip of my Guinness
and give a little laugh,
just so he knows I'm kidding.
The beer's bitter.
I should have gotten the Corona.

"Poetry . . . ," he ponders.

"Yeah," I say,
moving the plastic cup
of beer aside,
away from the edge
of the table,
". . . poetry."

Another man walks up
and asks if he can share the table.
He's wearing a green shirt, suspenders,
a green beret. All set for the Bloomsday
reading of episode seven from *Ulysses.*

Bag of wind, windbag, west wind,
wind in my sails, an ill wind.

The band in the courtyard
strikes up another Irish tune.

Three young ladies link arms and dance a jig.

The waiter brings the Irish stew
in a paper cup, a plastic lid on top.
I count the carrots and small pieces of meat.
I eat it with the plastic spoon.
It's not very good;
as Irish stew goes,
pretty bad.

After the reading I ask the Joycean scholar
a question, but she doesn't have an answer.
Pale vampire mouth to mouth.
The soul frets in the shadow of language.
This rough magic drowned in the book.
Love that speaks in the lizard's flash.
Do and do and done.
Courtesy of the inward light.
Fathers falling down.

Smooth Sailing

I don't think I've ever been hit with a bolt of inspiration.
It's just damn hard, trying to put something down.
Whether it's by hand in a journal,
watching the ink dry,
or on the old portable Royal typewriter
my dad got me when I was 11.
I learned to type on that thing using the *Ruth Ben'ry Touch-Typing* system
and wrote all those Inspector Peterson Murder Mysteries on it—
The Living Corpse, The Corpse Tells No Tales, The Corpse Takes Over.
On the IBM Selectric I wrote *A Savage Peace*
and *Seven Is a Frozen Number,*
and when I moved to L.A.,
I got that portable Smith Corona electric on which
I wrote most of *Breaking on Camera* and *Trees, Coffee* before I got a computer.
After a date, Lori and I would come home to the apartment
on Orange Street and have a glass of wine
and take turns writing a poem on that Smith Corona,
read them to each other, then make love.
But whether I'm writing in the backyard, or in a café, or in a coffee shop,
or in the kitchen, or at a picnic table, hell, it really doesn't matter,
it's just not easy.
The wind could be whipping up a storm
but I'd probably say something about the morning stillness.
Poetry does that to you, makes you lose your bearings,
makes you puff out your chest and put on airs.
High hopes, then it starts to fall apart
and the best you can hope for
is that you don't make a fool of yourself
by the last line.
You wave the white flag while you're still typing,
hoping for some sympathy from the gods.
I give up, I give up, but it's a false declaration.
You never really give up.
In this poem, maybe, where I can feel myself
thinking about throwing in the towel,
but there's always the next one, not to give up totally.
Prospecting for gold, hoping the parchment map is accurate.
Some deeper meaning you can hang your hat on.

Maybe I've been reading the wrong books.
I should get back to books with pictures.
But over the years,
I've grown this relationship
with the poem.
Bukowski said he duked it out,
and maybe Rilke breathed them from the storm,
and Whitman yawped his way through.
But me? 'Dunno. We're just old friends,
the poem and me.
I imagine us sitting on a swing on the front porch,
smoking a pipe or a cigar,
watching the passing parade.
The poem says, "The world stands revealed,"
and I say, "There's a squirrel there in that tree."
Then the poem says, "Makeshift ennui,"
and I say, "My wife makes our front yard
look so beautiful."
The poem says, "Lines of darkness run true,"
and I say, "My son is becoming a man,
bon voyage, my son, smooth sailing,
steer by the stars."
Then the poem closes its eyes,
and I close mine,
just a nap we're taking before dinner,
steamed broccoli and a piece of chicken.

FINE

My great fantasy when I was in my early teens was that my dad and I would go bowling on a Saturday morning, then go out to breakfast together. Maybe to one of those broken down waterfront joints next to the wharf. They served coffee in thick, white mugs. It would be just the two of us. We'd watch the big ships come down the Mississippi. He could tell me stories of when he was young, tramping around the country during the Depression, eating in places like this.

Why bowling? I don't know. Maybe because I thought I'd have him all to myself. The only time it was me and my dad was when he took me fishing. And even then, we didn't talk much. He'd wake me up at two in the morning, and I'd sit in the back of the car, half asleep, still in my pajamas. Every so often I'd open my eyes to see where we were. We're on the Airline Highway, passing the airport. We're driving through the bayous with cypress stumps sticking up out of the swamps. We're on a dirt road passing the shacks by the oil refineries. Fire shooting out of a big smokestack in the middle of the night. The car comes to a stop and we're in Grande Isle just as the sun's coming up.

By the time it was light, we'd be out on the water in the Gulf of Mexico with a bunch of men who were all grizzly and unshaven, loud and playful. The smell of diesel fuel mixed with the odor of fish heads used for bait. The boat went up and down, smacking the choppy waves that got higher and higher the further we got from land. Finally, we came to the oil rigs. When they cut the engine and threw anchor, I had to hold on as the boat rocked and rode the waves. The men were smoking and drinking and yelling back and forth, throwing their lines into the water, pulling up the fish. They seemed to come flying on board as if their fins were wings. Spade fish and red snapper. There wasn't time for my dad and me to talk in all that confusion. It was mostly the slime and blood of the fish, and my worrying that he was sneaking a drink and would end up drunk by the time we got back to shore. On the way home I watched how he drove the car, so that if he was so drunk he couldn't drive, I'd be able to get us home. I was eleven, and had no idea how to drive a car, but if I had to, I thought, I could figure it out. And I worried that my mother would yell and threaten divorce if she smelled the whiskey on his breath, and then maybe they'd fight and the mirror in the medicine cabinet in the bathroom would get broken again and Mom would start slapping us kids, and then Dad would go on a binge that would last for days and we wouldn't know if he would ever come home again.

So bowling seemed tame. Afterwards, we could get French Market doughnuts, maybe talk about his life before he met my mom, that life of adventure during the Depression when he "rode the rails and slept in hobo jungles," when he saw Dempsey fight Firpo and get knocked clear "outta the ring," and when he was a cowboy out west. I liked it when he told us stories of his days as a cowboy, getting shot in a gun battle and being nursed back to life by a Mexican woman named Juanita. I was 14 before I realized the cowboy stories were made up.

If my dad were alive today, I'd want to take him and my 12-year-old son bowling. I'd want my dad to know Josh, want Josh to know his grandfather. I'd want my dad to see how Josh and I go out every Friday night to see a play, that we've been doing this since he was 10, and how before that we went to the Silent Movie Theatre on Fairfax every Friday since he was eight. Josh always has more popcorn and candy than his mother would like, but what the hell. We've seen Shakespeare and Thornton Wilder, Chekhov and Neil Simon, Molière and Arthur Miller, Sophocles and Eugene O'Neill, Ibsen and Samuel Beckett, Ionesco and Bertolt Brecht, Neil Simon, Pirandello, and Edward Albee. It's better than bowling.

So anyway, Josh and I saw Strindberg's *Dance of Death* last weekend at the Company Rep in North Hollywood. An adaptation by Friedrich Duerrenmatt. A battle of the sexes, to put it mildly. The play figuratively takes place in the boxing ring of their living room. The husband enters the stage and sits up left while the wife enters and sits down right. An announcer steps into the center of the ring and says, "Round One, Conversation before Dinner." Then they sit there for five minutes saying absolutely nothing. Tick tock. Tick tock. Silence. I've never heard silence get such a laugh. It came in waves. Silence, then laughter, then tired silence. Waiting. You figure, okay, joke's over. But no, the silence goes on. Then laughter again. Then silence. Then laughter. Then silence and more silence. Acceptance of the profundity of their lack of communication. Everyone, actors and audience alike, finally lapsed into this sad and weary silence.

On the way home I told Josh about Strindberg's life, how he married several times, always to very young women.

"Sounds like he was a player," Josh said.

Last night Lori, Josh and I went to see De Sica's *Bicycle Thief* at the New Beverly Cinema. A bad print, and the bulb kept going out in the projector, but it was still exquisite. Father and son searching all over Rome for the bicycle stolen from the father that morning after he finally gets a job that requires a bicycle, the bicycle he got out of hock by selling all the family's linens. "We don't need sheets," his wife says as she strips the bed. Bruno is about 10 years old. So many moments in that film, silences between dialogue. The purity of De Sica's shots that seem more interested in the human face than cinematic composition. I don't want to give the end away for anyone who hasn't seen this masterpiece of Italian Neo-Realism, but at the end, as the film fades to black, the two walk away from us into the world awaiting them, a sad ending, surely, but to say the ending was sad would be to trivialize its profound complexity. Bruno takes his father's hand and we see them from the back as they disappear into the crowd, trudging their weary way homeward, leaving the world to darkness as the Italian word FINE appears in white on the black background. After having read the English subtitles throughout the film, there was an odd confusion when that final word appeared. As if De Sica were commenting on the ending, father and son walking off into the rest of their lives together, the son burdened at such an early age with the awareness of his father's desperation and imperfection—yet De Sica seemed to be saying that everything would be fine, not to worry. FINE. But no, you re-adjust. The word is Italian. It wasn't fine, it was FINE, THE END, FINITO. Everyone in the audience sat there, silent. No one got up to go. We sat staring at the black screen, at the word FINE. A long silence before one or two people began to clap. Then the slow, deliberate applause of everyone in the theater, then silence again, as we sat there, going nowhere. And why did we sit in the darkened theater without moving? Because we had lives to go home to, just as Bruno and his father had to face the rest of their lives, and it wasn't FINE, it wasn't the end. But for a moment, just for a moment, we sat there, in the silence of the theater, somewhere between the life on the screen and the life waiting for us outside.

When we left the theater, just before we crossed the street to our car, Josh took my hand. A casual kind of thing, something he hadn't done in years, since he was little and used to take my hand whenever we crossed the street. Hugs and small embraces had become rare, as Josh took off into that teenage macho thing. But there was his hand taking hold of mine. I wasn't sure how obvious I should be about it, so I just let my hand dangle a bit, let him hold me without me holding back. Then as we stepped off the curb, I grasped and entwined, and we crossed the street together, holding hands, like when he was a little boy. We continued to hold until we got to the car, talking the whole time about the film.

Josh has his bedtime ritual with his mom, and I still haven't learned the sequence, good night, good night, sleep tight, sleep tight, bed bugs bite, bed bugs bite, then these little sounds that are impossible to describe: hawwooo, hawwooo, uuuwaaahh, uuuuwaaaaah, weeeeoooh, weeeeooooh. It's like a song two animals might sing to each other. I've tried but never get the sequence right, so I'm not exactly allowed to do it. So he and I have our own ritual. It's a bit of a joke, and Lori always cracks up when we do it.

"'Night."

"'Night."

"Love you."

"Love you too."

Then there's a perfectly-timed pause, and both of us say at exactly the same time, "Just kidding!" Then we laugh, and it feels good. We get to be sentimental and mushy, but we get to undercut it as well.

So last night, after the movie, we did it again, all the way through the "just kidding" part. Maybe it was the movie, that heartbreaking movie, and the father and son thing. But after the "just kidding," I walked to the door, and just as I was closing it, said, "Love you," a frail whisper sent like a paper airplane into the darkened room, and he answered back, just as quietly, "Love you too."

I decided to wait, to see if he'd say "just kidding." We'd turned off the light so I couldn't see anything, just the shadow of him in bed, under the covers, his hands holding the duvet up to his chin. The dog's rustling into position at the foot of his bed. I could hear Lori in the kitchen close the dishwasher with that little snap. I waited another second, let the silence grow larger. Was he thinking the same thing I was thinking? Was he waiting to see if I was going to say "just kidding" again? I let the silence hang a bit longer, as if to clarify our joint decision not to say anything. We were both going to endure the silence, a silence that was not about separation or disconnection, but an affirmation of the love between us.

I closed the door, leaving that little crack as usual. Then into the kitchen to help Lori with the rest of the dishes.

"Don't bang the dishes," she said.

"No, I'll be quiet."

And we cleaned up around the kitchen, whispering to each other until we were sure he was asleep.

FINE

Paris Is So Parisian

The poets and writers sat in Parisian cafés because their apartments were cold and the cafés were warm and they could write. The philosophers sat in Parisian cafés because where better to spread the butter of existentialism than on the toast of Parisian *indolenté*. New Orleans is my mother; Los Angeles, my wife; and Paris, my mistress. I know, you don't have to tell me. There's Florence and London and Prague and St. Peterburg and Rome and Venice. But Paris calls me and calls me, and so I go. When Josh was ten years old, Lori and I took him to Paris. Eight years later, we dropped him off in New York for college, helped set him up in his dorm, and decided to keep going, avoid the empty nest, catch a plane for Paris. Once Josh got his classes set up, and he seemed to be having the time of his life. We didn't hear from him once, except when his food card wasn't working and he had to pay cash for his meals. So we get a call in Paris all frantic.

"You gotta give them your ID number," said Lori from our table at the small café across the street from L'Hotel Moderne.

"Oh," he said.

So unless he needed money and couldn't find his socks, we were barely a blip on his radar screen. And you know what, we were glad. If we had been back in L.A., we'd have worried every minute, how's he doing, what's he doing? All you do in the empty nest is walk around obsessing about your kid's comfort. But in Paris, you're in another life. So what if Josh doesn't call, we said. We get the news second hand, but it's okay. We find out that he's doing fine, has a wonderful roommate, made lots of friends at another dorm, which seems to be the hot spot, and has even made trips into Manhattan a few times. We knew all this because we heard it from a guy on the metro in Paris who heard more about what Josh is up to than we did. *C'est la vie.*

But Paris. What can one say about Paris? It's so Parisian. And the little kids are amazing. Even at an early age, they can speak French. Me, I'm still struggling. Or as they say in Paris, *Je m'efforce de parler français.* If I use the wrong verb or pronounce it wrong, I end up asking the lady at the café to give me a tennis shoe with hubcaps on the side. When I do say something in French passably well, they respond in French so fast I can't understand a word they're saying. I'm lucky if I catch one or two words. But I plunge in anyway. I love talking to people. I'm on the metro and I start talking to someone and I barely get what they're saying back, but I keep plugging away, and it's like we're having two different conversations.

"I'm from Los Angeles. Have you lived in Paris all your life?" (all this in French, of course: *"Je viens de Los Angeles. Habitez-vous à Paris depuis toute votre vie?"*)

"No, I was born in Antwerp, but my business takes me here."

"Oh, I had a dog once. Her name was Jessie. She died last year."

"We have two cats in Antwerp, Suzzzo and Peroni, 'cause she's an Italian cat."

"No, I've never been to the Isthmus of Panama, but one of my favorite books [*livre préféré*] is by Malcolm Lowry, *Through the Panama*."

"I've never heard of him. I read a lot of Jean Paul Sartre."

"Yes, I used to like sardines on my salad. But now I find them too salty."

"Well, here's my stop, I gotta go. Hope you enjoy your time in Paris." (in French, the word to make the most of one's time is *profiter*.)

"Yes, I made a big profit when I sold my car, thanks. *Au revoir* and *bonne chance* and *à bientôt* and *toute à leure*."

Lori and I had no schedule. We wanted to get to the museums, of course, you know, the Louvre and the D'Orsay and the Picasso and the Pompidou, not to mention the churches and cathedrals, Notre Dame, the Sacré-Couer high atop the Mountain of Martyrs, Saint Sulpice (still recovering from being featured in *The Da Vinci Code)* where we could check out the tempting boutiques that surround the church. For sustenance we stopped at La Maison du Chocolat on Rue de Sèvres where Lori got an exquisitely wrapped box of half a dozen little tasty yum-yum chocolate morsels and later, in front of the fountain in front of St. Suplice she asked, "Do I have any chocolate on my face?" and I answered, "No, don't tell me! You ate the whole box!"

We stopped into St. Severin on Rue St. Jacques and checked out the weird stained glass windows, and then of course speaking of stained glass windows how could we not check out Saint Chapelle and maybe even catch the metro that goes all the way up to Orry-la-Ville and see St. Dennis. And while we were at it, there was the Pantheon and the puppet shows in the Luxembourg Gardens where Gary Grant and Audrey Hepburn got together in *Charade*, and speaking of *Charade*, our hotel was right next to the Hotel St. Jacques where Gary Grant, in the same movie, takes a shower with his clothes on.

Then there's the Rodin Museum, works by the greatest sculptor since Michelangelo. In one of the rooms there's a short film of Rodin furiously working a block of marble, tapping the chisel with a hammer as fast as a woodpecker, moving the chisel as he goes, and slowly, a face emerges as little chips of marble lodge in his beard. By the end of the film, his beard is full of marble snowflakes. His sculptures are so smooth, you want to run your hand over the stone, but this little film reveals the brute in him; there he is, at that point an old man, yet his hands brutalized the stone to bring out the flower within.

And finally, that monstrous 1,000 foot-tall ornament, built a hundred years after the Revolution, serving no other function but to impress: the Tower that Eiffel built, a bridge-builder who beat out such rival proposals as a giant guillotine (imagine that, lovers!). Seven thousand tons of metal and fifty tons of paint and who knows how many iron rivets, yet so well-engineered that it weighs no more per square inch than a linebacker standing on his tippy-toes. So many artists of the time thought it was such a monstrosity that they couldn't wait for the thing to be torn down after the World's Fair, for which it was built. Guy de Mauppassant, the great French writer, hated the damn thing. He lunched in the tower every day because, as he said, it was the only place in Paris he wouldn't have to look at it. The negative criticism—it's all true. Compared to the cathedrals and churches, the Arc de Triomph, the museums, the cafes that ooze charm, why it's like Godzilla has perched on the left bank, opposite the beautiful Champs de Mars, and become metallically electrified.

Would that they had torn it down when they had the chance! And while they were at it, burned Van Gogh's *Sunflowers*, scraped off every once of paint from Monet's *Gare de Nord,* ripped up Manet's *Picnic on the Grass*—the painting that scandalized Paris and was relegated to the Salon des Refusés—and blown up Haussman's grand boulevards. It makes you wonder about art the art produced in one's lifetime. What kind of blinders do *we* wear? How could anyone with sophisticated taste have liked that tower? It *is* a monstrosity! It makes perfect sense to want it removed from the Parisian skyline. And yet, today, it's Paris. And it's beautiful, whatever beautiful means. It looks like nothing else in the world. Perhaps the Empire State or the Chrysler Building come close to defining a city, maybe London's Big Ben, St. Petersburg's Winter Palace, St. Peter's in Rome. But that tower, by day or lit up at night—you see it, and instantly, you know, it's Paris.

We won't always have Berlin, or Moscow, or Beijing, or New York, but we'll always have Paris. And yet, were we alive then and had the power to tear it down after the World's Fair, wouldn't we have done so? I'm afraid to say we might have. And what paintings, stories, sculptures, films, poems, are we tearing down now, this very minute?

Yeah, there's all that to do, see *this* and go *there*, but if you get sucked into the pace of it all there's no sitting around in the cafes like expatriate writers writing *Go Tell It on The Mountain* or *The Sun Also Rises* or *Invisible Man* or just poetrypoetrypoetry. So we made no plans. We were gonna step out of our hotel on a crisp Monday morning straight from the airport and *flanneur* our way through the streets of Paris. We were gonna sit in cafes all day and write in our journals and read our favorite French poets:

> Guillaume Apollinaire:
> *"A la fin tu es las de ce monde ancien."*
> —In the end you are weary of this ancient world;
>
> Paul Reverdy:
> *"Entendez je ne suis pas fou, je ris au bas de l'escalier devant la porte grande ouverte."*
> —Listen, I'm not crazy, I laugh at the bottom of the stairs before the wide-open door;
>
> André Breton:
> *"Ma femme à la chevelure de feu de bois."*
> —My wife whose hair is a brush fire;
>
> Paul Éluard:
> *"Toutes les transformations sont poissibles."*
> — Every transformation is possible;
>
> Antonin Artaud:
> *"Je ne conçois pas d'oeuvre comme détachée de la vie."*
> — I cannot conceive of work that is detached from life;
>
> Raymond Queneau:
> *"Les eaux bruns, les eaux noirs, les eaux de merveille."*
> —brown seas, black seas, seas of marvel;
>
> Aimé Césaire:
> *"D'en bas de l'entassement furieux des songes*
> *épouvantables les aubes nouvelles montaient."*
> — from the bottom of the furious piling up
> of appalling dreams new dawns were rising;
>
> and Breton again:
> *"La poésie se fait dans un lit comme l'amour."*
> —Poetry is made in bed like love.

But we were so close to the Pompidou, sipping a beer and a hot chocolate (guess who had the hot chocolate) at Au Temps des Cerises, a local wine bar with tight seating and lots of character (not to mention characters) and food and vin served by goateed Yves and his wife, Michele. The café was in a two-story corner building that was formerly an annex to a Celestine monastery and had escaped demolition and was now classified a monument. Just a few steps away from the Bastille. Its exterior walls covered with tiny ochre tiles. Inside, the authentic decor is enhanced with kitschy flea market treasures. They serve a good *petit Bordeaux*. Victor prepares the food. He dropped in one day for a drink on his way to an interview at another restaurant, Yves and Michele were looking for a chef, and voila! Chef Victor. Sitting there, you didn't feel like you were in Paris but in a country village. A café since 1910, it was originally called Trains Bonnet, named for Louis Bonnet, who founded the newspaper *L'Auvergnat de Paris*, with offices next door. Bonnet encouraged people to come to Paris from the Auvergne by the trainload, thus the name Trains Bonnet. His newspaper helped Auvergnats reduce their sense of isolation as they tried to adjust to the capital city, "the enchanted forest," wrote Balzac, "that all young provincals hoped to take by storm." Bonnet's newspaper helped combat prejudices against them.

We sipped and munched and thought, well, as long as we're so close to the Pompidou (in Paris, so close means a half hour walk), why not, we said, go there and look at some art and then have lunch. Three hours later we've "*bien mangeéd*" on art and are ready for onion soup and beer, a *mille six cent soixante-quartre* (1664). At the Pompidou, on our way to see the main exhibit, "Elle," we got sidetracked by the fully-collected in-one-place for-the-first-time works of Henri Gaudier-Breszka, who was killed at the age of 23 in World War I. If you've seen the Ken Russell movie *Savage Messiah*, you know what I'm talking about, and if you haven't, rent it ASAP. Thirty-five years later, and I still remember the scene where his lover, the older Polish woman (Breszka) chops vegetables in their tiny apartment. No one forgets that scene. No one forgets the sculptures, of course, but no one forgets the chopping the vegetables scene either. (You think I'm kidding, but see the movie, you'll thank me.) It was Gaudier-Breszka's death that haunted Ezra Pound all his life, he never got over it. He never got over the death of so many promising poets and artists killed in the trenches on the Marne. One could probably trace his anti-war and anti-capitalist crackpot views to the loss of Gaudier-Breszka in that Great War to End All Wars.

> Michel Deguy:
> *"Cri de corbeau des yeux qu'enfoncent les poings en deuil,*
> *cri de corbeau le même cri sous les paupières closes*

où le pâle hiver de mémoire sommeille."

—Crow cry of eyes that mourning fists grind into,
Crow cry the same cry under closed lids
where the pale winter of memory dozes.

But then we checked out the "Elles" exhibit, a presentation devoted to the work of women artists, the largest ever exercise of its kind and the first by any museum. It was quite astonishing and moving. But leave it to me to get egg on my face. When you walk into the exhibit, the first thing you see are rows of larger-than-life lapel buttons, mounted on a wall, with the names of famous male artists, feminized. So there's Andrea Warhol, Jacqueline Pollock, Francine Bacon, Pamela Picasso, Henrietta Matisse, etc. Quite prominent. But me, the first one I notice is MISS VAN DER ROHE, a joke on the famous Bahaus architect Mies Van der Rohe (he's the guy who coined the phrase "God is in the details."). So I'm thinking, they spelled his first name wrong. I didn't realize that all the buttons were jokes. So I dutifully marched into the main office to let them know. "It's Mies," I said, "Not Miss." Well, that's called *oeuf* on your face. I was licking it off for days. But the director and I had a little laugh, 'cause he told me most people thought it was a play on Mister Van der Rohe, not realizing his first name was Mies.

Robert Marteau:
"Pour l'âne don't les cartilages fleurissent le fossé pour le chien"
—For the ass whose gristle flowers the ditch for the dog.

After a few days we had this yearning for an American movie. So down the street from our hotel, next to a great little café and a fruit stand where I got my peaches at night, was a movie house with American films *V.O.— version originale*, which means in English with French sub-titles. So that's fun, we can practice reading our French. They're showing *Inglorious Basterds.* About the French and the Germans and the Americans in World War II. Perfect! Only problem is, 1/3 of the movie was in French, and another 1/3 of the movie was in German. In America, of course, the French the German parts would have subtitles in English. Only we weren't in America. So the parts in English had subtitles in French, *n'est pas*, pas de problem. And the scenes in French, well, there's no need for subtitles, *n'est pas*, since the French, who study hard and learn their verbs, can speak fluent French. And the scenes in German, well, of course those are subtitles, but in, what else, FRENCH! And the tiny theatre on the third floor was like a sauna, and the woman sitting in front of Lori, one seat over, slapped Lori's foot off the chair like she was slapping a fly with murder in mind. Inglorious Basterds for sure.

René Char:
"Je chante la chaleur B visage de nouveau-né, la chaleur désespérée"
—I sing the heat that is like a newborn babe, desperate heat.

Next day—or the day after, one loses track of time in Paris —we were in the Maillol Museum in the Odeon district, St. Germain, etc. A wonderful museum. An amazing sculptor, one of my favorites. But I had not realized how wonderful a painter he was. On the third floor they had an exhibit that took up four rooms, an artist who made paintings of American rock 'n' roll singers of the '50s: Chuck Berry, Fats Domino, Elvis, etc. And they were blasting the rooms with recordings of all those old rock 'n' roll songs. How can one not dance when hearing that. There was no one else on the floor but us. So Lori and I danced, and danced, through all the rooms on that floor, how can one not do the jitterbug to Fats Domino's "My Blue Heaven" ("when whipperwill come, and evnin' is nigh), or Presley's "Hound Dog," or The Platter's "Smoke Gets in your Eyes" (okay, that's a slow dance, so we slow-danced in the Maillol Museum, in Paris, on a smoochy mooochy rainy afternoon).

René Daumal:
"Le peau de lumière vLtant ce monde."
—the skin of light enveloping this world.

After the Gustave Moreau Museum we stopped at a little café in Montparnasse, on the corner of Montparnasse and Raspail Blvds called La Rotande. I ordered the *mille six cent soixante-quatre* (1664) beer. I could have ordered a Heinekin or a Peroni. Why go through all that trouble to say *mille six cent soixante-quartre*? Because that's the point. Try saying it out loud. It takes about 5 minutes. Order one beer and you sound like you're actually speaking French. *Je vourdrais le mille six cent soixante-quatre,* and then you add the *s'il vous plaît* and you've got a mouthful of French. *N'est pas?*

Now if you really want to impress someone—the waiter, the art dealer at the next table, or the woman sitting across from you, before gulping down your beer, study it. After all, it may be just a beer, and a *mille six cent soixante-quatre* at that, a Euro pale from Brasseries Kronenbourg in Strasbourg, founded in 1664 (a leap year), brewed with a unique blend including aromatic hops from Alsace, good with chicken, fish, shellfish, but now, now you can at least act like you know what the hell you're drinking.

Start with the Froth (or the foamy head). Is it dense and creamy with adherence and good stability, or does it deflate as soon as it's poured into a limp soggy mess. This one's got a fast falling head that leaves a small amount of lace on the glass, with lots of lively bubbles. "Great froth," you say.

Then you raise the class and inspect the Colour. Not too pretentiously, but with just enough mumble to seem an afterthought, you say, "Pale straw yellow, golden yellow, bright, crystal clear." Make sure you nod approval.

Now comes the Odour, not to be mistaken for the Aroma. Your *mille six cent soixante-quatre* has a medium intensity, a dominant odour of flowery hops and citrus fruits with a soupçon of malt, which itself has a touch of yeast, fruits, and pepper. This you announce, don't be bashful. Remember, you're passionate about what you drink and eat. No mere dockworker from Le Havre, there's a zest to what you do, and you're not afraid of letting others know it. Same for the Aroma. Go on, pronounce it: "Cereal, malt, spicy and flowery with a touch of honey."

And there's the Bubbles. Let's not forget the bubbles. Your *mille six cent soixante-quatre* is filled with tiny champagne bubbles struggling to support a full and pearly but unfortunately volatile and short-lived head. Keep this to yourself, no pronouncement necessary, but don't get too carried away with this show. The time to drink this beer is now, when it's cold and even a bit stiff. Art has its place, and you can loll all day in the luxury of a French garden with its geometric platitudes, but beer waits on no man. The time has come for action, *carpe diem*, seize the day! Gentlemen cry peace, but there is no peace! The next gale that sweeps from the north brings to your ears the clash of resounding arms. Why stand we here idle? Is life so dear or peace so sweet as to be purchased at the price of chains and slavery? Forbid it Almighty God! I know not what course others may take, but as for me, give me Liberty or give me Taste, Froth, Colour, Odour and Aroma!

It's time to drink. To Taste. The people at the next table have caught on. They look forlornly at their beers and wonder what they've missed. And you haven't even tasted your *mille six cent soixante-quatre* yet, but you're going to now. The moment is at hand. After extending the glass out so you can see the color and passing it under your nose to heft in the aroma, you now bring the glass to your lips and take that first sip, the crucial one, when everything is at its peak. You're done with looking and smelling, evaluating and considering. You're in the prime of your life, scooping up the best and the brightest, a writer inking up and facing life head on. Drink now or forever hold your peace. Merry or Die.

Bring the world to your lips. Swallow without fear or remorse. Now the liquid travels down your gullet, a fine bitter taste, just the touch of light acidic, and a nice smack of citrus hops. And another swallow to make sure, clean and crisp on a hot summer day . . . but you're not done.

There's the Mouthfeel. Ah yes, beyond the taste itself, there's the Mouthfeel. You're not afraid to look back. In this moment of plowing forward, you remember the feel of it all, how she looked in the moonlight when you kissed her, how she looks at herself stepping out of the tub, the feel of her skin as she lies next to you on the bed, the pin-ball laughs and tears, the memory of all that, no you can't take that away from me. So you feel the light sparkling bubbles prickling your mouth and gums. Little explosions, the fireworks of the revenge of living well, you've not forgotten a thing, you've savoured it all, the bitter with the sweet. Mouthfeel. Mouthfeel. Mouthfeel.

If there were no more, you'd stay here forever, perched on the edge of eternal Mouthfeel. But . . . you're not done . . . there's more. The revelation and the afterlife—the Aftertaste. That fine taste of bitterness with a flowery hop aroma and a touch of malt and light tannis. Just the right touch of bitterness, following a sweet floral start.

Had you world enough and time, this is how you'd do it. From Froth to Colour to Aroma to Taste to Mouthfeel to Aftertaste, each one a galaxy. But it's a hot day, all that walking and I can feel the sweat on my forehead. There's no time for tomfoolery. I want to be smacked awake by a cold, cold beer. That's the ticket this time. A life that blazes from start to finish like a comet. So I throw the whole glass down in six or seven gulps, each swallow of bubbles punching at the roof of my mouth and the back of my throat, no froth to evaluate, no color to savor, no aroma to enjoy, just the mad bad ingestion of everything at one time, the big bang carbonation exploding on the palette in a starburst of sensation. Ahhhhhh. *Mille Six Cent Soixante Quatre. S'il vouz plait? N'est pas? Mais Oui, Mais Oui, Mais Oui.*

Anyway, we decided to share, *partager*. I got the onion soup, Lori got the quiche. Lori pronounced it the best quiche she'd ever had. Same, I said, for the onion soup. We had onion soup everywhere in Paris, as if we were food critics writing a book on onion soup. But the onion soup at La Rotande was the best. By far. In Paris, that is. Almost—not quite—but almost as good as the onion soup we get at our little café a few blocks from our home on 3rd street, a place called The Little Next Door, 'cause it's next door to La Petite Porte, The Little Door, an expensive but good French restaurant. And the rain was coming down, and across the street was a beautiful cathedral, and everyone was rushing about carrying umbrellas, and it looked exactly like Gustave Caillebotte's magical painting "Rue de Paris, Wet Weather." Every time I see that painting, I'm convinced that *that* was what it was like on that particular afternoon in 1877, when the light was cool and bright and the rain fell in a fine drizzle. Despite his being more a well-to-do patron and hanger-on of the Impressionist scene, Caillebotte's work is stubbornly unromantic and clearly focused on the absolutely ordinary, the real world in all its drabness and lack of romance. Yet, that painting encapsulates the world of 19th-century Paris in a celebration of a wet street on a dull day. Without great visual excitement, it remains a picture of originality and beauty. And I look up from my beer and there's the same guy with the top hat walking by, the same woman holding his arm, both of them sharing the same umbrella. "Look," I say to Lori. And we look out through the plate glass window and the moment is timeless.

> Benjamin Péret:
> *"Va-t-il pleuvoir ciel de pendu s'il pleut je mangerai du cresson s'il ne peut pas de la langouste"*
>
> —Sky of a hanged man, is it going to rain? If it rains I'll eat watercress unless it rains lobsters.

But the rain was staged for us, timed by the gods to start just as we sat down to our onion soup and salad and quiche and beer. Paris gives to give each of us exactly what we need at the moment we need it. Like the couple Lori met in the laundromat, the pipes in their apartment having broken. So the next night we went to dinner with Claude and Susan at Chez René on Blvd St. Germain, and I had the suckling pig and Lori had the duck something or other. Or was it lamb? Then there was the waiter at the Italian café on St. Germain Blvd., the same waiter Lori met at the same laundromat a few days later, complaining that because of his dark skin he was often mistaken for an Arab and discriminated against and he wanted to know what we thought of Barack Obama. Then there was the wedding that was just beginning when we walked into St. Sulpice Cathedral. And then, the next day, at Place des Vosges, that beautiful square with the statue of Henri IV, "le verte gallante" — roughly translated as "gay blade," or "the old flirt"—now hidden by the leafy chestnut trees, and while we're sitting at Café Hugo (Victor Hugo's apartment is a few doors down) there's another wedding in the center of the square.

"That's the same couple," I say.

"No . . . "

"Yeah, take a look."

And like Caillebotte's painting, it seems we're seeing the exact same couple getting married again. She looks to be in her late-30s, and two men slightly older are giving her away, so we figure her parents are deceased and these are her older brothers. And when we go to Notre Dame later that evening, we walk in just as the evening mass is beginning. And over the next few days, we keep running into Susan and Claude, the couple from the laundromat.

"What are you two doing out and about?" we ask.

"Oh, we're meeting some friends for a quick bite."

"How are the pipes coming."

"We're still swimming around the apartment," Claude says, laughing.

"Well, maybe we'll see you at the laundromat."

And then we see them the next evening up near the Pantheon. Why, we could be back in L.A., running into old friends at a movie.

"What are you two doing here?" we ask.

"We're going to have an early dinner at our favorite little café, Descartes, just up the street." (If you know where the Pantheon is, you know up the street really means UP.) "Wanna join us."

The café is situated at one of those *carrefours* (crossroads) you find all over Paris where four streets come together and there's a soccer match on the TV inside and everyone's cheering and yelling, kind of a cross between an authentic old Parisian Brasserie and an American sports bar, so we sit outside and I have steak tartare *aller retour*, which means they flip it and cook it on one side for one minute and then flip it again and cook it on the other side for one minute. When you buy a ticket on the train you can get a one way, or *aller de retour*, to go and to come back, a round-trip ticket. *Aller retour* means round-trip. So the steak tartare is *aller retour*. Better than the suckling pig, better than the canard de quelque chose, better than the lamb quelque chose d'autre. And it came with French fries. I gotta tell ya, the French know how to make French fries. *Et pourquoi pas, n'est pas?*

Speaking of meals, the two best meals in Paris were at Atelier Maitre Albert where I had chicken and the creamiest mashed potatoes at the bar (for those without reservations), and a late late night hamburger at BIA, Breakfast in America, a little Johnny Rockets type diner a block from our hotel. The waitresses were all from America, young dark-haired girls seeking adventure in Paris. After closing, if we came back to our room late enough, we'd see them sitting on the sidewalk together after closing, backs against the wall and legs folded against their bodies, three of them chatting away as they puffed ravenously on cigarettes, like true Parisians. Their life was before them, but how could they appreciate that? As we walked past, I leaned down and said in French, "Mais, vous aurez toujours Paris." They looked up and smiled. I put my hand around Lori's waist and we skated back to our hotel, to our little room with the green suitcase jammed between the bed and the wall. *Nous en trains d'avoir Paris juste maintenant, maintenant et pour toujours.* [We're still having Paris, right now; right now and forever.]

In Montmarte, the next day, at Place de la Tertre, full of tourists and artists hounding you to let them paint your picture, I went up to one artist and asked him how much and he said 100 Euros but for you 40 Euros and then finally when I said no, he said, 20 Euros, and I said, in broken French, "Tell you what. I'll pay you 30 Euros if you let *me* paint *your* portrait." Which I did. Then he did mine. We had a nice chat, turns out he was a published poet, so we yakked about Baudelaire and Rimbaud and Marcel Marceau and Muddy Waters and Charlie Chaplin and Jesse Owens and Clyde Beatty, great poets all.

> Appollinare again:
> *"Aujourd'hui tu marches dans Paris les femmes sont ensanglantées"*
> —Today you walk in Paris the women are blood-red

Well, there's so much more we did in Paris, all the art and the cathedrals, especially St. Denis, which I'm writing about in my telephone book of a book on the history of poetry, and that little cathedral on Ile St. Louis where I ducked in out of the rain eight years ago when we were in Paris with Josh, and the Jacquemart-André art-strewn mansion which is now a museum housing the art this couple collected in their lifetime, and the house is more of an art work than all the art inside put together, a house as big as a shopping center, only there's no kitchen, 'cause all their meals were brought in, and afterwards, we sat in a little tea room around the corner on Boulevard Haussmann and wrote postcards. In the rain. It seemed to be always raining in Paris. I thought of Vellejo's poem, "I Will Die in Paris in the Rain." I had the beer, Lori had a *citron pressé* (they bring you a glass with the juice of one or two lemons just squeezed, then another smaller glass with ice, and a little carafe of water, and two sugars. It's up to you to mix and stir and make your own lemonade. It starts out too sour, then it's too sweet, then it's mostly water. I got *limonade*, which is not lime-aid, but carbonated lemonade, kinda like a Seven-up or a Sprite, only sweeter. The label on the bottle says PSCHITT! There's several other limonade bottlers, but I can't resist this one. Every time I go to a café I say, *"Je prends une biere et une bouteille de Pschitt!"* And while they say "Oui," Lori cracks up.

And so in Paris, we make each other laugh. Josh is far away, and so is our home on Colgate. But our home is between us, our home is each other. For thirty years we've made a home in each other's hearts. I'd been in Paris when I was eighteen, and Lori had never been, so ten years ago we went together with Josh, and that was all part of phase three. And now, it's phase four, and we continue to love each other in the simple act of writing postcards in a tea room on Boulevard Haussmann named after Baron Haussman who tore up and did away with close to 100 streets to make medieval Paris into19th Century post-Industrial Revolution Belle Epoque Paris. So the streets we made in our youth that we remade in our marriage raising our son are being remade once again in this city of light.

Despite the people-watching while sitting in cafes, and all the *flanneuring* we did walking aimlessly and letting one street lead into another rue and a tinier rue lead into a larger boulevard, and then the whole stroll blooming into another carrefour (*de routes* or *de la vie*), there's only so much you can do to resist the pull of history and art and architecture, not to mention the touristy things that just seem *de rigueur* unless you're going to stick your nose up and pretend you're too sophisticated to ride the Bateaux-Mouches up the Seine at 10pm to see the Eiffel Tower light show. Lori and I were not too sophisticated. If having a cognac at the Café Metro on Place Maubert after a dinner of chicken and mashed potatoes at Atelier Maître Albert is a bit touristy and unsophisticated, so be it. I came to Paris to be unsophisticated, to be a tourist in the biggest amusement park in the world. The guy at the next table was having an omelet and turned out he was from New York, attending the Sorbonne. Later that night, across from Shakespeare & Company, we climbed down the steps and bought a ticket for a boat ride and sat up front to get the cold night wind, forcing us to cuddle.

"Aren't you cold?" Lori asked.

"It's Paris," I said, "One doesn't get cold. Always, the fire within."

That's a quote from Bernie Goldfarb, a true Parisian. Of course, at one point, Lori got cold, so she went into the boat's center cabin, but the diesel fumes got to her and she came back out. Meanwhile, I was trying to have a conversation with a couple from Spain. They couldn't speak French, so I had to resort to the Spanish I remembered from high school. *Yo quiero* and *tengo que fumar* and *con mucho gusto.*

"De dónde eres?"

"Yo vengo de Los Angeles. Y tu?"

"Nosotros venimos Huesca, en España."

It was another one of those parallel conversations. But there's something elemental about people trying to communicate when language is not enough to pry open the window of humanity. It doesn't matter what you're trying to say. There's a desire to communicate, to share a common experience. They're from Spain and we're from Los Angeles and there we were, strangers on a boat on the Seine in Paris, all of us lost in the midst of something so big it's indescribable.

Most of us who come to Paris walk around in a bubble. This unfathomable city stretches out in time and space and there's no way to comprehend it all. We talk to each other, but remain insular. After awhile, there's a hunger to connect.

"We're from Cologne, where are you from?"

"Minnesota."

How do you reconcile the Paris of Gershwin with the imperialism of small shopkeepers annexing the sidewalks, and all that with the Bastille which is no longer there or the Latin Quarter which is mostly a shadow of its former bohemian self? The streets close to the river across from Notre Dame are more Tunisian, Greek, and Woolworth's than old-time Paris. Isn't that what we're in search of, old-time Paris? In the film *Amélie*, cars were digitally removed from the streets to create an old-fashioned Montmartre. Perhaps the sensuousness and the poetry and the life we find there is what we bring to it, an illusion we carry within ourselves. A desire to discover another way of living. We want the Paris in the paintings, John Singer Sargent's elegant couple strolling in the Luxembourg Gardens, Utrillo's views of the tranquil village streets of Montmartre, Caillebotte's street of Paris in wet weather. Or we want the bigness of the museums and cathedrals, a way of finding God again, God who has become so small, a windmill on a deserted plain poked at by despairing philosophers. We come upon St. Denis or Notre Dame or St. Sulpice as those in the surrounding village might have come upon a towering façade. It's all there in Paris, everything is there for us. And finally, on a boat going up the river, it's not the buildings or the art or the monuments we need, but each other.

"We're from Budapest, where are you from?"

"El Paso."

But now we're home, and glad to be home, though I truly miss Paris. I don't know why. We all have our favorite cities. New York certainly gets into my brain and makes me feel like writing all day. San Francisco calms me down, makes me want to paint. New Orleans, the city I was born and raised in, with its above-ground cemeteries, returns me to my brooding inner self, a stray dog peering out from under the running board of an abandoned car. But Paris, I'm in love with her, though I know she's a slut and a whore, fucking everyone who loves her. But she makes you think you're the ONLY ONE. When you arrive, she says, "Mon cheri, I've missed you so much." And she wraps her arms around you and you rub your face along the skin of her face and neck, and run your hands over her body from head to toe. God, you're dizzy with the love you feel in the streets and the cafes and the people reading books on the metros and the street musicians (who turn out to be British) on the Pont Neuf or the Pont des Arts, so you buy their CD, why? Because you're in love with everything! and even the carnival barkers on the Rue de la Huchette you love, and you go into Shakespeare & Company and you feel like you've made love a thousand times to every book and there are more books on the second floor, books everywhere, and there's the Henri Guimard metro station at Abbesses where you get off to see Sacré-Coeur.

You're in love with Paris and she loves you back and then you get in the taxi to go to the airport and already you see another cab drive up to the hotel and someone gets out and they raise their arms and Paris springs into action, "Mon Cheri, where have you been, I've missed you so much," and you see all this looking out the back window of the cab, that slut, that whore! You're sullen on the plane the whole way back, through customs, in line to change planes in Washington, in the line to get your baggage at LAX. You try to blot her out of your mind, try not to see all the others she embraces, but you know you're hooked. Next time, every time, you'll forget about the others, you'll walk into her embrace and fall for every line she utters from her red and sensuous lips:

Apollinaire:
"Et tu bois cet alchool brûflant comme ta vie,
Ta vie que tu bois comme une eau-de-vie."
—And you drink this alcohol burning like your life,
Your life that you drink like spirit of wine.

Passport to Paris, City of Lights

We went back to Paris again, this time to help Josh get set up (*installer*, to use the French verb) at the Cité Universitaire, for his Junior Year Abroad, and we decided to spend a few days together with him before he got swallowed up by classes and classmates, giving us a week or so in the city of lights. We visited a few museums for the first time (the Zadikin, a real charmer, the L'Orangerie, a delightful surprise); we re-visited some old standbys (the Louvre, the Pompidou, where Josh and I did an impromptu performance in front of the Brancusi exhibit, freezing in a sculpted pose against a white wall for 20 minutes, attracting lots of people who couldn't figure out if we were part of the exhibit or not. They gaped, walked away, came back, took pictures, trying to figure out what the hell we were. A dozen young people from Italy speculated on what we signified, until at one point, they all turned their heads and Josh and I shifted poses, I grabbed his leg and he stretched forward as if to fall. When the students looked back, they squealed with delight. "Look, it's moved!" Then we held that pose for a while. Finally, one guy from Germany, after much deliberation, walked up and joined us, hooking one arm in mine and assuming his own pose.); we discovered new churches and cathedrals (St. Eustache, a few blocks up from the Pompidou, and the St. Louis-en-I'lle), ran into delightful back alleys and cobblestone hide-aways, found a few new eateries (*Le Train Bleu* in the Gare de Lyon train station, a belle epoque mind-blower), rapped with four young rappers on the Place Dauphine who had set up shop on a park bench where they took turns toking on a hookah the size of a large espresso machine. All in all, I adjusted my relationship to the city. No longer young lovers, not quite an old married couple, something in-between, settling and unsettling just what this city meant to me.

My love and fascination for Paris goes back to when I first went there at 18, imagining myself Hemingway (who wrote *Sun Also Rises* at La Coupole in Montparnass), Jean-Paul Sartre (who wrote much of *Being and Nothingness* in Café Les Deux Magots), or James Baldwin (who wrote *Giovanni's Room* ensconced in Café de Flore), or any number of beat poets like Ted Joans or Harold Norse shooting up on Rue Git Le Coeur, that little alley right off Rue de la Huchette.

But on this trip, one night, around midnight, I had trouble sleeping and went down to Deux Magots to get something to eat and write in my journal. Just as there are Platonists and Aristotelians among philosophers, when it comes to café society, there are *Magotistes* and *Floreurs*—those who prefer Café deux Magots and those who wouldn't be caught dead anywhere but in Café Flore. While I'm a Platonist as a philosopher, my leanings toward Café scribbling are more pedestrian. Sorry to say, I'm a Magotiste, not a Floreur—*quel horreur!*. The streets were still wet from a sudden shower, but the tables on the terrace were crowded, it was a Saturday night, and there was a lot of hustle and bustle going on. I went inside where it was easier to get a table, since there were only a few people inside.

Over in the corner, two young ladies were sharing a glass of wine; I couldn't tell if they were college lassies *bavardaying* about their boyfriends, or lovers themselves. They clinked their wine classes a few times, leaned in and touched foreheads, then took a delicate sip, followed by a more rambunctious one, throwing half the glass of wine down in one gulp. I half-expected them to smash their glasses against the wall. Made me want to get a glass of wine too, but I settled for a beer, my favorite, a Mille Six Cent Soixante Quatre—1664.

At the long table by the door, three French intellectual types–late thirties, early forties—a man and two women, were yapping and gesturing, maybe discussing French philosophy, but probably just arguing about what color to paint the walls of the dining room in their Latin Quarter apartment. And there I was, sitting near the cashier, who was perched high on a stool behind a glass partition, taking checks from the waiters who were all talking at one time, raising a racket to go with the racket from the kitchen, the clanking of plates, glasses, and silverware. The lights were bright, made even brighter by the mirrors along the walls. Compared to the Parisian night outside on the terrace, it was garish, more like a coffee shop than a romantic café. But I was writing, I was giving it a go. I was being Kerouac or Ginsberg, ranting about the road and the best minds of my generation; I was Albert Camus or Alain Robbe-Grillet, a post-modern modernist chic with alienability; I was an unknown poet, just out of college, filled with T. S. Eliot's fire and Robert Frost's brimstone, writing the Great American Poem.

And then, between bites of a club sandwich that cost about $25, it hit me. I could be in Denny's on La Cienega or Canter's on Fairfax back in L.A., and it would be the same thing. The garish lights, the clinking of dishes, the smell of fried eggs and hash browns. Except I'd be eating a pastrami sandwich for $12. Except for the *je-ne-sais-quoi* slipped into your consciousness like the accent *aiguë* over the "e" in a word like *café* or *Polynésie* or slipped into your subconscious like the accent grave over the "e" in a word like *polystyrène* or *ascète*, it was all the same. I didn't need to be in Paris for this, I could be anywhere, writing in my journal, grabbing the muse by the throat and begging her for one more good line.

So sad to say, the dream was over. Paris and I had turned a page. Does this mean I no longer love her? Of course not. Every time I go, she takes another little piece of my heart. It's an old heart, too. I've given so many pieces of it away, who knows how much is left to give. New Orleans, of course, she's got a nice chunk of it, rolling along in the mighty, muddy Mississippi. New York, Greenwich Village, the troubadours and poets of Washington Square, like the rebels in Shakespeare's Henry IV, they continue to divide up the map of my heart. And what can I say about L.A.—city of the Hollywood sign, city of the Hollywood Bowl, city of Hollywood Park Race Track, city of plastic, city of despair, city of reruns—my heart is so splattered on the boulevards you're probably stepping on a piece of it now.

But like I said, it's an old heart, and there always seems to be another piece to give away. I don't need to give them to cities, I can give them to the waitress at Canter's, or to the teller in my bank on Wilshire, or to the mechanic on Pico, or to the petite Latina at the pharmacist on San Vicente, or to you, I can give a piece of it to you. Isn't this what this life is supposed to be about, giving out pieces of your heart, not holding onto them as if they were savings bonds or antique candlesticks. Paris will always be there for me, but I have to be there for her as well, willing to change, willing to re-imagine love, willing to do the can-can in the kitchen with my wife who has all the cities of the world within her, who is the one great city of my life for whom no passport is required.

The Impossible Fountain

Perché la vita à breve	Because life is short
et l'ingegno paventa a l'alta impresa,	and my wit is afraid of the high undertaking,
né di lui né lei molto mi fido	in neither wit nor life do I have much confidence.

—Francesco Petrarch, Rime Sparse, Poem #71 (1374)

Petrarch's father was exiled from Florence,
as was his father's friend Dante.

Had he studied law as his father did,
he might have accumulated some wealth,
and not squandered the wealth his father left him,
though he claims his father's executors
cheated him of his inheritance.
Who knows?
What it comes down to,
is, he wrote poetry—
what foolish boys do,
whose fathers practice law,
whose fathers labor in the fields,
whose fathers work daily selling household gadgets.
All my life I have understood how foolish it is
to write poetry.
As I said in a previous poem,
"poetry not much."
I try not to complain,
but alas, there is always the need,
to justify, at least, the enterprise,
that sweat forms at the brow
shaping a single line of poetry,
though not as much sweat as does
sawing a piece of wood or pushing a plow.
Though with poetry,
one is always starting over.
There's always the fear that the reader
has gone on to other pursuits
as I write this line, this one here, right here.
One is constantly reminded

by those who work in buildings
made of steel and glass
that we have somehow missed the boat,
that we're reading the wrong books,
that life is going to pass us by,
if it hasn't already done so.
The scientists are more blunt:
If you speak with eloquence,
the eloquence disassembles;
if you speak as a child, no one listens;
if you speak as the shopkeeper,
no one cares.
Words will not save you.
Better to keep your mouth shut.

It is in this silence the poet lives.
But it is Sunday, and down the street
someone is starting up their car,
someone passes by my house
walking her dog.
I should go out and empty the fountain,
so when Eric comes it will be good and dry
for him to paint.
Then we can fill it up again
and listen to its lovely gurgling.

I have come this far,
my seventieth birthday a few months away.
I didn't study law,
I didn't run my father's business,
I didn't sell household gadgets.
My son talks with his friends in the kitchen.
My wife and I laugh before going to bed.
Whether or not I have poetry matters little.
What I have is this life
that I have lived *with* poetry,
my personal gadget, my own plow,
the elemental particles of my life's blood.

I have come this far,
and as you can see,
I am still trying to fill

the impossible fountain,
still trying to shout
something meaningful
from out of the silence.

Small Craft Warnings

Maybe it began with a curse.
Someone needed to do more
than mouth the word,
someone needed to write it down.

So they thought about what the mouth does
when speaking
and scratched something on a scrap
of something and said the word aloud again,
only this time, as song,
heroic song, epic song,
the song of the word,
carrier of meaning,
a linguistic unit,
an utterance,
a quarrel,
a scripture,
a city,
cities within cities,
inescapable cities,
bronze iron steel glass,
small craft warnings,
doorways leading to broken rooms,
history & battlefields
mock apple pie
the great throb of continuous hope,
the glacial weight of it,
the delusions of paradise,
political crimes,
the curveball,
the currency,
the flow
the bedrock.

The Naked Eye

Got my microscope here looking at microbes,
got the telescope by the window looking
at stars or the moon, whichever comes first.
I don't know much, other than the fact
that the Earth's round and there are little
things that swim around on the slide that I can't see
with the naked eye.
It's the dogs sitting on people's front porches,
the cats that hang out in my yard
who run off when I approach.
Sometimes, I just stand there looking at them.
And they look at me.
If they only knew how kind I'd be to them.
But they're not taking any chances.
One step in their direction, and off they go.
How they jump up on top of the wall!
It's almost like they're flying.
I'm basically a dog person, but cats
have a special place in my heart too.
Cleo used to crawl up on my chest
when I was lying on the sofa reading.
She'd look at me, just look at me.
Boy, those cat eyes.
This is not the place to go into how she died,
that's another poem,
but I stayed up all night with her on the floor
and I think it was about 3am when I felt her body
and knew that she'd gone.
It wasn't until the next morning that I cried.
Big heaving heaps.
I think I was crying for my father, finally;
but that's another poem, too.

One evening, Glenn came by with his telescope.
Not like mine, this one was big and sophisticated.
We brought it outside, set it up on the corner
and found Jupiter and Venus,
not far from the moon—

a superior conjunction if ever there was one.
When people came walking down Orlando
we asked them if they wanted to look in the telescope.
Most said yes, but a few didn't seem interested.
They just kept walking.
This intrigued me the most.
Glenn was looking at stars or planets,
and I was watching the people
who just kept walking
without looking.
What planetary objects!
What stellar phenomena!
What we should have done was set up a table
next to the telescope with the microscope on it.
Give people a choice.
The big or the small,
the vanishing or the swimming,
the explosions of fire or the search for food.
My son could have set up another table and sold lemonade,
like he did when he was ten.
My wife could have come out and worked in the garden.
I could have brought out my book of poetry
and read the poem "Still Life."
Here, I'll quote a bit of it for you:

> *And we are so alone in this inscrutable palm,*
> *that presses against the other*
> *palm*
> *of exact passion   ready to curl*
> *to the sweet fist of science.*

So like a door that won't stay closed.
Or as Rilke says:
Eine blind Welt un rings umgiebt.
A blind world surrounds us.

Madness

Callimachus says our madness is most
acute at the start, then—if I get his meaning
correctly—it tapers off as time goes by.
Which means, I suppose,
that I am approaching sanity.
Complete and awful sanity.
Yet some kind of madness is needed
to venture forth,
to embark on the kind of adventure
mad for the taking, made perfect, as Orestes says,
by suffering.
Yet we continue to build cities
in the rain
as others weep
at the feet
of great monuments for the dead.
When Prometheus molds you,
the voyage on clay feet
continues to define you,
as the warp the loom,
the thread the cloth.
All this knowledge is enough to make
anyone mad, but sanity creeps up on you
like a . . . [fill in metaphor]. . . in the night.
Soon enough, dear friends,
everything makes sense—
every gesture perfect,
every amplitude of intellect
mapped out by the oscillations of time,
until—like Ishmael—you find yourself
knocking people's hats off just to feel alive.
I was mad enough once to dance in subways,
to burst into song in supermarkets,
to babble in French in French cafes.
Now I stare at my plate of tomatoes
cut into perfect wedges,
sprinkled with balsamic vinegar,
each placed expertly on my tongue.

I crush the meat between well-capped teeth,
letting the juice trickle down my gullet.
A generous tip for the waiter,
a stately walk to my car,
then the sane ride home
to the well-placed stones
and sophisticated bric-a-brac
on my mantelpiece.

Summer Night

After the Bloomsday reading at the Hammer
I retreated to my cubicle
surrounded by those old friends, my books.

Lamplight on desk. Lights in the garden
I can see through the window.

If snow were to fall, I'd listen to it,
but there's only the sound of the water
gurgling in the fountain, an occasional
car blaring loud music.

Older now, I sleep less and less.
I get up in the night and read
about the Hittites,
their iron artifacts and storm gods,
their chariots and mysterious language,
but even that's not enough
to send me back to sleep.

Forget the mind. How else
can one get past the silence
of history and great slabs of memory
like beef hanging in the brain.

Such a steadfast world.
How it goes on and on,
regardless.   No rhyme.
No reason.

Night: this favorite time of day.
Everything unto itself.

This Life

My wife is getting dressed,
rushing off to see her clients.
She puts a top on that comes down past her navel,
barely covering her pubic hair.
But when she sits on the bed to pull up socks,
the chemise rises up, exposing hair between her legs.
She puts one leg up, resting her heel on the bed's edge.
Her legs a few inches apart.
Her pubic hair and mound clearly visible.
It's enough.
This altar. This sacred, secret, sanctified,
whatchamacallit.
I stop by the TV and ask her
when she's coming home,
do I pick up Josh today,
are we going to David & Gina's for dinner on Saturday,
should I get bread and milk at J-Market
or what?
"What," she says.
I'm talking, she's got her head down working on the sock,
—no, I think it's panty hose or tights,
something like that,
something complicated that requires her full attention—
I'm talking but I'm really looking at her pubic hair, her sacred
whatchamacallit, that is . . . . and is not . . . . her,
the embodiment of everything,
the symbol of nothing but itself.
This is when . . . I think . . . maybe not . . . but probably so . . .
this is when I love her the most,
when she's putting on socks, half-naked,
paying little attention to me.
"What?" she says.
She's not even listening to me.
"Should I pick up Josh," I say,
"and what about the bread and milk?"
Actually, I'm not really talking to her, either.
I'm looking at her pussy
while she struggles with this complicated long sock or something,

her head down, working it fold by fold past her heel
and ankle, then up the calf, over the knee,
up the thigh, finally standing
and jumping up and down, small little jumps,
as she tugs the last part above her pubic hair,
above the navel.
She rims the elastic with her thumb,
gives it a snap, then looks up at me,
finally. She gives her head a shake,
straightening her hair for her clients,
getting all neat and composed and psychotherapeutic,
her sacred whatchamacallit covered by a gauze curtain,
and in a minute, by the dress.
I'm looking at her,
thinking of that Grecian pottery
where Aphrodite rises from the sea,
her sandstone naked body
gravelly and glistening in its classical flesh.
"What?" she asks.
"Do I pick up Josh today?"
"Yeah. Is that okay?"
"Yeah."
We stand there, holding everything
unsaid that seems to float along with the dust motes
made visible finally by the first light of the morning
coming through the blinds.
When you coming home?" I ask.
"6:30."
"Don't forget my class starts at 7."
"I won't."
Then she's off, rushing from one room to another,
grabbing necessities.
I catch up to her at the door.
She kisses me.
I kiss her back. A little piece of sweet lip
in her sweet breath. I keep my eyes open
so I can see her face close-up.
"Love you," I say.
"Love you, too."
I stand on the front steps and watch her

get in the car, buckle-up, start the engine,
make a U-turn and come to a stop at the stop sign
at our corner. I walk to the mailbox
on the corner and give a little wave.
She sees and waves back,
then pushes off for her day, her clients.
I have things to do, too.
Have to xerox poems for my students, my fellow poets.
The sun's not out yet; by noon, the clouds'll break,
and it'll be a sunny day,
and the sun will shine
on my wife
and on my students
and on this blessed,
sacred, sanctified life.

Teaching the Angels

I'll miss Sundays after I'm dead.
I'll miss all the days, I suppose.
Summers especially, the idea of vacation, the whole family packed in
the car, my mother yelling, "Leave your brother
alone or we're stopping this car this minute and we'll sit
here all day if we have to and you'll never get to Miami
and nobody's going swimming!" Outside, the Everglades,
nothing but cypress trees and alligators.
Christmas I'll miss too. The lights on the tree, and the Chanukah
candles burning on the table.
I'll miss it all. I won't get to read in the paper who won the ball game,
how the Dodgers are doing, who won the big fight, will
the quarterback throw that last pass to win the game
before he quits forever. Not much sports in Heaven.
Angels—7
New Arrivals—1
Not very competitive.
No one'll write poetry up there, either. What's to write about?
Bliss. Peace. Oneness.
Not exactly themes you can sink your teeth into.
I could always teach the angels how to write.
"Write like you talk."
"We don't need to talk."
"Okay, follow the transformation line."
"We've already transformed. There's nothing to follow."
"Right, Okay. Just give me image moment."
"That's all there is," they'll say. "The world comes, stays a
moment, then goes away. Image. Moment."
"All right. How about things? No ideas but in things. William
Carlos Williams, a very famous poet, said that."
"Oh, him. He changed his mind. He says it's the other way
around. He's sleeping over there, in that car. Besides, there are
no things here. Just ideas."
I look over at the car. It looks familiar—a gray '47 Dodge.
Sure enough, there's Williams, in the back seat, sitting up,
sleeping.
"Okay," I say, "just tell a story. A simple story."
"I thought this was a poetry class. Now you want stories."

"Look, a poem, a story, it's all the same thing. Writing's
writing."
Now the angels exchange glances. They want a refund.
"Christ!" I say.
"Oh, he's in the car with Williams, in the front seat."
Sure enough, there he is, hands resting on the steering wheel.
Beautiful, long fingers.
"Hey, that's my father's car!"
"Of course," they say, "It's *your* heaven."

Yes, I'll look down and miss it all.
All the things. All the talk.
All the transformations.
I'll miss sitting in the kitchen, watching the cars go by
on Orlando. Josh, coloring a picture on the floor, industriously
snapping the caps back on the markers; Lori, in her robe
reading a book, slurping her coffee; and me, writing this down,
finishing this poem,
returning to the world I so dearly love.

John 16:24

It's a funny thing about the universe.
You can't hog tie it,
you can't whip it into shape,
you can't bully it,
you can't demand, cajole, negotiate, or plead.
But you can ask:
for poems,
for love,
for meaning,
even,
perhaps,
for salvation.
Whether it be from
the cosmos
or from the god who created it,
or from those who are a part of it,
answers always come.

Just ask.

I asked for you,
didn't I?

And here you are.

Requiem

I guess when you get old
you tally the deaths, the ones
who went before you:
Martin Shapiro when I was twelve,
Leon Zilberman's father when I was sixteen,
Elton Cigali when I was eighteen—
the rich kid with the sports car
who died in a head-on collision.
It was the big drama in high school that year,
the golden boy, star quarterback,
fleet-footed track star,
doomed like Achilles.
Then Dad, when I was nineteen,
then Mom,
a few years later.
Then Jerry Pinero, from 5th grade,
whose father owned a fruit stand
on Carrolton Avenue.
I wrote about him in another poem.
There were others, some I remember,
some I forget.
Clifford Janoff about ten years ago,
of a heart attack.
I have a picture of the four of us,
Cliff, Allan, Paul and me,
high in the Sierras, in a bank of snow,
naked.
We thought it would be funny.
With our scraggly beards,
we looked like mountain men
impervious to the cold.
It took us ten seconds to take the picture,
but we froze our butts off.
"Twenty years from now," we said,
"this'll be funny."
Twenty years later, Clifford found the photo
and sent me a copy as a reminder.
I laughed. It *was* funny.

And of course the L.A. poets,
those I knew and read with
when we were all young and ambitious:
Leland Hickman, Linda Backlund,
John Thomas, Philomene Long,
Bob Flanagan, to name a few.
And yesterday, just yesterday,
I got an email from Paul
that Evelyn Klein had died
after a long bout with cancer.
Evelyn was a tall, beautiful brunette
with dark, deep set eyes,
whose father had been a Commie back in the '30s,
and I spent hours talking to him,
a frail old man
holed up in his house in Lakeview,
hounded by the FBI agents
parked on the street.
Evelyn would never have given me
the time of day, except that she was smart
and had no time for football players
or the blond Adonis with the tennis racket.
She liked her men smart.
I can't explain it, but there are people
who fit into categories.
Evelyn fit into none of them.
And in my mind,
though I haven't seen her in fifty years,
she's still twenty, dazzling, smart,
talking to smart men,
talking to me.
Now she's gone, too.

Mostly though, I've been celebrating
those still alive,
not just friends,
but plants, animals, things.
It's a checklist I keep in my head,
going through it several times a day:
the road's still here: check;
the washing machine, still here;

the dog next door, still here;
Peter behind bulletproof glass
at J-Market, still here.
This pair of scissors: check.
My old calculator: check.
This pen: check.
There's so much that is still alive,
it seems wrong not to notice it,
celebrate it.
That's the problem.
Who has time to celebrate the living?
And if you're really alive and living,
who has time for the dead?
So I've made some time,
here in this poem,
and then, when I'm done,
I'll go back to the daily routine,
filling up my car with gas,
getting food at Ralph's,
going to the bank and the post office.
Making my list.
The little Japanese fountain in my front yard: check.
The metal gate with the broken handle: check.
The cigar that I smoked halfway,
still in the ashtray in the back yard: check.
I sit down on the bench by the firepit.
That damned Chinese elm
that fills the yard with debris,
tiny leaves and orange dust,
I thought I hated it,
yet I check it off: still here.
And the belly I never could get rid of,
my corns,
my aching hips
and that muscle in my calf
that refuses to heal: check,
check, check,
check.

Sagittarius

When I park my car after class,
I sometimes glance at the stars
in the night sky—maybe there's a full moon,
or maybe I'll catch Jupiter next to Venus.
I've seen the sky a thousand times,
not looking for a UFO
or a shooting star, though I've seen
a few of those too.
I know enough about the cosmos
to know how far from me they are—
those white holes in the fabric of space.
I don't truck much with all that astrology
stuff; some days, I read someone
else's horoscope just to see how it
applies to me.
When I'm munching on a sandwich
I'll read just about anything,
including some nonsense about the alignment
of the stars and its impact on my daily life.
And no, standing by the gate in front of my house,
looking up at the sky, I'm not contemplating
the great mysteries of the universe, either.
Let's face it, those points of light
are just great balls of fire.
But still, I get out of my car,
walk to the front gate,
look up, and take a moment to feel
immensely small.
I'm this speck, and not a person out there
is able to see me, except Mr. You-Know-Who,
Mr. Astrology, Mr. Quantum Physics,
Mr. Electro-Magnetic Gravitation.
To tell you the truth, I do this little bit
of star-gazing for one reason—
to prepare myself for home.
Small though I may be,
I still have a place in the universe.
Then I walk through the door,

yell out, "I'm home," and empty my pockets
before going into the bedroom
to give my wife a kiss.
"Whatcha watching?" I usually ask.
"Nothing," she says, "just some dumb show."
"I'm gonna have a bite," I say.
I cut an apple, get a few crackers,
sit down in the kitchen to read the paper.
She joins me, makes small talk,
takes one of my crackers when I'm not looking.
"I saw that," I say.
"Saw what?" she says.
"You know what," I say.
Then, when I'm not looking,
she slips it into her mouth and starts chewing.
I move the plate of crackers out of her reach.
After a few crackers, I read from her horoscope:
"You have a mighty purpose today,
to make people laugh."
She swipes the paper from me
and reads mine:
"In some way, you are far from home,
but you'll make your way back
through the course of the day."
I swipe the paper back.
"Lemme see that."
I scan the constellations—
Aries, Gemini, Aquarius—
and land on Sagittarius.
"You read the wrong horoscope," I say,
"that was Sagittarius."
"All the same," she says,
"that one was yours."
Then I cut the last wedge of apple,
place it on the last cracker,
and enjoy the last chew
before bedtime.

The Man in Charge of Watering

The summer sun, strong and bright,
sits down on the bricks in the front yard.
Cars which have nothing to do with bricks
go by on the street heading home.
It's Wednesday afternoon,
middle of the week,
when you can put everything you'd planned
on Monday
back on the back burner.
A lady goes by; I nod and smile and say hello.
She's carrying a bag of groceries.
I think she lives down the block.
I should go back inside,
the sun's hot on my face,
and I'm not wearing my hat.
Lori admonishes me,
"Don't forget to wear your hat."
I came outside to fill the fountain
and forgot to wear my hat.
Now, I'm just standing here,
looking around, saying hello
to the neighbors as they pass by.
When we first bought this house
when Josh was two years old,
I used to go outside after the sun had gone down
and hose the grass on the front and side lawn.
Such a peaceful time, and the back spray from the hose
cooled everything down.
I was Mr. Homeowner watering his lawn.
There are flowers blooming here
that Lori knows the names of, but I can't
seem to remember their names—
jasmine, bougainvillea, true geraniums—
I can't keep track of them all.
I've tried, but the names elude me.
Even the grass has a name,
but I've forgotten that too.
This is what heaven will be like.

Anytime I want, I'll be able to water the lawn.
All my friends will walk by,
I'll nod, say hello, watch them pass along
going wherever people go in heaven.
I won't have to do anything but water the lawn.
And the water, you should see the water in heaven.
Crystal clear, light as a feather, so to speak,
diamonds of light.
The back spray will cool my face and head.
And the grass. You'd think grass
in heaven wouldn't need watering,
but you're in for quite a surprise.
Everything up here needs watering.
Even the bricks, the bricks that sit in the sun
getting hot.
Even God, who soaks up all our prayers.
Even God will need a spray or two
to cool down.
I'll be the waterer.
The man in charge of watering everything
and everyone,
the man spraying water in heaven.
That'll be my job.
When God comes by, asks how I'm doing,
I'll say, "Fine, just fine."
Then I'll turn and ask,
"Need a little watering?"
And God will nod,
say, "Sure, soak me down, just
don't wet the groceries."
And I'll give God a good spray.
That'll be my job—
the man in charge
of watering God.

Everlasting

The dog is the dog is the dog.
Everlasting.
The moon is the moon is the moon.
Everlasting.
Day to day, this is how it goes.
My son and his friend stand in the kitchen,
putting tattoos on their bodies.
Sunlight comes through the window.
The same sunlight that goes through
your window on a slow, everlasting Saturday.
And here we are,
alive here on this slow everlasting Saturday,
bread on the kitchen counter,
my wife humming
as she fools with the toaster oven.
March 18, 2000. A slow Saturday.
The dog is the dog is the dog.
Everlasting.
The moon is the moon is the moon.
sweet sweet sweet sweet life.

Afterword by Bill Mohr

"Just Temporarily Alive": The Transmission Poetry of Jack Grapes and the Stand Up School of Los Angeles Poets

Bill Mohr

Exhibiting an almost insolent courage, Peter Schjeldahl gave a talk in Chicago in 2011 in which he categorized that city as a "receptor city." Prominent collections of modern and contemporary art and a substantial roll call of noted indigenous poets, writers, and theater companies notwithstanding, Schjeldahl unhesitatingly relegated the Midwest capital of the United States to an urban crossroads of consumption rather than a "transmission city," an accolade he reserved for the places where evolutionary developments in art and literature originate and mount the runways of public visibility. According to Schjeldahl, Los Angeles ranks alongside London, Paris, and New York City as a transmission city, and if that is the case, then one of its most accomplished poets must certainly be Jack Grapes, who was born and raised in New Orleans, and brought the Beat-inflected artistic knowledge he gleaned from magazines such as *The Outsider* to the West Coast in the late 1960s; among other feats in the decades since, he made himself one of the founding members of a Los Angeles-based school often referred to as Stand Up poetry.

In this process, Grapes has attained the virtues associated with transmission—audacity, reinvention, and variety—through his stalwart commitment to a mordantly comic legibility within the larger cultural discourse. Part of his whole enterprise includes a career within the industrial production arena of Hollywood and the microcosm of little theater that keeps it well-supplied. He tweaked that portion of life with half-serious affection in the title of one of his earlier collections, *Breaking on Camera.* Becoming a transmission poet in a city that primarily vets the oscillating image mechanics of popular culture requires that one simultaneously keep that industry's larger audience in mind while in-

[1] Schjeldahl might well be correct in his assessment of Chicago, but isn't that city the starting point for what became known as "slam poetry"? Perhaps it might be more useful to think of major and minor transmission cities. New Orleans, for instance, which is the setting for many of Grapes's most memorable and poignant poems, would have a difficult time qualifying for a rank among the major transmission cities, yet can one really imagine the transformation of jazz into an art form with a global presence without bringing New Orleans into the discussion? The other factor to keep in mind is that a major transmission city will also most likely have an underground scene that in some way resists the most obvious armatures of transmission.

structing others as how to hear that which is not being broadcast on an hourly basis.

The Naked Eye makes it demonstrably clear what those of us who had the good fortune to hear Jack Grapes read his poetry in the 1970s in Los Angeles knew all those many years ago: he has an almost instinctual ability—akin to that of a master actor—to shape dramatic metaphors into the enduring substance of "a local habitation and a name." If the mind's ear can almost automatically begin to intone the poems in this collection on a reader's tongue, this felicitous transmission takes place because Grapes has at his command the ability to remain palpably present within the poem's domain and yet to absent himself from any need to control the poem's outcome. When Grapes is at his best—and that is far more often than even an above-average poet is entitled to perform at the rate of—he reminds me of Paul Valery's comment about the process of being a biographer:

> I wonder if anyone, when writing a biography, has ever tried at each moment to know as little of the following moment as the "hero" of the work himself knew at the corresponding moment of his career. In other words, to restore the element of chance that entered into every moment—instead of building up a coherent sequence that can be summarized, and a causality that can be formulated (*Analects*).

It is easy enough now to look back through the decades of poetry on display in *The Naked Eye* and perceive an almost gratuitous ineluctability that somehow guided Grapes through far more daunting risks than one finds in the poems published in the *American Poetry Review.* (Grapes deliciously takes the fashion-plate posing of that magazine down a couple notches in one of his early poems, "Poem without Picture for Picture without Poem.") His sense of discomfort with the predictable and familiar reveals itself in a poetics of permeating contingency that summons the reader to take concomitant leaps. Not that the reader isn't adequately warned. Yes, the poet's soul is "always for the asking," or at least Grapes hankers for that to be as true as any wish might be. But he cautions us about our selfish motives continually: "Listen, what are you reading this for? / Haven't you got bills to pay?", even as he invites to accompany him up the extension ladder. "Trying to Get Your Life in Shape," for instance, transmits a self-portrait of the poet engaged in home improvement, only to find himself pinioned to the roof, without any potential way off his existential promontory; nevertheless, he savors the alternative with rejuvenated irony:

You sit back,
you contemplate this new richness
come into your life,
and shiver on the roof
knowing it could be worse.
Why, you could be inside.
Warm by the fire.
Sipping sherry.
Shoes off.
Just
temporarily
alive.

Richard Kostelanetz once commented in a talk at the recently closed Bowery Poetry Club in New York City that a major poet was someone who had memorable poems in a book other than the title poem. Grapes has well over a dozen poems in this volume that merit being serious contenders as title poems for a standalone volume. In fact, given the manifest quality of the poems in *The Naked Eye*, one would expect to find a generous selection of his writing in anthologies that make claims to present contemporary poetry within a national scope. Unfortunately, I have serious doubts that this book will change the mind of any future editor working on an anthology associated with a university press. Instead, *The Naked Eye* will most probably remain present as an indefatigable rebuke of the ability of academic poets and editors to make fine distinctions within larger increments of poetic schools and movements.

If Grapes is to be considered primarily within the context of Stand Up poetry, one immediately runs into numerous obstacles, not the least of which is that—like Language writing—Stand Up poetry is easier to cite than to delimit. Popular misconceptions about Language writing and its so-called "difficulty" are eerily parallel in a flip-side manner to the alleged accessibility of Stand Up poetry and its supposed "easy" quality. Dana Gioia once insouciantly claimed that the problem with Los Angeles-based poets is that they lacked "standards." Yet one looks at the standards held up by academic critics and wonders how it is that the multiple-choice quiz ends up being such a closed set. Linda Gregerson portentously claims that "Form has modulated in multiple, and often extravagant, directions, but the formal imperative of most consequence in contemporary American poetry has a single, recognizable center: one must learn something new in the course of writing the poem" (*Negative Capability*).

It's difficult to restrain from rolling one's eyes. One only has to recall Frost's admonition, "No surprise for the writer, no surprise for the reader" to realize how little originality Gregerson actually brings to her critique, basking as it does in predictable selections: her lineup of poets favored to receive her notice amounts to a roll call of all-too-familiar names: Mark Strand, John Ashbery, William Meredith, Louise Gluck. One might ask of Gregerson to apply her rule to criticism: "One must learn something new about American poetry in the course of writing the review."

The Naked Eye provides us with an opportunity to learn something new about American poetry since World War II. Few critical tasks have been as egregiously neglected as the examination of the development of a group of poets parallel to the Beats. Grapes's volume remains one of the crucial testaments. The term "post-Beat" has recently come into use, but the chronology of any such designation disintegrates almost upon contact. The only way to understand a group of poets born between 1940 and 1955 whose work is a direct response to the first cluster of Beat poets but is not itself primarily aligned with the major tenets of Beat poetics is to foreground those poets in Southern California associated with Stand Up poetry, a label derived from the title of one of Edward Field's earliest collections, *Stand Up, Friend, with Me.* While a sense of humor and a voluble capacity to entwine performance with popular culture are signature elements of Stand Up poetry, the manifold ways that Grapes's poetry differs from Stand Up poetry, however, are probably as important as the way his poems inform the movement's first years of coalescence. With the possible exception of Laurel Ann Bogen, Grapes's poems are far more willing to engage with themes that are imbued with morbidity and desolation than most other Stand Up poets. Consider one of Grapes's earliest dramatic monologues, "The Count's Lament," which is probably the best single poem any textbook could juxtapose with Keats's "This Living Hand." If Keats's poem is seen as a frag-

[2] Richard Howard opened a long review of a pair of books by Edward Field by noting "the extreme resistance to the habitual conventions of literature" and goes on to say that Field's subversive excess "has produced a canon of successful poems without meter, without rhyme, without music, without images, without any of the disciplines and strictures we think of as constituting that share—at best the lion's, and at the very least some jackal's scrap—of poetry required by verse." (*Alone with America* 143). Howard overstates his case, in much the same way that Donald Allen vastly exaggerated the non-academic qualities of the poets in *New American Poetry.* Even so, critical writing that undertakes to analyze the differences between Field's poems as Stand up models and the writing of such poets as Gerald Locklin, Wanda Coleman, Laurel Ann Bogen, Bob Flanagan, Charles Harper Webb, Manazar Gamboa, Michael C. Ford, Elliot Fried, Suzanne Lummis, and Ray Zepeda has been sorely lacking.

ment, then Grapes has taken the spiral of energy launched by that poem and glided like a master surfer in its proleptic, death-rattle cliff-hanging gauntlet to produce an enduring encounter with thanatos as self-effacing imagination. Of how many poems can it be said that a posthumous recrudescence meets a blowtorch of nihilistic visceral revulsion? Grapes would deserve an entry in the canon simply for this verbal performance alone.

The complexity of Grapes's poetry is perhaps too easily overlooked. Maybe such close reading has become impossible at a time when the sheer quantity of contemporary poetry has turned the canonical selection process into a lottery subsidized by contest entry fees. How many judges keep in mind the trajectory of Emerson's influence on the development of American poetry, faded though it has into the evanescence generated by post-modern and the post-avant? If Grapes's title nudges us as a reminder of his vulnerable magnitude, his poems also serve almost as a cruel rebuke in delimiting that transition from an Emersonian poetics into the turbulent quickening of an utterly new era. Let's look briefly at one of Emerson's most notorious proclamations:

> Standing on the bare ground, my head bathed by the blithe air, and uplifted into infinite space, all mean egotism vanishes. I become a transparent eyeball—I am nothing; I see all; the currents of the Universal Being circulate through me—I am part or particle of God. The name of the nearest friend sounds then foreign and accidental: to be brothers, to be acquaintances—master or servant, is then a trifle, and a disturbance. I am a lover of uncontained and immortal beauty ("Nature").

In contrast, Grapes's "naked eye" strips away all lingering idealistic naivete (cf: hippies and all too many new-age movement recidivists) and cajoles us into admitting our complicity with a dystopic planet: "we are the thing told and like it" ("Greenhouse Effect"). Eros and thanatos go head to head in Grapes's poetry and each quotes Muhammed Ali to the other: "You can run but you can't hide." In poems such as "The Beast and The Dreamer," the refrain of "Comingtagetcha" reiterates its insidious temptation to readers: admit your complicity. Grapes is the one of the genuine progeny of Baudelaire. Transmission poets must be willing to pay the price for engaging in seduction, for transmission requires a willing audience. One cannot hold the mirror up to the experiments of self-invention most favored in modernity without an audience that craves to find out how thorough a reversal awaits its wakening. Grapes is one of the best in contemporary poetry in making the audience pay the price of admission to its desire for the poet to be its substitute protagonist. Eliot said of

Shakespeare that he had a "terrifying clairvoyance." There are touches of that quality in Grapes's poetry, too, which is perhaps not that unexpected, given that Grapes co-wrote a hit play, *Circle of Will*, that conjured up a version of the young playwright as a genius whose imaginary panoply of character was like a universe whose galaxies had yet to cool off enough to begin the stage of planetary formation.

As substantial and enduring as the poems in the first half of Grapes's output may be, all poets face a crisis at some point in their work in which they begin to interrogate the premises upon which they have built their achievements. Some resolve it without any apparent substantial alteration in their work. The point of the crisis is to avoid any complacency that might set in after the long trek to artistic mastery has finished its initial outpouring. For Grapes, the "card poems" in the Lucky Finds section constitute that moment when he examines the underpinnings of his poetics and finds out what it means for "each letter" to constitute "an attack upon the universe." The letters floating around the sentences have the effect of an anti-ABCdarian poem. The poet who might well have been the most interested in this particular project, if he had had the good fortune to know of it, would be the late Scottish poet laureate, Edwin Morgan. If you are not familiar with Morgan's work and how it might be useful in talking about this particular portion of Grapes's writing, then it's time for you to get to work. Sad to say, I've met very few American poets who seem to have the slightest idea of Morgan's work.

All too many considerations of a poet's work ignore the hard-won delicacy of the poet's music. Grapes has as deft a touch with the free verse line as one can hope for, but my appreciation for it is reinforced immensely when I come across a line such as "The fully mortal laugh of all his teeth" ("And This Is My Father"). That's one of the most solid lines of poetry ever written. If I were trying to teach a young poet how a line of iambic pentameter can still undulate with gorgeous resonance, then I would cite this line. Note how the "l"s play out in liquid felicity, and that the secret is how the unstressed fifth syllable lends itself to that chain. The caesura picks up the second major intonation in the line, so that the dipthong of "laugh" prefigures the conclusion of the line's monosyllable, "teeth." The "skipping iambs" of the first portion of the line "The fully mortal laugh" set the line in a fluttering equilibrium with the second portion: "of all his teeth": each increment of this line measures and counter-measures the total impact of its sonic vulnerability.

What would be my hope for this book? It should be required reading for anyone who is putting together an anthology of poetry that would claim to be national in scope. Any anthologist of such a project in the next quarter century who fails to read this volume should immediately be regarded as suspect. One hesitates to name names, but did Barbara Hamby bother to read any of Jack Grapes's poetry before she put together *Seriously Funny*? Her book is a blatant rip-off of the conceptual framework of Charles Harper Webb's three volumes of *Stand Up Poetry*. Grapes was one of the dozen of the original fifteen poets to appear in all three volumes, the last of which was published by the University of Iowa Press. The time for accounts of contemporary poetry to be forthright about where credit needs to be given is long overdue. If one were to name a dozen poets who have been the most significant within this decidedly non-academic, pre-Slam, pre-Spoken Word, Jack Grapes is more than merely one of the all-star poets in this core group; he fulfills the role of masterful mentorship through a body of work that would serve to inspire anyone on the West Coast who might take up the challenge of writing poetry in the coming decades. The scope of Grapes's work, however, will prove to be the most daunting aspect of anyone who decides to make a foray into this extraordinary complex assemblage of poems. He has not made it easy for anyone to grasp the full measure of his artistic journey.

In one of my favorite aphorisms by Paul Valery, he comments, "The best work is the one that keeps its secret longest. For a long while no one even suspects it has a secret." There are secrets in *The Naked Eye* that even I have yet to suspect as to the nature of their presence. I entrust them to you for their safekeeping in remaining so.

Bill Mohr has a Ph.D. in Literature from the University of California, San Diego and is an associate professor at CSU Long Beach. His monograph, *Holdouts: The Los Angeles Poetry Renaissance 1948–1992*, was published by the University of Iowa Press in 2011. His poems, prose poems and creative prose have appeared in dozens of magazines during the past 40 years, including *5 AM, Antioch Review, Beyond Baroque, Blue Collar Review, Blue Mesa Review, Caliban (On-line), ONTHEBUS, OR, Santa Monica Review, Skidrow Penthouse, Sonora Review, Spot, Upstreet, Wormwood Review*, and *ZYZZYVA*. His writing has been featured in over a dozen anthologies of poetry, prose poetry and non-fiction, and has been translated into Japanese and Spanish. Individual collections of his poetry include *Hidden Proofs, Vehemence*, and *Bittersweet Kaleidoscope*. Between 1974 and 1988, he devoted himself to working as the editor of Momentum Press, a publishing project that was supported by four grants from the National Endowment for the Arts. In 1997 he was a Visiting Scholar at the Getty Research Institute in Los Angeles.

www.ingramcontent.com/pod-product-compliance
Lightning Source LLC
Chambersburg PA
CBHW022047160426
43198CB00008B/149
9780941017008